Legislative Reform

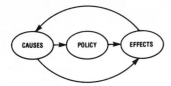

Policy Studies Organization Series

Legislative Reform

The Policy Impact

Edited by
Leroy N. Rieselbach
Indiana University

Lexington Books
D.C. Heath and Company
Lexington, Massachusetts
Toronto

Library of Congress Cataloging in Publication Data

Main entry under title:

Legislative reform: the policy impact.

  Bibliography: p.
  Includes index.
  1. United States. Congress—Reform—Addresses, essays, lectures.
I. Rieselbach, Leroy N.
JK1061.L34   328.73   77-223
ISBN 0-669-01436-2

Contents

42052

Legislative Reform

1

Introduction:
Reform, Change, and
Legislative Policy Making

Leroy N. Rieselbach

Glendower: I can call spirits from the vasty deep.
Hotspur: Why, so can I, or so can any man;
But will they come when you do call for them?

Shakespeare, *Henry IV*, Part I, Act III, Scene I

Political reformers, including those concerned about legislative change, are like Shakespeare's wily Welshman, Owen Glendower: they can evoke, from the depths of their experiences and expectations, visions of better forms of political organization and practice. Moreover, they have seen some of their proposals accepted and acted upon. Academic observers, by contrast, tend to be more careful and circumspect. Like Hotspur, they prefer to deal in concrete results, not speculative ventures; they seek to assess the extent to which reform visions accomplish their stated objectives. This book, an outgrowth and extension of the *Policy Studies Journal* "Symposium on Legislative Reform" (Rieselbach 1977b), approaches the issue of legislative change from Hotspur's perspective. The chapters here attempt to look carefully at the policy impact of political change; they seek to determine what have been the results, whether or not intended, of a wide variety of reforms that Congress and state legislatures have adopted. These empirical assessments present a cautionary tale: There is surely no guarantee that reform will have any, much less the desired, impact on representative assemblies.

A major problem, of course, is that promoters of legislative change do not always articulate their visions. (Even Glendower did not specify *which* spirits would respond to his summons.) When reformers are explicit, frequently they focus solely on one or another aspect of the legislature's duties. Thus, even in the heightened reformism of the post-Vietnam, post-Watergate period, changes aimed at enhancing legislative representational, oversight, and lawmaking capacities have been advanced, adopted, and implemented, often without discussion of, to say nothing of agreement on, which of these legislative functions most requires attention. For instance, to improve the citizen-assembly linkage—to make it more open, more visible, and less subject to abuse—a variety of changes have been introduced. Toll-free telephone "hot lines" now enable the ruled to contact their rulers directly; "sunshine laws" obligate legislators to do their work in public, in full view of interested persons and the mass media; ethics codes,

1

with financial disclosure requirements, make it more difficult for legislators so inclined to put private interests ahead of the commonweal.

To impose more meaningful control on executive agencies, legislatures have provided themselves with more staff and vastly improved information resources; they have, in some cases, explicitly asserted their obligation to exert "continuous watchfulness" over executive departments. To enlarge their policy-making capacities to regain authority "lost" or willingly ceded to chief executives, legislatures have adjusted their structures, rules, and procedures and have sought to impose new restrictions on executive power. Thus, for example, Congress has reorganized its committee system, enacted a War Powers resolution, and created a new budget process—all in the hopes of reinvigorating its policy process, the limitations of which were clearly revealed in the Vietnam-Watergate era. In sum, legislative reformers have seen a variety of visions; and while each may have a distinct view of the best of all possible legislatures, collectively reform has proceeded incrementally at best or haphazardly at worst.

Even with respect to policy making, where executive failure and malfeasance have encouraged legislative resurgence, reformers have responded to differing visions of the assembly's proper role. Some (Burnham 1959; de Grazia 1965) argue for a modern-day version of legislative supremacy in which the elected representatives dominate policy making and the executive plays a clearly supporting and subsidiary role. This view, however, appears impractical, ill-suited to twentieth-century developments, and additional possibilities have appeared at center stage. Other observers, less sanguine about legislatures' policy-making potential, have proposed that assemblies accept subordination to the executive and his/her political party (Huntington 1973; Burns 1963, 1965). This script calls for legislatures to accept, to confer legitimacy on, executive policy proposals and instead to devote their energies to serving the citizenry (representation) and overseeing the bureaucracy. Like the legislative supremacy vision, this executive superiority scenario has engendered little enthusiasm; events in the Johnson and Nixon administrations have undercut its appeal.

In consequence, much of the contemporary reform drama has revolved around efforts to revive legislatures' status as coequal makers of public policy, as institutions able, in Fenno's (1975) term, to "counterbalance" political executives. This is a reasonable view because, as Jones (1975) reminds us, legislative change, when it occurs, originates almost inevitably within the assembly; outside forces can urge reform, but they cannot compel reluctant or unwilling senators and representatives to adopt it. In addition, because legislatures are neither eager to abdicate their power to executives nor naive enough to believe that they can supplant executives, the reforms they enact are likely to aim at enlarging the legislative role, at making the legislatures more—not less—competitive with executives.

Here, of course, practical change may depart from the broad visions of theoretical reformers. The lawmakers, who must debate and ultimately implement any reform, tend to have at least some vested interests in the status quo. Predictably, they appear reluctant to make wholesale changes in legislative operations; they prefer to "buy retail," making piecemeal changes where they have little to lose and where they can persuade their colleagues to go along. In seeking to find acceptable formulas for reform, they have made small, but not necessarily insignificant, steps in the direction of several, not necessarily compatible, visions of the "better" policy process. The changes they have approved have seemed simultaneously to move legislatures in differing directions; these alterations have reflected pragmatic political and personal considerations, not careful planning about future consequences. To strengthen their policy-making capacities, legislatures have undertaken reforms of three general types: (1) altering internal structures and procedures to enhance their ability to produce effective policy decisions efficiently; (2) legislating to improve their positions vis-à-vis the executives; and (3) seeking to improve their standing, and thus their influence, with the American citizenry. Obviously, these practical steps need not necessarily square with any long-term, broad-gauge vision of legislative change. Indeed, given the motivations underlying those changes, it is unrealistic to expect them to do so.

In short, legislative reform, however current and fashionable, remains in a muddled condition. There are Glendowers, anxious to articulate and impose sweeping visions of desirable states of legislative affairs; needless to say, these visions do not always look in the same direction, much less coincide significantly. There are legislators, those who actually adopt reform, less concerned to implement ideal schemes than to protect their own positions; the changes they introduce reflect their short-run interests. And there are Hotspurs, skeptical and critical, eager to specify the meaning, to evaluate the concrete results, of reform efforts. What is needed, perhaps, to sort out these various perspectives is to step back and place change in context. The writing to date on reform (see especially Ornstein 1975b; Welch and Peters 1977; and Dodd and Oppenheimer 1977b) has raised, but not answered conclusively, a series of fundamental questions about legislatures and legislative politics. The answers to one query go far to structure the responses to subsequent ones:

Do we want vigorous policy-making legislatures, capable of counterbalancing executives, or assemblies that commit their efforts to nonpolicy functions such as oversight of administration or representation?

Can we devise a set of structures and procedures—involving committees, political parties, and rules—that facilitates the appropriate policy-making stance?

Can the legislatures establish appropriate relationships to the executives, ones that will allow them to exert the degree of policy-making influence they desire?

Can the legislatures attract the kinds of public support that will let them employ their policy-making powers most effectively?

Can the legislatures mobilize their political courage to follow the policy-making courses they set for themselves?

Not surprisingly, legislators have overwhelmingly answered the first question in the affirmative; they prefer to see assemblies capable of exerting substantial influence over policy outcomes. The authors represented in this book, implicitly at least, share this preference. They accept the reality of legislative assertion (or reassertion) of policy control and focus their attention on the subsequent queries relating to the effectiveness of changes intended to enhance legislative policy-making capability. Yet such analyses must be read with caution. It is not at all certain, as David Rohde and Kenneth Shepsle make clear, that any single type of change—in legislative personnel, legislative structures and procedures, or external political circumstances—inevitably leads to altered policy outcomes. Indeed, on the contrary, they contend that policy change may come either with or without concomitant changes in legislative membership or rules. In short, they demonstrate that "political change is a messy business," and we should be wary of seemingly simple explanations of change as well as of overoptimistic expectations about the potential impact of reform.

E. Lee Bernick and Charles Wiggins pick up one of Rohde and Shepsle's themes, but from the perspective of state legislatures give it a sort of "reverse twist." If in Congress too little turnover—too small infusions of new legislative blood—inhibits policy change, then at the state level, so Bernick and Wiggins argue, too much turnover undermines expertise and, in turn, effective policy formulation. The problem in the states is to retain a cadre of experienced and competent lawmakers. To that end, reformers have proposed increasing legislators' perquisites to make continued service more attractive. These proposals, Bernick and Wiggins' data suggest, miss the mark; they do not deal with the real causes of state legislative turnover, which are largely intractable and not easily treated by any available reforms. This analysis reminds all reformers, whatever their vision, that not all problems will be amenable to solution and that what is a vice in one legislature may be a virtue in another.

Many reform efforts take the personnel of the legislature as given and instead turn to "institutional tinkering," adaptation of structures and rules, to improve policy making. The venerable seniority system in the United States Congress, long the *bête noire* of reformers, lost its hold as the exclusive criterion governing assignment to congressional committees and choice of committee and subcommittee chairpersons. Beginning in the 92d Congress, House Democrats instituted reforms that undercut seniority, presumably to give younger members greater access to the chamber's decision-making centers. Then, more dramatically, at the start of the 94th Congress, the Democratic Caucus actually deprived three elderly Southern oligarchs of their full committee chairs, ostensibly because the Caucus, its ranks enlarged by 75 freshmen, heavily liberal in outlook, felt the need to replace these senior conservatives. John Stanga and David Farnsworth explore the relationship of the House rules changes and seniority. They find the consequences minimal: in the postreform period, junior representatives were neither assigned in increasing proportion to important committees nor succeeded more rapidly to subcommittee chairs on most panels. In short, they suggest that the seniority principle has not lost its sway, that younger, perhaps ideologically distinct, members have not moved into the more powerful leadership positions in the House. John Berg explores the immediate impact, on committee policy making, of the ouster of the three senior chairmen. He concludes that, in the short run, "there has been little if any immediate change" in committee performance under the new chairpersons. Again, reform seems to have had less effect than its proponents desired.

Replacing chairpersons is only one, albeit a dramatic, way to seek to alter committee behavior. Many congressional committees have changed, or been changed, by intent as well as by events. Fred Kaiser, Catherine Rudder, and Bruce Oppenheimer—studying the House International Relations, Ways and Means, and Rules Committees, respectively—underscore Fenno's (1973) sage reminder that committees vary widely in the ways they conduct their affairs and, by extension, in the ways that reform affects them. The contrast between International Relations and Ways and Means is instructive. The former, modified subtly, has, Kaiser tells us, enhanced its policy-making position; the latter, drastically restructured, has, so Rudder's analysis indicates, lost its ability to dominate its policy domain. In contrast, reformers seeking to "tame" the Rules Committee have, as Oppenheimer demonstrates, clearly succeeded; the panel has become a much more reliable arm of the majority party leadership in the House.

Other efforts to strengthen the political parties, however, have had curiously mixed effects, as Eric Uslaner points out, resulting from the newer and young House members' ambivalent views about the proper role of the congressional party. On the one hand, reform-oriented junior representatives seek to exercise "policy entrepreneurship," to advance their own favored policy alternatives. On the other hand, these same members want to use party procedure to promote their preferred policies; that is, they want intraparty democracy that fosters individual members' policy initiatives. Not surprisingly, these contradictory goals have led to contradictory reforms, leaving uncertain the fate of the party as a centralizing institution capable of formulating and enacting policy.

Finally, and more straightforwardly, legislators may seek to change assembly procedures to improve legislative performance. In Wisconsin, Ronald Hedlund and Keith Hamm discover that procedural innovation achieved its stated goals: changes made the state Assembly both more productive and more expeditious in treating legislation. All in all, then, numerous efforts in varying legislative contexts to reshape structures and processes have met with differing degrees of success. As observers, we should be aware that the results of reform are unlikely to be easily predicted.

A second set of reformers, as noted, has moved beyond structural change, focusing instead on ways to strengthen the legislature's position vis-à-vis the executive. For one thing, they have sought to improve legislative oversight capacity and performance. David Price explores the effect of change on the House Commerce Committee's subcommittee on Oversight and Investigations. Echoing Rohde and Shepsle, he finds the subcommittee's performance to have altered in response to a mixture of structural reform, the accession of new members to positions of influence within the panel, and changed environmental circumstances. Reform may improve oversight, but will not necessarily do so in the absence of members committed to oversight and/or conditions conducive to its exercise.

Another, and more dramatic, front on which legislatures have attempted to advance against the executive force is the area of budgetary politics. The most visible of such assaults is, of course, Congress's passage of the Budget and Impoundment Control Act of 1974. The national legislature reformed its procedures to recapture a major, if not the dominant, position in federal financial decisions. James Thurber and William Munselle assess the initial impact of the two chief features of the act. The former suggests that the act's budgetary provisions have clearly enhanced Congress's position as an independent actor in fiscal politics: Armed with substantial informational resources of its own, Congress has been both willing and able to impose its own priorities in the budget. The ultimate impact of this success on the substance of policy, however, remains unclear. Munselle finds, similarly, that the anti-impoundment title of the act has enabled Congress to restrain the President's ability to undercut legislative spending decisions, but it has not necessarily maximized "Congress's ability to make and control public policy."

Another aspect of legislative-executive relations to which assemblies have addressed themselves with increasing frequency is the information advantage that regularly inheres in the executive. Congress, in particular, has moved to increase its own information resources. Susan Hammond documents the growth of congressional staff and indicates clearly that more personnel permit the legislature to provide assistance to more of its members, who can devote that aid both more broadly and more deeply to a wider variety of activities, including but certainly not limited to making public policy. With respect to reassertion of legislative policy-making influence, then, assemblies have achieved much, but not as much as the visions of some reformers call for.

A third broad goal of legislative reform has been to restore assemblies—eclipsed by executives and sullied by scandal—to their place in the sun. Only legislatures that merit public approbation, so the argument runs, can expect to realize their full policy-making potential. To that end, reformers have sought to expose all legislative activities, including elections, to public scrutiny; legislators inhibited from pursuing self-interest should act more consistently in the public interest. For example, if candidates for office must make prior policy (or other) commitments to secure campaign funds, their freedom to pursue sound policies may be limited severely. To forestall such dangers, Congress enacted the Federal Election Campaign Act in 1971, and refined it in 1974, to restrict the amounts that congressional candidates can spend in seeking office. Immediately, critics of the legislation asserted that the law merely masqueraded as reform when, in fact, it protected incumbents by imposing such stringent limits on campaign spending that challengers had no genuine opportunity to unseat sitting members. Gary Copeland and Samuel Patterson test the proposition that the limit on candidates' total spending (a limit the Supreme Court invalidated in 1976) worked to the detriment of electoral challengers, and find it without foundation. Of course, whether disclosure statutes and limits on individual contributors' donations to single candidates (which the Court approved) will advance broad national interests is another matter.

In the same vein, Congress has enacted numerous reforms in recent years to open to public view most of, if not all, the legislative process—from subcommittee to conference committee. The intent of these reforms, as Charles Bullock describes it, was to inform the public, in the hope that publicity would deter wrongdoing, promote popular accountability, and ultimately reduce the influence, which could flourish in the shadows, of powerful self-serving interests. The reforms, Bullock speculates, have been at least partly successful; they have reallocated influence to the benefit of legislators' constituents, and perhaps of their staffs as well. At the same time, however, the changes may have produced some unintended and, to some at least, undesirable consequences. Publicity may make members more wary, hesitant to act in ways offensive to the "folks back home" who are now able to look in on legislative deliberations, even when they believe that popular sentiment is misguided. Again, these analyses point a clear moral: change is predictable only with great difficulty; it may bring the good or it may not; it may produce the desirable, or it may lead to the unintended and unwanted.

Nonetheless, this unpredictability need not deter the would-be reformer, visionary or more pragmatic. As Raymond Tatlovich graphically demonstrates, "good" legislatures produce "quality" legislation. If the standards of the Citizens Conference on State Legislatures denote criteria of legislative quality, then to move legislatures toward those standards should, over the long haul, improve the policies that the assemblies enact. Moreover, the movement need not be dramatic; any steps, however small or halting, toward a "better" legislature may ultimately enhance the quality of the legislative product. More fundamentally, however, the lesson of the studies in this book is less optimistic: While, like Glendover, we may summon our visions, broad and narrow, from the "vasty deep," we must, like Hotspur, remember that these spirits may not come at all or, if they do, they may appear in different guises than we imagined.

2 Thinking About Legislative Reform

David W. Rohde and
Kenneth A. Shepsle

Over the past decade, a substantial number of people have voiced dissatisfaction with many of the policies produced (or not produced) by the United States Congress, calling for more "progressive" or "liberal" solutions to perceived national problems. These people, however, have disagreed among themselves about the remedy. Some have taken the position that the "problem" is largely structural and that alteration of congressional procedures would produce different policies (see, for example, Clark 1965; Bolling 1966). Others (for example, Orfield 1975) have held that procedural change is of minor import and that the crucial element in producing new policies is to change election outcomes, substituting new "liberal" decision makers for the older, "conservative" ones.

We argue that both these views fall wide of the mark by establishing two propositions: first, at times significant policy changes can occur without being preceded by either membership or procedural change; second, membership and procedural changes (either separately or together) do not guarantee alterations in policy outcomes. In other words, we contend that membership change and procedural change are neither *necessary* nor *sufficient* conditions for policy change.

Are Membership Change and Procedural Reform Necessary or Sufficient for Policy Change?

In order to assess the validity of our propositions, let us consider the following cross classification:

		Membership Change	
		Yes	No
Procedural Change	Yes	a	b
	No	c	d

9

Here we conceive of membership turnover and procedural reform as simple yes-no events and seek to determine how various combinations of these events produce (or fail to produce) policy change (as recorded in cells a through d). The following logical conditions on the cross classification are deduced in a straight-forward fashion:

1. If *procedural change* is *necessary* for policy change, then cells c and d must contain "no's"—no procedural reform implies no policy change. If *procedural change* is *sufficient*, then cells a and b must contain "yes's"—procedural change implies policy change.
2. If *membership turnover* is *necessary* for policy change, then cells b and d must contain "no's"—no membership change implies no policy change. If *membership turnover* is *sufficient*, then cells a and c must contain "yes's"—membership change implies policy change.
3. If *both* are *necessary* for policy change, then cells b, c, and d must contain "no's"—the failure of either procedural reform or membership turnover to materialize implies no policy change. If *both* are *sufficient*, then cell a must contain a "yes"—procedural and membership changes imply policy change.

The following illustrations should convince the reader that neither procedural reform nor membership turnover (nor both) is necessary or sufficient.

Procedural Change Is neither Necessary nor Sufficient

To show that procedural change is unnecessary as a general rule for policy change, we must uncover instances of "yes" in cells c or d. Many instances can be cited in which changes in the nature of the membership without alterations of the rules (cell c) produce different policies. One example is the Voting Rights Act and the host of other liberal legislation that passed the 89th Congress as a result of the large group of freshmen swept into the House by the Johnson landslide. Another example, which exhibits the effect of membership change over a longer period of time, is the demise of the House Internal Security Committee (HISC). In 1961 only 6 liberals opposed funds for HISC (née HUAC), while 412 members supported funds. Over the years, however, support deteriorated as subsequent funding votes show:

1963: Funding passed 386-20.

1965: Funding passed 360-29.

1967: Funding passed 350-43.

1969: Funding passed 305-51.

1971: Funding passed 300-75.

1973: Funding passed 289-101.

In December 1974, the Democratic Steering and Policy Committee presaged the end, assigning only Richard Ichord (the sitting chairman) to HISC, and in January 1975, the Democratic Caucus killed the committee by voice vote.

Though more difficult to discover, instances of policy change associated with membership and procedural *stability*—"yes" in cell d—do exist. One of the most dramatic is the 1964 Civil Rights Act. Before President Kennedy was shot, the bill was almost certainly dead. During the Congress there were no procedural changes that affected the bill; nor was there significant intra-Congress membership change. Yet after the assassination, the bill passed. Here changed circumstances and changes in executive leadership, not congressional reform or membership change, were the bases for significant policy change.

These examples undercut the necessity of procedural reform for policy change. Other illustrations prove the additional fact that the former is not always sufficient for the latter. That is, there exist instances of "no" in cells a and b. Agricultural policy in the 94th Congress illustrates how procedural changes (and, as it happens, membership change) did not produce notable policy departures—"no" in cell a.[1] Few parts of the Congress have seen so much change in so little time as the Agriculture Committee of the House in 1975. First, it had seen tremendous membership turnover. Only 6 of the Democrats (out of 27) and 2 of the Republicans (out of 14) had been members of the committee in the 91st Congress. Indeed, a majority of the Democrats and half the Republicans were new to the committee in 1975. These were, moreover, different kinds of members. In 1970, Southerners accounted for 14 of the 19 Democratic seats (74 percent); by 1975, Southerners comprised only 37 percent of the Democratic membership. The mean conservative coalition support ratio dropped from 70 to 45 for Democrats and from 78 to 56 for the full committee between the 91st and the 94th Congresses. Reform also struck the committee. The Democratic Caucus deposed the old and conservative William Poage of Texas as chairman and ratified in his place young and liberal Thomas Foley of Washington. The new chairman and the committee's Democratic majority produced a new set of rules which democratized the committee's operations and incorporated all the main provisions of the "Subcommittee Bill of Rights" (Rohde 1974) passed by the Caucus in the previous Congress.

Despite these changes, the behavior and policy output of the committee changed little. Unlike a number of other committees in the 94th Congress, there was (with the exception of a single subcommittee) little change in the level of activity on Agriculture. There was also little evidence of policy innovation or different policy outcomes in committee. One major reason for the lack of change is that the jurisdiction of the committee remained narrowly confined to agricultural issues. The new members, while liberal on other issues, retained the same parochial interests with respect to agriculture as their conservative predecessors had. The old members had been able to satisfy these interests within the old committee structure, and the new members did the same, despite procedural reforms.

Democratic committee assignments in the 1960s and 1970s serve as another illustration of the insufficiency of procedural reform for policy change—"no" in cell b (Shepsle, 1978). From the revolt against Speaker Cannon to the 94th Congress, these assignments were made by the Democratic members of the Ways and Means Committee. In December 1974, however, the Democratic Caucus transferred the committee assignment authority to the Steering and Policy Committee, made up of elected representatives of geographic zones, members of the party leadership, and appointees of the Speaker. The faces were different on the two committees (only one member served on both), and the makeup of the two committees differed somewhat in terms of ideology, party support, and seniority. Nevertheless, the motives of the respective members of the two committees regarding the making of committee assignments, the environmental constraints on the two committees, and their respective decision-making procedures remained virtually identical. The consequence? Secular changes in Democratic committee assignments, begun before the procedural reform, continued and few departures in actual assignments that could be traced to the reform were visible in the 94th Congress (Shepsle 1978).

Membership Turnover Is neither Necessary nor Sufficient

To dispose of the argument that membership turnover is necessary for policy change, we illustrate instances of "yes" in cells b and d. A significant procedural change, in the absence of much membership turnover, occurred in the 94th Congress with the alteration of Senate Rule XXII, the rule governing cloture. The requirement was changed from two-thirds of the membership present and voting to three-fifths of the entire membership (60 votes). On the basis of one year's performance, it appears that the new Rule XXII has had a substantial impact, although there was no marked change in the nature of the Senate's membership as a result of the 1974 elections. One analysis argues that cloture has been attempted more frequently and has been achieved proportionately more often under the new rules. "Senators know that the 60-vote burden is easy to overcome. As a result, they tend to more readily vote for cloture. The filibuster has lost its power" (Mondale 1976). Here, then, is a rules change that had an effect without prior substantial or significant membership change.

The passage of the 1964 Civil Rights Act—"yes" in cell d—is another illustration that contradicts the claim that membership turnover is necessary for policy change.

The sufficiency of membership turnover is contradicted by "no's" in cells a and c. The lack of change in agricultural policy discussed above again illustrates the insufficiency of membership turnover in spite of procedural changes that were expected to have policy import ("no" in cell a). A resounding "no" in cell c is found in the frustration of liberal legislation by an "unreformed" Rules Committee in the 86th Congress, despite the swelling of liberal ranks in the 1958 elections.

Membership Turnover and Procedural Reform (Jointly) Are neither Necessary nor Sufficient

A "yes" in cell b, c, or d is required to reject the necessity of the joint changes in membership and procedures for policy change. The changes in Senate Rule XXII, the Voting Rights Act of 1965 (or the demise of HISC), and the 1964 Civil Rights Act, respectively, satisfy that requirement—the joint change is not necessary for significant policy change. Nor is the joint change sufficient for policy change, as the absence of change in agricultural policy in the 94th Congress demonstrates ("no" in cell a).

Discussion

In general, policy outcomes are the consequence of three factors: the rules under which decisions are made, the preferences of the decision makers, and the situations or circumstances in which the decision makers find themselves (Rohde and Spaeth 1976). In any given area of decision, the rules divide the set of conceivable outcomes into those that are feasible and those that are not. Some results are made easy to achieve, while others are rendered virtually impossible; the preferences of some actors are advantaged, while those of others are disadvantaged. Similarly, the changing preferences of actors (or replacement of the actors themselves) are important in determining outcomes in different policy areas. Finally, varying circumstances can lead the same decision makers to one outcome at one time and to another at some other time.

Thus, each of these three factors—rules, preferences, and circumstances—has an effect on outcomes. Of course, this does not imply that each is equally important in every issue area, nor even that each is of consequence in all policy realms. To the contrary, our point is that the impact of each of these factors—their decisiveness in determining outcomes—will vary from one area of decision making to another, as Table 2-1 suggests. The case of the oil depletion allowance repeal, on the one hand, and the absence of change in agricultural policy in the 94th Congress, on the other, reveal the two extreme cases in which membership change, procedural reform, and propitious circumstances produce very different results.

Table 2-1
The Absence of a Systematic Relationship between Procedural and
Membership Changes and Policy Change: Some Examples

		Policy	
Cell	Condition	Change	No Change
a	Membership and procedural change	Repeal of oil depletion allowance in 1975	Agricultural policy in the 94th Congress
b	Procedural change	Change in Senate Rule XXII	Democratic Committee assignments in the House
c	Membership change	Voting Rights Act of 1965; Demise of HISC	Liberal legislation in the 86th Congress bottled up in House Rules Committee
d	Neither membership nor procedural change	1964 Civil Rights Act	Aid to Education in 1950s

The oil depletion allowance had long been a *bête noire* of liberal legislators. Yet, while they had been able to reduce its impact, they had not been able to get an up or down vote on the allowance on the floor because most bills from Ways and Means came to the floor under a rule prohibiting amendments (Manley 1970). But, in 1973 the Democratic Study Group proposed a new rule, approved by the Democratic Caucus, requiring a special Caucus meeting to be called if a committee chairperson is seeking a closed rule for a bill and 50 members of the Caucus file notice that they wish to offer an amendment. If the Caucus votes to support the petitioning members, the Rules Committee Democrats are obliged to vote to make the amendment in order on the floor. William Green (D-Pa.), a member of Ways and Means, invoked this procedure when he proposed an amendment to repeal the oil depletion allowance entirely in February 1975. The Caucus voted 153-98 to order Rules to permit floor consideration of the amendment, and two days later the House passed the Green amendment, 248-163. Of 73 freshman Democrats voting, 67 (or 92 percent) supported the amendment, while only 54 percent of nonfreshman Democrats and Republicans voted for it. In the 1974 elections, the Democrats won 49 seats that were previously occupied by Republicans. Among these Democrats, the vote on the amendment was 47-2 in favor. If they all had voted nay, the amendment would have lost. While it may be unlikely that all would have opposed the amendment, it does seem probable that with a large share of these votes against the amendment, enough additional votes could have been acquired to defeat it.[2] Therefore, it would seem reasonable to conclude that the rules change regarding the closed rule, the membership change in the 1974 elections, and the poor political circumstances in which the oil companies found themselves all combined to produce repeal of the oil depletion allowance.

The opposite occurred in the case of agriculture. Despite compliance with the "Subcommittee Bill of Rights," major personnel change on the House Agriculture Committee, and relevant political circumstances such as spiraling food prices, questionable overseas grain sales, and a mobilized consumer interest, agricultural policy displayed no new departures.

A Modest Proposal

To give some theoretical content to the proposition that reforming rules and/or membership is neither necessary nor sufficient for policy change, we must provide some logical links between institutional structure, membership preferences, and policy outcomes. In this concluding section, we offer a modest proposal to that end. Our proposal provides some analytical leverage at the expense of oversimplification; but, as in most other complex endeavors, one must learn to walk before one can run.

Let us suppose that a *policy choice* is characterized by a choice of level on each of n dimensions, so that it may be represented by a point in an n-dimensional coordinate system. Figure 2-1 represents the space of alternative policy choices for $n = 2$. By arbitrarily setting the status quo at the origin, 0, the point (x_1, y_1) represents an alteration of the level of policy on both dimension X and dimension Y, while $(x_2, 0)$ and $(0, y_2)$ represent changes in policy affecting only the X and Y dimensions, respectively.

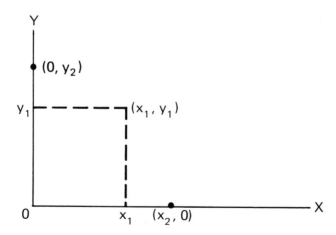

Figure 2-1

The *preferences* of each individual member may be represented in the policy space by his/her optimum (or most preferred) point and indifference contours. It is considerably simpler, though technically problematic (see McKelvey 1976; Plott 1976),[3] to suppose that member preferences are aggregated (normally by majority rule) into a membership preference relation. Thus, in Figure 2-2, a dominant coalition prefers any point on III-III' to any point on II-II', and any point on II-II' to any point on I-I', but is indifferent among the points on any one line (say, *a* and *b* on line III-III'). Membership preferences *may* change—producing membership indifference contours of different shape or slope from those of Figure 2-2—through membership turnover or a change in procedures. Replacing conservatives with liberals, Republicans with Democrats, or members with one set of policy priorities with those with another will, upon aggregation, generate a different membership preference relation (providing, of course, the new members actually have different preferences—hence the emphasis on "may"). Procedural changes may accomplish the same effect by empowering a different class of dominant coalitions.[4]

Procedural rules have another effect. They partition the space of outcomes into those that are consistent with the rules and those that are not.[5] The rule that requires the appropriation for a given policy not to exceed the authorization level for that policy is an example of this type of *partitioning rule*. In Figure 2-3, a legislative committee has authorized K dollars for a particular policy area consisting of two activities—X and Y. The rule relating appropriations to authorizations restricts the appropriations committee in the obvious way: it may appropriate no more than K dollars to activity X (in which case it purchases *a* "units" of X and none of Y), no more than K dollars to activity Y (in which

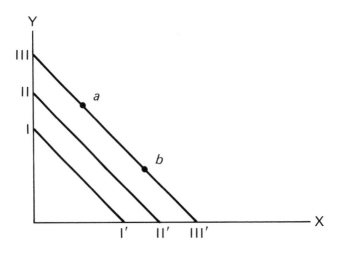

Figure 2-2

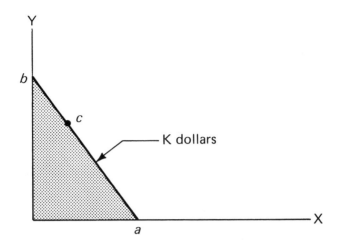

Figure 2-3

case it purchases *b* "units" of *Y* and none of *X*), or some mix of the two activities so long as the amounts spent do not sum to more than *K* dollars (as is the case at point *c*). The shaded region in Figure 2-3 defines the set of *rule-constrained feasible outcomes*.

Figure 2-4 provides another illustration where, in this case, several rules qua constraints are operative. The arrows point in the direction of feasibility, and the shaded region gives the set of points that is compatible with *all* the constraints simultaneously.

We may now combine Figures 2-2 and 2-4 to represent both feasible alternatives (as defined by the rules qua constraints) and membership preferences (as defined by the aggregate indifference contours) in the same diagram. This is accomplished in Figure 2-5. The optimum point is that point in the feasible set lying on the highest indifference contour.

With these concepts we are now prepared to inquire into the effects of changes in rules and changes in membership preferences.[6] Since we presume a modicum of rationality on the part of members, our principal concern will be with the effect of preference and rules changes on the location of the optimum. Throughout we maintain the most elementary structure—linear constraints and linear indifference contours in two dimensions—though the analysis can easily be extended to more complicated arrangements.

First, consider the effect of membership turnover. It should be noted immediately that membership turnover and changes in the aggregate membership preference relation are *not* equivalent. Members may change; but their goals, objectives, and interests may not. The preferences of the representative of Iowa's

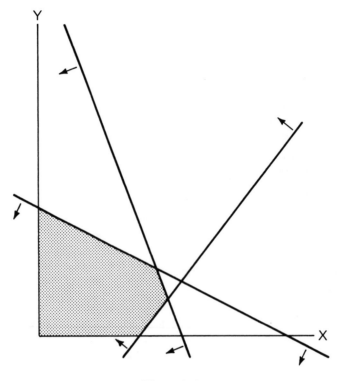

Figure 2-4

3d district did not change dramatically in many policy areas when Charles Grassley replaced H.R. Gross.

Second, even when the aggregate membership preference relation does change, it may have no effect on the optimum. In Figure 2-5, the indifference contours may be rotated in a counterclockwise direction by an angle as large as θ_1 without affecting the optimum; it may be rotated in a clockwise direction by an angle as large as θ_2, again with no change in the optimum point.

These two points, then, serve as a basis for the conclusion in the earlier part of this chapter. Membership turnover is not a sufficient condition for policy change because that turnover may either leave the aggregate membership preference relation intact or not alter it enough to "pick up" a different optimum.

Nor is membership turnover necessary for policy change. The feasible region of Figure 2-5 is reproduced in Figure 2-6 as the area bounded by the line segments 0a, ab, bc, cd, and d0, with the optimum at b. Now suppose that the rule represented by constraint ab is relaxed. That is, it is shifted vertically to

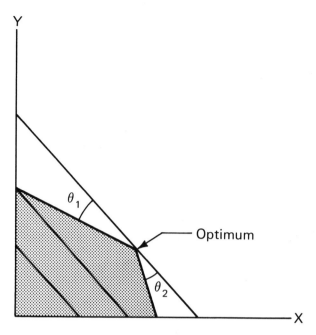

Figure 2-5

$a'b'$ so that, after the "reform," the new set of rule-constrained feasible points is the area bounded by the line segments $0a'$, $a'b'$, $b'c$, cd, and $d0$. Membership preferences remain fixed, but the point b is no longer optimal. Rather, the point b', lying on a higher indifference contour, may now be reached. The conclusion? Membership turnover is not necessary for policy change.

The same kind of analysis may be used to demonstrate the relationship between rules changes and policy outcomes. Returning to Figure 2-5, notice that the optimum falls at the intersection of two of the three constraints. The third constraint, then, is *nonbinding* and may thus be altered in a variety of ways without changing the optimum. In fact, for the more cynical, it is the obvious candidate for "cosmetic reform"—a change in rules that leaves the status quo intact! Even the two binding constraints can change without affecting the optimum. The upper constraint can be rotated clockwise by an angle as large as θ_1, and the lower counterclockwise by an angle as large as θ_2, with no apparent change in outcome. Thus, reforming the rules is not sufficient for policy change.

Figure 2-7 demonstrates that rules reform is not necessary either. With the same rules as in Figure 2-5 in effect, a slight rotation in the aggregate membership indifference contours changes the optimum point from b to b'.

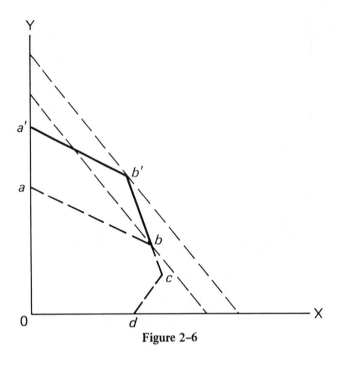

Figure 2–6

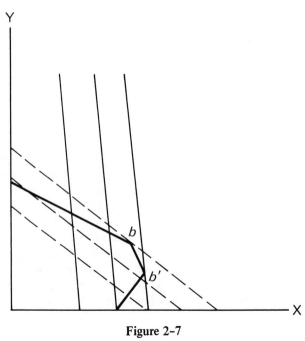

Figure 2–7

Conclusion

Policy change, for whatever purposes, cannot be ensured in a complex arena like the Congress by simple changes in rules, personnel, or circumstances. Sometimes these factors may conspire to produce change; sometimes they will fail. While we may have been unfair to the authors cited in the introduction who argued in behalf of structural or personnel change, and while our own analysis and examples have been very simple, the basic point of this brief chapter stands: political change is a messy business; it is often difficult to understand and almost always challenging to engineer. Whether the game is understanding or engineering, the observer ought to take a theoretical look before leaping. We believe the constrained maximization approach presented here provides a promising theoretical format for thinking about legislative reform.[7]

Notes

1. This discussion is adapted from Ornstein and Rohde (1977).

2. Recall that there were 98 votes in the Democratic Caucus against permitting the amendment to be offered, while there were only 69 negative votes from Democrats on the floor.

3. As is well known, most rules for aggregating "well-behaved" individual preferences do not produce "well-behaved" group preferences. In particular, the problem of cyclic group preferences—a majority prefers a to b, b to c, but c to a, so that no point is undominated—is a very strong prospect. In this case, a transitive membership preference relation does not exist; nor do the membership indifference contours of Figure 2-2.

4. This was the effect of the change in the definition of cloture in the Senate. In the case of House Democratic committee assignments, too, a new dominant coalition was created not by membership turnover but by procedural change.

5. Rules, of course, do other things as well. In particular, rules constrain *behaviors* (for example, no proxy voting on the floor) that have indirect impact on membership choices. In this chapter, however, we confine ourselves to the class of rules that restricts outcomes directly.

6. Our discussion remains abstract, but particular congressional activities are easily accommodated. Shepsle (1975) uses this approach to model committee assignments and Shepsle (1978, chap. 11) adapts this approach to examine the effect of increasing resource endowments on legislative oversight activities.

7. A theory of legislative outcomes underscoring the varying effects of rules, preferences, and circumstances is still not in sight, though scholars have begun nibbling around the edges. For an overview of approaches, see Ferejohn and Fiorina (1975).

3

Legislative Reform and Legislative Turnover

E. Lee Bernick and
Charles W. Wiggins

Membership turnover traditionally has been viewed as undesirable for state legislatures (Rosenthal 1974; Ray 1974). Rapid turnover is thought to result in inadequate use of legislative manpower and to contribute to deficient lawmaking. The importance of turnover is such that in its tenth anniversary report, the reform-oriented Legis 50 (formerly the Citizens Conference on State Legislatures 1975, pp. 18-20) pinpointed turnover as a major ailment of state legislatures and endorsed efforts to determine the forces "which shape turnover." As it stated (p. 20), "The area [legislative turnover] is admittedly broad and poorly explored, but it is central to continuing efforts to strengthen people working in the legislative system and to build general public support for that system."

Our present understanding of the major factors associated with state legislative turnover is based upon aggregate data analysis, much of which comes from Rosenthal's (1974) systematic work. Rosenthal found wide variation in the rate of turnover between and within the 50 states during the period under study (1963-1971) but determined that 30.4 percent was the average rate of turnover. He found party system variables (such as party competition and party integration) to have some importance, but electoral factors (that is, frequency of elections and reapportionments, election-to-election voting variations, etc.) were substantially more important causes of instability in legislative membership. While some political institutional factors—size of legislature and length of legislative session—were important, lawmaker compensation was the most important factor associated with legislative turnover.

In a related study covering 1897-1967, Ray (1976) examined the turnover rates for eight states. He concluded, like Rosenthal, that the rate of turnover has been on a gradual but steady decline. Moreover, Ray found a decline in the number of legislators who voluntarily retire. In fact, in five of the eight states, electoral defeat was a more important cause of departure than voluntary retirement.

An unfortunate aspect of much research on state legislative turnover is its heavy reliance on aggregate data. Such data may well hide important underlying factors that explain why individual lawmakers do not continue their state legislative careers (Ranney 1962). Therefore, we analyze the roots of legislative

This is an updated version with an expanded data base of our earlier article, "Legislative Turnover Reconsidered," *Policy Studies Journal*, 5 (1977).

turnover by examining individual nonreturning lawmakers' personal assessments of their failure to continue legislative service. On balance, our aim is to ascertain whether legislative reform directed at correcting insitutional factors as well as improving personal rewards will significantly alter the level of legislative turn-over.

Methods and Data Collection

In 1975, 98 nonreturning state senators in 11 diverse American states were identified.[1] Questionnaires were subsequently sent to the 95 living senators who had served during the 1973-1974 sessions but who were not sworn in for another term in 1975. Follow-up communications resulted in a final return rate of 84 percent (80 of the 95).[2]

The questionnaire consisted of both open- and closed-ended items designed to determine why nonreturnees did not continue their legislative careers. The initial question ascertained whether the nonreturnees had been defeated in a reelection bid or had not sought reelection to his/her other legislative seat. Those reporting primary or general election defeats were classified as involuntary nonreturnees (along with those who had passed away). An additional open-ended question directed at those who reported voluntary retirement asked them to relate the major reason(s) for their voluntary departure. Next, the voluntary nonreturnees were asked to indicate on a 5-point scale the relative importance of a battery of factors frequently cited as major reasons for lawmakers' decisions not to continue legislative service (Rosenthal 1974; Keefe and Ogul 1973, pp. 127-30). (See Table 3-2 for items.)

Besides ascertaining the legislators' attitudes toward legislative life, additional personal background information from each legislator in the sample was collected to understand why solons leave the legislature. Included were questions concerning the legislator's political socialization, partisan affiliation, and the standard demographic variables (sex, education, occupation, place of residence, and term of office). Each legislator's assessment of the balance of power between the executive and legislative branches was also determined, since unhappiness with the legislature relative to the governor may color a legislator's opinion of the utility of legislative service.

Discussion

The figures in Table 3-1 reveal that in 1974 a little more than one-third (36.4 percent) of all the senatorial seats to be filled were vacated. This level corresponds closely to Rosenthal's (1974) previous findings. Again, like Rosenthal, we found a wide range in the level of turnover within the 11 states—the lowest,

Table 3-1
Pattern of Turnover in Eleven State Senates, 1974-1975

	Contested Senatorial Seats[a]	Number of Nonreturnees[b]	Number Defeated for Election	Number Who Voluntarily Withdrew to:		Number of Respondents[c]
				Seek Another Office	Return to Private Life	
Florida	20	11	3	3	5	9
Idaho	35	8	2	2	4	8
Iowa	25	7	1	4	2	6
Michigan	38	16[b]	7	2	5	10
North Dakota	27	8[b]	2	0	6	7
Oklahoma	24	10[b]	6	1	2	8
Oregon	15	10	5	2	3	9
Pennsylvania	25	6	2	0	4	5
Texas	15	4	1	3	0	4
Vermont	30	10	4	2	4	9
Wyoming	15	8	2	1	5	5
Totals	269	98	35	20	40	80

[a]These figures represent the actual number of seats up for election in 1974 for each state.
[b]Two senators in Michigan and one in Oklahoma died; thus, the total potential senators in the sample is 95.
[c]These figures represent the number of respondents to the mail survey of living nonreturnees.

24 percent, in Pennsylvania and the highest, 67 percent, in Oregon. Of the 98 seats vacated, a sizable number of nonreturnees leave the legislature involuntarily through defeat or death. Out of the 98 nonreturning legislators 38 (or 39 percent) did so involuntarily, including, of course, the 3 who passed away.[3] In 3 of the 11 states—Oklahoma, Michigan, and Oregon—involuntary departure accounted for at least half the turnover. The magnitude of forced retirement confirms earlier findings that this mode of departure must be given serious consideration in evaluating legislative turnover (Ray 1976). Moreover, it highlights a first and important consideration in attempts at legislative reform: a large portion of the turnover problem will *not* be affected, simply because of the dynamics of the electoral process.

Despite this large group that leaves involuntarily, a substantial percentage (61.2 percent) leave voluntarily. What are the major reasons given by these nonreturnees for leaving the legislature? And how do these explanations relate to reform proposals often discussed?

Answers to our open-ended question reveal that legislators leave office voluntarily for two general reasons: to pursue other public office or to return to private life. Of the voluntary nonreturnees in our sample 33 percent gave as their primary reason for departure a decision to seek other public office, while the remaining 67 percent expressed their desire to return to private life. While those two categories of responses provide a general impression of why individuals leave the legislature voluntarily, they fail to specify the basis of any underlying dissatisfaction with legislative life, or those factors essential to an adequate evaluation of legislative reform proposals.

The battery of close-ended questions, shown in Table 3-2, tap specific sources of satisfaction or dissatisfaction among the voluntary nonreturnees. The items are grouped into four general categories: institutional, legislative efficacy, career, and personal. An examination of the responses suggests that institutional, legislative efficacy, and career considerations are rather unimportant in the lawmakers' decisions. More specifically, there was no item within the three categories that a majority (or even 35 percent) of the legislators considered important in their decision to discontinue legislative service.

In contrast to these three categories is the personal dimension. On two items, personal financial burden and interference with personal family life, there were substantial minorities (45 and 47 percent, respectively) who believed they were important considerations in their decisions not to return. Most important in lawmakers' deliberate decision not to return are the personal business demands placed upon them. One could argue that the 67 percent who responded affirmatively to this item were merely expressing their dissatisfaction with the financial rewards of legislative work. Increasing the legislators' salaries may appear initially to be an appropriate remedy for this concern; however, data in Table 3-2 regarding institutional factors reveal the relatively insignificant role that salary plays overall in the decision of voluntary nonreturnees to forgo further legislative service.

Table 3-2
Voluntary Nonreturnees' Attitudes toward Components
of Legislative Life (Percentages)

	Very Unim- portant				Very Im- portant	
	1	2	3	4	5	
Institutional						
Salary too low	39	16	11	9	25	N=45[a]
Length of session too long	41	17	15	15	12	N=43
Poor staffing of legislature	51	19	10	12	7	N=44
Legislative Efficacy						
Inability to accomplish desired goals	45	21	17	12	5	N=43
General frustration with job	43	17	21	17	3	N=43
Public support too low	47	21	7	9	16	N=44
Career						
Never intended to serve any longer	36	14	26	10	14	N=43
Chance for a better public office	50	10	12	5	24	N=42
Personal						
Personal business demands	21	7	5	17	50	N=43
Poor health	70	11	9	2	7	N=45
Personal financial burden	33	16	7	12	33	N=44
Interference with personal family life	21	19	14	21	26	N=44

[a]The N's vary as a result of missing data.

Correlates of Turnover

What factors appear to be associated with the voluntary nonreturnee's decision to leave? The ensuing analysis will look first at the personal characteristics of the legislators to determine if the nonreturnees form a distinctive group. As one might expect, there was a definite tendency for the nonreturnees to be male rather than female (less than 6 percent were women). However, this finding is of little significance since an overwhelming number of state solons are male (Jewell and Patterson 1977, p. 72). Similarly, the former legislators had high educational attainments (74 percent with a B.A. or better), but this is also insignificant since legislators tend to have higher than average levels of education (Jewell and Patterson 1977, pp. 70-72).

We looked next at the length of legislative service of the nonreturnees, expecting to find that the former legislators had long tenures in office. Unhappiness with legislative life, it was hypothesized, is a slow and gradual process and, as a result, former legislators would be individuals who had served a long time—five or more terms in office. The actual tenure distribution of the voluntary nonreturnees, however, is primarily bimodal; consequently, it does not completely support our assumption. Of the nonreturnees 23 percent served the expected five or more terms, but another 23 percent had served only one term! One possible explanation for the bimodal tenure distribution would be that the first-term nonreturnee group consists mostly of those who sought another political office, but the data do not completely support this. Of the first-term nonreturnees 45 percent sought another office, but the remaining 55 percent returned to private life. Apparently disenchantment with legislative life can be acquired very quickly. (The reason that the first-term retirees most often cited was a desire to return to private business.)

The residency pattern of the nonreturnees was the next characteristic evaluated. We expected the former solons to come mostly from rural districts. As the legislature becomes more professional, rural legislators were expected to be less willing to give up the time necessary to continue in office. Another group of rural legislators was expected to retire voluntarily to seek higher political office. The opportunity structure to run for other political offices is usually greater in rural areas and, as a result, the voluntary retirees seeking another office would be composed largely of rural solons (Jewell and Patterson 1977). However, the data do not support such expectations. While there was a slight tendency—51 percent of the nonreturnees were from rural districts—the difference was so insignificant that firm conclusions cannot be made. Moreover, a majority of solons seeking another office were from urban constituencies—only 43.7 percent came from rural districts. With both the expectations rejected, this variable must be dismissed as a factor explaining legislative turnover.

What role does political socialization play in the legislators' decision to retire? Individuals socialized early should be more tolerant of the political process. On the other hand, an individual socialized later in life would have low tolerance for the process and, therefore, have a tendency to withdraw more easily. Consequently, we expected to find more of the former legislators to have been socialized later in life. Contrary to this expectation, there was no significant tendency for the former legislators to have been socialized later; instead, they appear to have been politicized at varying stages of their life cycles.[4] On the whole, the background characteristics of the legislators have not proved to be fruitful in explaining why people leave the legislature voluntarily.

Three additional variables were explored for their ability to explain turnover: the nonreturnees' attitude toward executive-legislative relations, their majority-minority status, and the professionalism of the legislature. It was believed initially that former senators might be distinguished by their attitude toward the balance of power between the chief executive of the state and the legislature. Legislators who perceive the legislative branch to be dominated by the governor, and as a result weak and ineffectual, will not see the efficacy of continued legislative service and, as a consequence, would resign or pursue another office. With this in mind, we asked the nonreturnees to indicate whether they thought a proper balance existed between the two branches when they were in the legislature.[5] Surprisingly, 80 percent of the former senators agreed that there was a proper balance; in fact, the nonreturnees have a slightly higher level of agreement than the senators currently serving (75 percent of whom found the balance acceptable) (Bernick and Wiggins 1977). Thus, few solons leave to express their low esteem of the legislature vis-à-vis the governor's office.

The second variable, majority-minority status, focuses on the partisan attachments of nonreturnees. Legislators may decide to leave as a consequence of inequalities in treatment resulting from their partisan identification. More specifically, minority-party members may not receive all the perquisites of office (for example, secretarial assistance, office space, committee assignments) afforded majority-party members. In a system where minority-party members "walk" while majority members "ride," it may not take the former long to yield to the other pressures of office (for example, "personal business demands") and, as a consequence, leave.[6] Therefore, we expected more of the nonreturnees in our sample to come from the minority party than from the majority party. After ascertaining the party identification for each of the nonreturnees, we determined the majority-minority status for the entire sample. Most nonreturnees do not actually come from the minority party, as we had expected. In fact of the senators who voluntarily left office in our study, 79 percent came from the majority.[7] Coming from the minority party, in and of itself, is not sufficient cause for voluntary retirement. A more plausible notion is that voluntary nonreturnees may be a part of a frustrated faction within the majority party. The legislators' realization that they may be unable even to accomplish their own personal goals as members of the majority party may frustrate them and encourage them to withdraw from legislative life. This is an interesting supposition that should be tested in greater depth in the future.

The last variable deals with the professionalism of state legislatures and its effect on legislative turnover. Our assumption was that the setting of the unprofessional legislature would offer fewer inducements for continued legislative service, resulting in a legislator's decision not to return. Conversely, the more professional the legislature, the less likely lawmakers are to submit to outside pressures and not return. The proportion of nonreturnees in professional and nonprofessional legislatures in the study was compared to the number of seats contested in 1974 to test this hypothesis.[8] The number of voluntary nonreturnees as a percentage of the contested seats in the less professional legislature was 17.4, while in the more professional legislature the figure was 22.5 percent. With a significantly higher proportion of nonreturnees coming from professional legislatures, the hypothesis must be rejected. In sum, none of the factors expected to explain legislative turnover proved satisfactory, further confirming the complexity of the turnover problem and the unsatisfactory nature of present-day reform proposals.

Office Seekers versus Returnees to Private Life

So far we have looked at the voluntary nonreturnees and have found their motives for leaving were ones not easily remedied by reforms offered in the literature. Furthermore, our inability to explain legislative turnover with a variety of independent variables does not offer much encouragement to those who seek an easy solution to this difficult problem. While the research, to this point, has not been very encouraging to legislative reformers, an additional question should be investigated before we dismiss reform as futile.

A sizable minority (33 percent) of the nonreturnees left to pursue another office. Our task is to determine if this group is significantly different in their attitude toward legislative life from the other voluntary nonreturnees. More specifically, do the two groups differ on the closed-ended items used previously (see Table 3-3)? If significant differences are present, they might have implications for our evaluation of previous reform proposals. We might, for example, find that legislators seeking another office have attitudes toward legislative life that reforming the size and structure of the legislature can change.

Little or no differences (less than 10 percent) were found between the two groups on five items (length of session, public support too low, poor staffing, interference with family life, and personal financial burden) (see Table 3-3).

A difference of 10 to 20 percent was found between the groups on four items, with those seeking other office more concerned about their inability to accomplish desired goals and those returning to private life more concerned about their personal health, private business demands, and general frustration with the legislative job. Differences greater than 20 percent were found on three items. Other office pursuers attributed more importance to salary and (of course) their chance for better public office, while a larger proportion of those returning to private life indicated they never intended to serve an extended period in the legislature.

The three items with the greatest difference have differing implications for this study. First, the 22-point difference on the "never intended to serve any longer" item is deceptive from the standpoint that neither group believed it was important—30 percent of those returning to private life as compared to 8 percent of the "office seekers." Second, the difference (60 percentage points) for the "chance for a better public office" item was to be expected since it taps the reason one group left; in fact, it is surprising that the difference between the two

Table 3-3
Attitudes toward Components of Legislative Life, Controlling
for Mode of Voluntary Departure (Percentages)

	Seeking Another Office[a]		Return to Private Life	
Institutional				
Salary too low	50	(N=12)[b]	28	(N=33)
Length of session too long	25	(N=12)	26	(N=31)
Poor staffing of legislature	16	(N=12)	20	(N=32)
Legislative Efficacy				
Inability to accomplish desired goals	25	(N=12)	13	(N=31)
General frustration with job	8	(N=12)	23	(N=31)
Public support too low	25	(N=12)	25	(N=32)
Career				
Never intended to serve any longer	8	(N=12)	30	(N=31)
Chance for better public office	70	(N=12)	10	(N=30)
Personal				
Personal business demands	58	(N=12)	70	(N=31)
Poor health	0	(N=12)	12	(N=33)
Personal financial burden	50	(N=12)	42	(N=32)
Interference with personal family life	50	(N=12)	·43	(N=32)

[a]These figures represent the percentage of each group who believed the item to be important or very important.

[b]The N's reflect the total number of respondents in the group answering the item and vary from item to item because of missing data.

groups was not greater. The third item, salary too low, has implications for reform that we discuss below.

At least 50 percent of the "office seekers" found five items (personal business demands, financial burden, interference with family life, salary too low, and a chance for better office) to be important in their decision to leave. As one might expect, the "chance for better office" had the highest percentage for this group (70 percent) while "personal business demands" was important to 58 percent. Meanwhile, 50 percent of the former legislators thought interference with family life to be an important consideration.[9] As noted previously, these are disincentives for continued legislative service that researchers have not adequately broached, and as a result, these findings offer legislative reformers little comfort.

It appears from the data that, while some legislators may leave solely for ambition, there are a number who seek other offices for financial reasons. Of the voluntary retirees who sought another office 50 percent believe low salary and personal financial burdens were important factors in their seeking another office. For these legislators, a better office means a better salary. This would seem to confirm, to a point, Rosenthal's (1974) finding that salary was the most important reason for legislative turnover. However, we must remember that we are merely talking about 50 percent of a group that comprises only a third of all the legislators who leave voluntarily. (In other words, if 100 legislators leave voluntarily, only 17 would have left because of the poor salary.) In short, for a small minority, if legislative life were made more attractive financially, their proclivity to leave might be reduced.

For the nonreturnees going back to private life, only 3 out of the 12 items had any widespread impact as reasons for leaving. Of these former solons 43 and 42 percent believed interference with personal family life and personal financial burdens, respectively, had an important effect on their decision not to return. "Personal business demands" was, by far, the most important item for this group, with 70 percent finding it important. As previously mentioned, personal business demands should not be equated with low legislative salary especially since only 28 percent believed low legislative salary was important. Thus, the burden placed on personal business reflects not merely low financial rewards, but also a more complex phenomenon. To our knowledge, purposeful reforms to alleviate the private business concerns of many American state solons have yet to be developed by engineers of legislative modernization and improvement.

In sum, there are no substantial differences between the two groups of voluntary nonreturnees. The only exception was the somewhat greater emphasis placed on financial rewards for a small percentage of other office seekers.

Conclusion

The implications of this study for legislative reform directed at decreasing legislative turnover are twofold. First, frequently proposed legislative reform will have only a minor impact in terms of reducing the overall turnover rate of legislative personnel since a considerable amount of the turnover (59 percent) results from electoral defeat, death, or the legislative position having been used as a necessary and sometimes repugnant stepping stone to higher office. Certainly it is outside the bounds of reasonableness to suggest that we might meddle with the electoral process to reduce legislative turnover. Nor is it responsible to constrain artificially an individual's personal political ambition. On the other hand, for a small group of nonreturnees increased salary may be sufficient to induce them to continue in office. On the whole, purposeful reforms enhancing the perquisites of legislative officeholding will have only marginal consequences in reducing the overall turnover rate.

Second, the disincentives lawmakers cite as reasons for their voluntary departure argue against the effectiveness of the changes often espoused in the reform literature. Personal business concerns and interference with family life are complex social problems that are difficult to incorporate into present frameworks of legislative reform. We believe personal business demands will continue to be very salient to solons until being a legislator becomes a full-time position.

When legislators leave the state capitol (upon completion of the session) and return home with six to nine months of the year left, they most assuredly will work in some profession. Short of prohibiting the active participation in any other occupation while in office or making the position full time, there does not appear to be any viable solution. And even these solutions are not entirely satisfactory.

On the other hand, the potential benefits of not tampering with turnover should be recognized. Having one-third of the contested seats filled by new people at each election may be very healthy for the political system. Individuals with new ideas and new hopes can be brought into government. Further reduction of turnover may weaken seriously our basic concept of representative government.

In conclusion, the need to develop a new reform framework, or at least to reevaluate currently popular proposals, is the major implication of this brief and admittedly limited analysis of state legislative turnover.

Notes

1. The eleven were selected to represent a wide range of states with regard to party competition, political culture, region, level of urbanization, and other environmental factors.

2. After all the surveys were returned, we contacted local state officials to make a final determination about the data regarding the defeat and career patterns of the nonreturnees.

3. The number of incumbents defeated probably is somewhat greater than normal because of the idiosyncratic influence of the Watergate issue on the 1974 election. In addition, two of the states had just reapportioned, a factor previously found to be important in legislative turnover.

4. The former legislator's political socialization was assessed with the following question: "When did you become interested in politics?"

1. In elementary school
2. In high school
3. In college
4. Working on your first job
5. Recently
6. Don't remember

5. The question used to tap the nonreturnees' opinion on this matter was, Do you think there is a proper balance between the legislature and the governor?

6. This hypothesis was suggested by Larry Margolis, Executive Director of Legis 50, in personal correspondence with the authors.

7. One could argue that more nonreturnees come from the majority party simply because it has more senators. However, the majority held, on the average, only 67 percent of the seats in the 11 state legislatures.

8. Based upon slight modification of an index developed by John G. Grumm (1971),

High Professional: Florida, Michigan, Oregon, Pennsylvania, Texas

Low or Nonprofessional: Iowa, Idaho, North Dakota, Oklahoma, Vermont, Wyoming.

9. Finding interference with family life to be important to former solons seeking another office would appear to be contrary to what one might expect. However, the other office being sought may allow for a more stable family life. This would be especially true for any position that would not demand the former solon and his/her family to be separated (even if one ran for Congress, the entire family could travel to Washington).

4

Seniority and Democratic Reforms in the House of Representatives: Committees and Subcommittees

John E. Stanga, Jr. and
David N. Farnsworth

In recent sessions of the House of Representatives, Democrats have reformed their rules and procedures regarding both the assignment of members to committees and the selection of committee and subcommittee chairpersons. This chapter examines the effect of these reforms on the traditional seniority system.

Surface indications suggest that the reforms have done much to modify what Fenno (1965, p. 71) calls the "seniority-protégé-apprentice system." A new committee assignment procedure in the 94th Congress led to the selection of seven freshmen for seats on the Ways and Means and Appropriations Committees. Such action seems to be an abrupt departure from past practices which required members to serve apprenticeships of two or more terms before becoming eligible for assignment to elite committees (Fenno 1973, p. 19). An even greater violation of strict seniority rules occurred in the 94th Congress when Democrats removed three standing committee chairmen.

Although they received less public attention than the reforms of the 94th Congress, reforms in subcommittees, effective in the 92d and 93d Congresses, also appear to have weakened the seniority system. These reforms prohibit members from holding more than one subcommittee chair and require a vote by committee Democrats to fill vacant subcommittee chairs.[1] Preliminary evidence suggests that the new rules on subcommittees have resulted in the awarding of subcommittee chairs to younger, less senior members (Ornstein 1975a, p. 102).

It is important to examine the effect of the Democratic rules on seniority because seniority is related to institutional characteristics of the Congress since 1910. Seniority rules foster both the decentralization of power within the House and the norm of subject-matter specialization. Hence, modification of seniority rules may lead to a different method of allocating institutional power in which committee autonomy and expertise are relatively unimportant.

In addition, the seniority system is frequently associated with the lack of congressional responsiveness to public opinion. Masters (1961, p. 348), for instance, describes the old system of making committee assignments as "ill-designed for flexibility and responsiveness to electoral changes and public

We are indebted to our colleague Jim Kuklinski for valuable suggestions.

opinion trends" and compares it to "a firmly entrenched bureaucracy capable of considerable resistance to any pressures placed upon it." Similarly, Eulau (1967, p. 224) asserts that senior members of important committees "can afford to be irresponsive [sic] —being safe and senior, they can elude the wrath of the electorate." If Masters and Eulau are correct, then it is reasonable to expect the modification of seniority rules to lead to a more responsive Congress.

We are unable here to assess whether reform has undermined the system of expert, subject-matter standing committees or has led to more congressional responsiveness to public opinion. However, we are able to examine several hypotheses dealing with the effect of reform on seniority. Because certain assumptions about the seniority system underlie notions regarding congressional decentralization and responsiveness, our findings should aid in interpreting studies of the broader effects of reform on congressional policy and the policy-making process.

Freshmen Assignments: Hypothesis 1

Hypothesis 1 holds that freshman Democrats will have received "better" standing committee assignments in the 94th than in earlier Congresses. This hypothesis could be tested by examining the percentage of freshmen assigned to various types of committees over time. Percentages could be based on either the best assignment each freshman received or the total number of freshman assignments made, but neither procedure reveals anything about the success of freshmen in getting good assignments as compared with their numerical strength. Accordingly, we employ a measure of over/underrepresentation to test the hypothesis.

Table 4-1 indicates that in the 94th Congress freshman Democrats constituted nearly 10 percent of all Democrats on exclusive committees and about 31 percent of those on semiexclusive committees.[2] Although considerably higher than comparable percentages for prior Congresses, these figures do not reflect freshman numerical strength as do the indices of over/underrepresentation. These indices show freshmen to be (1) consistently underrepresented on exclusive committees and only slightly less so in the 94th than in the 90th or 93d Congresses; (2) overrepresented less on semiexclusive committees in the 94th than in any of the three previous Congresses; and (3) overrepresented on nonexclusive committees in the 94th Congress, even though they were underrepresented on them in five of the previous seven Congresses. While providing modest support for hypothesis 1, the data do not reveal a markedly better pattern of freshman assignments in the 94th Congress than in the previous seven Congresses.

Freshman assignments were not "better" in the 94th Congress because they were already good in previous Congresses. The reformed procedure largely

Table 4-1
Indices of Under/Overrepresentation of Freshman Democrats on House Committees, 87th to 94th Congresses

	87th	88th	89th	90th	91st	92d	93d	94th
Exclusive Committees								
Representation Index[a]	-100	-100	-86.3	-68.4	-100	-73.6	-68.2	-62.9
Percent of Freshman Democrats on Exclusive Committees	0.0	0.0	3.3	1.8	0.0	3.4	3.4	9.6
(N)	(55)	(55)	(61)	(55)	(55)	(58)	(58)	(73)
Semiexclusive Committees								
Representation Index	0.0	16.4	14.5	17.5	35.4	32.6	24.3	18.1
Percent of Freshman Democrats on Semiexclusive Committees	6.9	16.3	27.6	6.7	11.1	17.1	13.3	30.6
(N)	(189)	(178)	(206)	(178)	(180)	(182)	(180)	(216)
Nonexclusive Committees								
Representation Index	8.7	-11.4	-22.9	-70.1	-50.0	-13.2	6.5	14.7
Percent of Freshman Democrats on Nonexclusive Committees	7.5	12.4	18.6	1.7	4.1	11.2	11.4	29.7
(N)	(106)	(121)	(140)	(120)	(122)	(152)	(149)	(182)
All Committees								
Representation Index	-13.0	-10.7	-13.3	-26.3	-14.6	-1.6	3.7	6.6
Percent of Freshman Democrats on Standing Committees	6.0	12.5	20.9	4.2	7.0	12.7	11.1	27.6
(N)	(350)	(354)	(407)	(353)	(357)	(392)	(387)	(471)
Democratic Freshmen as a Percentage of All Democrats	6.9	14.0	24.1	5.7	8.2	12.9	10.7	25.9
(N)	(263)	(258)	(295)	(248)	(243)	(255)	(243)	(289)

[a] A negative sign indicates underrepresentation. See S. Verba and N.H. Nie, *Participation in America: Political Democracy and Social Equality* (New York: Harper & Row, 1972), p. 96. The index was computed as follows:

$$\frac{\text{Percent of freshmen of all Democrats} - \text{Percent of freshmen of all Democrats by type of committee}}{\text{Percent of freshmen of all Democrats}} \times 100$$

symbolized changes already underway. Gertzog (1976, pp. 695-700), for example, found that the prospect of freshman assignments to semiexclusive committees has risen sharply in the postwar period. The reformed committee assignment procedure may accelerate changing patterns of freshman assignments; it did not precipitate them.

Improved freshman assignments may be a function of the leadership's tendency to increase committee size and to award more dual committee assignments to accommodate demands from members (Westefield 1974, pp. 1595-96). Interestingly, Table 4-1 reveals that freshman Democrats have been overrepresented on standing committees since the 93d Congress. Should such a pattern continue, freshmen would be virtually assured of assignment to at least one semiexclusive committee.

Overall Seniority as a Criterion for Assignments: Hypothesis 2

Hypothesis 2 holds that the overall influence of seniority on committee assignments was less in the 94th than in previous Congresses. Hypothesis 1 treated seniority as a dichotomous variable by comparing freshmen with nonfreshmen. Hypothesis 2 treats seniority as a continuous variable measured in years of uninterrupted congressional tenure. If seniority was less important in the 94th than previous Congresses, members of Congress newly assigned to high-status committees in the 94th Congress should have less seniority than those newly assigned to such committees in previous years.

To determine the overall effect of seniority on committee assignments, the 89th and 94th Congresses are compared. The two are comparable in that both had unusually large freshman classes. The influx of large numbers of new members alone may mean that freshmen would receive relatively better assignments and veterans relatively less prestigious assignments than in sessions with few freshmen (Asher 1975, pp. 221-222; Fenno 1965, p. 71). The comparison of the the 89th and 94th Congresses allows a test for the effect of the new committee assignment procedure while "controlling" for any bias associated with large freshman classes.

In comparing the two Congresses, mean seniority was calculated for Democratic members assigned to each standing committee. These means were in turn converted into standardized Z scores to account for intersession variations in overall House Democratic seniority or committee seniority levels. A two-way analysis of variance was used to analyze the data, with the Z scores constituting the dependent variable. Congressional session (89th, unreformed; 94th, reformed) and type of committee (exclusive, semiexclusive, nonexclusive) constitute the nominal independent variables. Table 4-2 indicates that the only statistically significant F ratio is for the type of committee.[3] The data fail to support hypothesis 2.

Table 4–2
Two-Way Analysis of Variance for Seniority of Democratic
Committee Assignees by Session and Type of Committee

Sources of Variance	df	F Ratio	P
Congressional Session	1	.307	n.s.
Type of Committee	2	10.777	.001
Interaction	2	1.182	n.s.
Within (error)	33		

Seniority of Subcommittee Chairpersons: Hypothesis 3

With certain limited exceptions,[4] the new Democratic rules prohibit members
from chairing more than one subcommittee. Beginning with the 92d Congress,
the reform apparently was instrumental in increasing the number of Democrats
chairing subcommittees. Table 4–3 indicates that the practice of holding dual
subcommittee chairs was virtually eliminated with the 92d Congress. The number of members chairing subcommittees rose from 97 in the 87th Congress to
127 in the 94th Congress. The percentage of Democrats chairing subcommittees

Table 4–3
Members Chairing Two or More Subcommittees before and after Reform[a]

	Prereform					Postreform		
	87th	88th	89th	90th	91st	92d	93d	94th
Members Holding Two or More Chairs (N)	16	18	22	20	22	0	0	4[b]
Subcommittee Chairpersons (N)	97	93	95	107	98	111	117	127
Number of Sub-committees (N)	116	113	119	133	123	111	117	131
Subcommittee Chairpersons as Percentage of All House Democrats	36.8%	36.0%	32.2%	43.1%	40.3%	43.5%	48.1%	43.9%

[a]Because it was exempted from the subcommittee reforms, the House Administration Committee is not included in these tabulations. All other subcommittees of standing committees
are included.
[b]Three of the four dual chairs were held by members of the Small Business Committee
which became a standing committee in the 94th Congress. The committee was exempted
from the subcommittee reforms for only the 94th Congress.

was greater in every postreform Congress than in any prereform Congress. The increased opportunities Democrats have to chair subcommittees in recent reformed Congresses should mean that subcommittee chairpersons do not have to wait as long for their chairs and that they should be less senior than their counterparts in earlier Congresses. Hypothesis 3 holds that the reforms produced subcommittee chairpersons with less congressional seniority than such chairpersons in "unreformed" Congresses.

The first method of testing the effect of the subcommittee reforms on seniority is simply to compare the percentage of subcommittee chairpersons with five or fewer terms of congressional seniority in "reformed" and "unreformed" Congresses. To control for overall levels of seniority in the House, this percentage is also expressed as a ratio to the percentage of all House Democrats with five or fewer terms of service. If seniority is becoming less important in the awarding of subcommittee chairs, the percentages should rise over time while the ratios should increase. Table 4-4 indicates support for hypothesis 3. The percentage of junior subcommittee chairpersons has risen in each reformed Congress, and the ratios are also higher in the reformed period than in the unreformed.

While it seems that the subcommittee reforms have had at least a short-term effect of producing less senior subcommittee chairpersons, the mere fact that the overall seniority of subcommittee chairpersons has declined says nothing about their seniority on particular committees. Even if all committees have been affected by the reforms, the effects may not be the same. Indeed, starting with Fenno's (1973) observation that all standing committees are not alike, Ornstein and Rohde (1977) show that different committees react differently to change.

Table 4-4
Subcommittee Chairpersons with Five or Fewer Terms of Congressional Service[a]

Subcommittee Chairpersons with Five or Fewer Terms of Service	Prereform					Postreform		
	87th	88th	89th	90th	91st	92d	93d	94th
As Percentage of All Subcommittee Chairpersons	28.5%	31.9%	28.6%	25.6%	29.3%	31.5%	37.6%	38.2%
As Ratio to All Democrats with Five or Fewer Terms	.47	.52	.43	.43	.47	.55	.66	.60

[a]The House Administration Committee is not included in these tabulations.

Hence the second test of hypothesis 3 begins with the assumption that congressional reform does not have uniform effects for every committee.

In this second test, we employ the following three measures to examine subcommittee seniority by parent committee for reformed and unreformed Congresses: (1) the percentage of subcommittee chairpersons with five or fewer terms in the House, (2) the mean seniority of subcommittee chairpersons, and (3) the variability of subcommittee seniority. The third measure is the mean coefficient of variability for both the five unreformed and the three reformed Congresses (see Blalock 1972, p. 88). The smaller the coefficient, the more homogeneous a committee's chairpersons for that particular grouping of congressional sessions, that is, the more representative any individual of mean subcommittee seniority. While the mean coefficient of variability cannot be used in isolation to test hypothesis 3, it is an interpretative aid. One or two exceptionally senior subcommittee chairpersons, for instance, can contribute to a high committee mean that masks the entry of junior subcommittee chairpersons to a committee. In such cases, the mean coefficient of variability should rise and provide a clue as to what is happening.

Reporting the above three measures, Table 4-5 indicates that mean subcommittee seniority was less in reformed than unreformed Congresses for eight committees. Too much should not be made of this change, however, for at least three committees. The change in seniority for the Armed Services Committee is negligible. The Science Committee was low in seniority for both periods, fourth lowest for the unreformed and second lowest for the reformed. And an examination of mean seniority by individual congressional sessions indicates that the decline in seniority for the Merchant Marine Committee began in the 88th Congress, long before the reforms.[5]

Of the remaining five committees for which subcommittee seniority declined, the change is clearest for the District of Columbia, Agriculture, and Judiciary Committees. The drop in mean seniority for the latter is partly a result of Emanuel Celler's defeat, but this alone does not account for the increase in the percentage of junior subcommittee chairpersons. For the District of Columbia and Agriculture Committees, an examination of seniority patterns by individual sessions indicates that the trend toward declining seniority began at least in the 91st Congress. This trend, however, became markedly evident for both committees in the 93d and 94th Congresses. Junior subcommittee chairpersons have outnumbered veterans on Agriculture since the 91st Congress and on District of Columbia since the 92d.

For the Banking and Currency and Public Works Committees, decreases in mean seniority have been accompanied by increases in the mean coefficients of variability and the percentage of junior subcommittee chairpersons. Seniority has declined on Banking and Currency, despite the fact that Wright Patman chaired at least one subcommittee during each of the eight Congresses. Both the percentage of junior chairpersons and the mean coefficient of variability increase

Table 4-5

Seniority of Subcommittee Chairpersons, by Committee, for Unreformed (87th to 91st) and Reformed (92d to 94th) Congresses

| Committee | Unreformed Congresses | | | | Reformed Congresses | | | |
	$\bar{X}$ (yr)[a]	$\bar{X}$ Varia- bility[b]	Percent Junior[c]	N of Sub- committees	$\bar{X}$ (yr)	$\bar{X}$ Varia- bility	Percent Junior	N of Sub- committees
Agriculture	16.9	.48	27.5	69	12.0	.91	66.7	30
Appropria- tions	20.8	.32	7.6	66	22.7	.33	2.6	39
Armed Services	21.3	.26	9.8	51	21.2	.36	0.0	21
Banking	20.4	.50	16.1	31	18.5	.58	25.0	24
District of Columbia	16.2	.49	26.9	26	6.3	.62	87.5	16
Education and Labor	9.5	.33	66.7	36	14.9	.23	13.0	23
Government Opera- tions	15.3	.37	27.5	40	16.4	.36	9.5	21
Interior	10.8	.38	56.7	30	11.9	.33	38.1	21
Interna- tional Relations	13.4	.26	30.0	50	16.3	.43	33.3	30
Interstate Com- merce	15.6	.22	8.0	25	18.7	.16	0.0	16
Judiciary	20.7	.47	7.9	38	15.7	.55	36.9	19
Merchant Marine	14.3	.34	25.0	28	12.6	.37	37.5	16
Post Office	7.8	.58	77.4	31	9.3	.34	68.4	19
Public Works	16.8	.21	6.7	35	14.4	.44	36.9	19
Science	11.1	.56	61.4	22	8.6	.44	66.7	18
Veterans	9.6	.49	55.6	27	9.7	.72	80.0	15

[a]Mean seniority of subcommittee chairpersons by parent committee.

[b]The mean coefficient of variability.

[c]Subcommittee chairpersons with five or fewer terms in Congress.

sharply for the Public Works Committee in the reformed period. Of the nine junior subcommittee chairpersons on the committee during both periods, seven served during the reformed Congresses.

While Table 4-5 indicates that subcommittee seniority on a few committees has declined since the subcommittee reforms, perhaps the most striking aspect of the table is evidence of the trend toward *increasing* seniority for subcommittee chairpersons on some committees. The most striking case is the Education and Labor Committee: two-thirds of its subcommittee chairpersons were junior members during the unreformed Congresses as compared with only 13 percent during the reformed period. Although less obvious, similar trends appear under-way with the Commerce and International Relations Committees, and perhaps even with the Interior and Government Operations Committees. While subcom-mittee seniority is also higher for the Appropriations and Post Office Commit-tees, the seniority ranking of these committees is similar in both the reformed and unreformed periods.

In summary, then, Table 4-5 suggests that the effects of reform are far from clear. Indeed, the fact that seniority has increased on some committees may indicate that seniority patterns have less to do with internal reform than with changing patterns of policy concerns among members of Congress. Education and Labor, for instance, may be rising in status as the House becomes more liberal. Its activist subcommittees (Fenno 1973, pp. 101-105) and a stabilized chairperson's role should make the committee especially attractive to liberal careerists. Similarly, liberals may have developed an increased awareness of the importance of congressional oversight, perhaps reflected in the rising number of freshman requests for assignment to the Government Operations Committee (Ornstein and Rohde 1977, pp. 197-99). And the desire to have the House play a larger role in foreign policy making may make International Relations popular, at least for those relatively free from an electoral sanction. Thus, it may not be that the subcommittee reforms reflect the abandonment of seniority rules as much as a manipulation of those rules to benefit Northern liberals rather than Southern conservatives (compare Orfield 1975, pp. 29-34). If so, committees like Education and Labor, International Relations, and Government Operations may become prime examples of the "liberal" bias of the seniority system.

What is needed to clarify these mixed feelings is to link changes in seniority patterns directly to the subcommittee reforms. Logically, the reforms should have their greatest impact on committees whose subcommittee chairpersons frequently held dual chairs before the reforms. Accordingly, Table 4-6 attempts to relate committee patterns of subcommittee seniority to the frequency of holding dual chairs. The holding of dual chairs is measured in two ways. First, for members holding dual chairs on the same committee, we divide the number of subcommittee chairs available on a committee during unreformed Congresses by the number of committee members actually chairing subcommittees. The result is the average number of chairs held per chairperson, by standing commit-tee. Second, for members holding dual chairs on different committees, we divide the number of outside chairs held during unreformed Congresses by the number of subcommittee chairpersons on the parent committee. The result is the per-centage of a committee's subcommittee chairpersons who chaired subcom-mittees outside their parent committee. In addition, Table 4-6 indicates the difference in mean seniority of subcommittee chairpersons between reformed and unreformed Congresses.

Table 4-6 does suggest a connection between the frequency of holding dual chairs and a subsequent decline in subcommittee seniority, particularly for com-

Table 4-6

Dual Subcommittee Chairs, Internal and External, by Standing Committee

Committee	Average Number of Internal Chairs per Chairperson, 87th to 91st Congresses		Percentage of Subcommittee Chairpersons Holding External Chairs, 87th to 91st Congresses		Difference in Mean Seniority between Reformed and Unreformed Congresses
Judiciary	1.41	(38)[a]	7.4	(27)[b]	−5.0
Armed Services	1.31	(51)	2.6	(39)	−0.1
Agriculture	1.30	(69)	11.3	(53)	−4.9
Public Works	1.30	(35)	14.8	(27)	−2.4
Science	1.16	(22)	5.3	(19)	−2.5
Banking and Currency	1.11	(31)	39.3	(28)	−1.9
Merchant Marine	1.04	(28)	29.6	(27)	−1.7
Appropriations	1.04	(66)	1.6	(63)	+1.9
Interior	1.03	(30)	34.5	(29)	+1.1
Government Operations	1.00	(40)	50.0	(40)	+1.1
District of Columbia	1.00	(26)	46.2	(26)	−9.9
Veterans Affairs	1.00	(27)	33.3	(27)	+0.1
International Relations	1.00	(50)	26.0	(50)	+2.9
Post Office	1.00	(31)	22.6	(31)	+1.5
Commerce	1.00	(25)	16.0	(25)	+3.1
Education and Labor	1.00	(36)	2.8	(36)	+5.4

[a]N is the total number of subcommittee chairs available.

[b]N is number of subcommittee chairpersons.

mittees with a history of internally held dual chairs. Those committees for which subcommittee seniority declined during the reformed period tend to be those on which internal chairs were frequently held. The exception is the District of Columbia Committee. While this committee has no history of internally held chairs, nearly half of the committee's chairpersons held chairs on other committees. And 11 of the 12 outside chairs were on clearly superior committees such as Foreign Affairs, Agriculture, and Banking and Currency. Yet the holding of external subcommittee chairs does not appear to be generally related to declines in seniority. The Government Operations Committee, for example, had the highest percentage of chairpersons holding outside chairs, but the seniority of its subcommittee chairpersons rose.[6]

In summary, there is some empirical support for hypothesis 3, but the hypothesis must be modified substantially. The subcommittee reforms had the greatest effect on committees whose members frequently held two or more internal chairs. Committees that did not award dual chairs seemingly were not affected by the reforms, at least insofar as the seniority of subcommittee chairpersons is concerned. Again, the reforms may be less than they seem because many standing committees were already reformed.

Conclusion and Implications

This chapter has analyzed the effects of two sets of Democratic reforms on seniority in the House of Representatives. Neither the committee assignment nor the subcommittee reforms have resulted in abandonment of the seniority principle. Freshmen continue to be underrepresented on the most influential committees; multiterm apprenticeships remain the usual prerequisite for assignment to them. Exclusive committees remain largely the preserve of senior members. Similarly, there has been no dramatic decline in the seniority of subcommittee chairpersons on most standing committees; such decline as exists is largely restricted to a few committees. The seniority of subcommittee chairpersons on most committees has remained stable or has increased.

It is, of course, possible that we have observed the reforms for too short a period to detect their effects. Should they remain in force long enough, the reforms might substantially modify the "seniority-protege-apprentice system." It is more likely, however, that the effects of reform have been diluted not by lack of time but by informal adjustment of seniority rules before the legal reforms occurred. In contrast with earlier Congresses, freshmen in recent years have not been disadvantaged in receiving assignments to semiexclusive committees. The committee assignment reforms, from one perspective, merely recognized the preexisting right of a member to obtain at least one good, if not top, committee assignment. Similarly, the subcommittee reforms did not affect seniority more because most standing committees had an equitable internal distribution of subcommittee chairs before the reforms. Committees on which dual internal chairs were common were those most affected by the reforms. Finally, even before the reforms, the probability that a member might chair a subcommittee was quite good. Not including the House Administration Committee, about 37 percent of Democrats chaired a subcommittee in the 87th Congress. And close to 29 percent of subcommittee chairs were held by junior members.

There are also some indications that change occurs more through the reform of political values than through the manipulation of legal rules. As the House has become more liberal, the pecking order of committee desirability may be changing. If so, this may account for the rise of subcommittee seniority on a committee like Education and Labor. A new set of political priorities may help explain why subcommittee chairpersons on some committees became more senior during a period when rules changes were designed, in part, to undermine seniority.

What do the formal and informal reforms portend regarding the future of the House? The development of the seniority system and of expert, subject-matter standing committees has helped enable the House to play a major, if frequently negative, role in shaping public policy (Polsby 1971; Polsby, Gallaher, and Rundquist 1969). The decline of seniority as an important criterion for assigning members to semiexclusive committees and the practice, increasing in frequency, of awarding members dual committee assignments may prefigure an attendant decline in the norm of subject-matter expertise. If so, such a decline may enhance the relative influence of the bureaucracy and the President in policy making.

Another possibility is to interpret the new pattern of House committee assignments as evidence of a nascent system of congressional party responsibility (compare Uslaner 1974). With power centralized in the Democratic Caucus and the formal leadership, the House could develop a more positive, innovative policy-making role without losing influence vis-à-vis other policy-making institutions. Aside from the constraints of divided government and a decentralized party system, this prospect seems unlikely, however, because of the decentralizing effects of the subcommittee reforms (compare Dodd 1977, pp. 269-307; Dodd and Oppenheimer 1977a, pp. 33-37, 40-49).

While the subcommittee reforms have created incentives for further decentralization of the House and thereby make a centralized party-responsibility system unlikely, it is by no means certain that the subcommittee reforms will preserve the norms of subject-matter expertise. The decline of the traditional, seniority-based committee system, the changing nature of political priorities in the House, and the exacerbation of decentralization as a result of the subcommittee reforms are more likely to portend policy individualism and what Mayhew (1974a, pp. 61-73) calls "position taking" than either a party-responsibility system or the old pattern of governance through expert, subject-matter standing committees. After all, a subcommittee chair provides a good forum for position taking, particularly on committees like Education and Labor.

If this structured speculation is correct, then, as Cover and Mayhew (1977, p. 70) observe in another context, the reformed House may be one "that looks more like the Senate—weak party leadership, nonhierarchical committees, a vast number of subcommittees in which congressmen can do their own thing, an ethic of member equality and member individualism." Insofar as the House is changing to meet this description, that change seems to have been wrought not so much by new rules as in spite of old ones.

Notes

1. The subcommittee reforms are described in Rohde (1974); Ornstein (1975a); and Dodd and Oppenheimer (1977a).

2. Freshmen include those resuming interrupted service but not those taking office after initial committee assignments were made. Because of their special nature, the Official Conduct and Budget Committees were excluded from analysis.

3. The Official Conduct, Budget, and Small Business Committees were excluded from analysis. A new committee in the 94th Congress, the latter had the highest mean seniority of assignees of any regular standing committee, even

though 10 of the 14 assignees were freshmen. To include it in the analysis produces results only slightly weaker than those reported in Table 4-2. Having moved from semiexclusive to nonexclusive status between the 89th and 94th Congresses, the Science Committee was classified as nonexlusive for the analysis of variance.

4. The House Administration Committee was exempted.

5. In addition to the three measures reported in Table 4-5, we also examined the ratio between mean subcommittee seniority on a committee and the mean seniority of all House subcommittee chairpersons. These ratios suggest the same findings as our other measures. For the Merchant Marine Committee, for instance, the ratios indicate that only in the 87th Congress was the mean subcommittee seniority greater than the mean seniority of all subcommittee chairpersons.

6. The coefficient of determination (R^2) between the frequency of holding *internal* chairs and mean change in subcommittee seniority is .20; the coefficient between mean change and the holding of *external* chairs is .05.

5 The Effects of Seniority Reform on Three House Committees in the 94th Congress

John Berg

Political reformers in the United States have sought for many years to modify or abolish the congressional seniority system. At the same time, some students of Congress have held that such a reform would make relatively little difference (Hinckley 1971). Long frustrated, the reformers won a partial victory at the start of the 94th Congress when the Democratic Caucus in the House removed three committee chairmen, replacing them with less senior members (Table 5-1). This reform victory makes it possible to compare seniority with a real alternative and to evaluate its effects empirically. This chapter is a preliminary effort at such an evaluation, based on the three committees' activities during the 94th Congress.

Before starting, we need to clarify two issues. First, what did the reformers expect to achieve? The answer varies; speaking broadly, there were three groups of reformers and three goals. Liberals wanted Democratic chairpersons to be

Table 5-1
Age and Seniority of New and Old Chairmen, Three House Committees, as of January 1975

Committee and Chairmen	Seniority Rank before Change	Years in Congress	Age
Agriculture			
Old: W.R. Poage (D-Tex.)	1	38	75
New: Thomas Foley (D-Wash.)	2	10	45
Armed Services			
Old: F. Edward Hebert (D-La.)	1	34	73
New: Melvin Price (D-Ill.)	2	30	70
Banking and Currency			
Old: Wright Patman (D-Tex.)	1	46	81
New: Henry Reuss (D-Wis.)	4	20	62

subordinate to the majority of the Democratic Caucus, which was and is liberal. "Good government" supporters wanted to get the most competent chairpersons possible, or at least to eliminate those who were plainly incompetent. And junior members of Congress wanted to increase their own opportunities for job satisfaction, power, and favorable publicity. The first two groups provided most of the intellectual rationale for changing seniority; the last group provided the votes.

Second, what good features were claimed for seniority? It minimized intra-party conflict by making chair selections automatic; it kept party leaders from becoming bosses (and had been adopted for this purpose early this century); and since it rewarded prolonged service on the same committee, it encouraged specialization and the development of expertise on the part of committee members, which in turn helped Congress to keep abreast of the executive and the bureaucracy (Hinckley 1971; Price 1971; Blondel 1973). Whether these features are really advantageous can be debated—a strong leader can do good or ill, and specialist-dominated committees can serve the public or private inter-ests—but is beyond the scope of this study. (See Lowi 1969 for some of the argument.) Here we limit our concern to the actual effects of the change.

The changes are unlikely to have had significant policy effect unless, as a minimum, the new chairmen were significantly different from those they re-placed. How different were they? The were all Northerners, replacing South-erners. Ideologically, they were more liberal; Table 5-2 shows the scores of each, for the 93d Congress, on various *Congressional Quarterly* voting indices. There were marked differences between the old and new chairmen.

However, the *Congressional Quarterly* (*CQ*) indices may exaggerate the relevant differences. Each index includes votes on a wide variety of issues. They are good measures of overall liberalism and conservatism, but few members of Congress are consistently liberal or conservative in their voting. In particular, since each committee tends to attract members with similar viewpoints and interests, and these similarities among committee members are reinforced by interaction within the committee (Fenno 1973), it is possible that old and new chairpersons may have agreed with one another more often on the issues their committees dealt with than on other issues. Ornstein and Rohde (1977, p. 230) make the same point about a chair change in one of Agriculture's subcommit-tees:

While David Bowen of Mississippi (who chairs the Cotton Subcommittee) may not have a great deal in common with Thomas Abernethy, his congressional district predecessor (who also headed that subcommittee), their differences do not extend to legislation affecting cotton.

To the extent that this point applies to the chairmen of our three committees, the differences in their *CQ* scores will have relatively little relevance to their handling of the committees' work.

Table 5-2
CQ Voting Scores for Old and New Chairmen, 1973 and 1974

Representative	Conservative Coalition Support/Opposition		Party Unity Support/Opposition		Presidential Support/Opposition		
	1973	1974	1973	1974	1973	1974 Nixon	1974 Ford
Poage	81/12	83/3	41/54	24/63	54/42	60/32	57/30
Foley	23/70	13/75	81/12	80/9	37/57	51/36	50/44
Hebert	45/12	39/3	22/36	15/28	35/25	55/17	17/9
Price	20/80	29/71	94/5	88/11	33/66	55/45	50/50
Patman	30/29	35/38	50/13	51/20	26/36	45/21	41/33
Reuss	9/89	3/94	88/12	84/11	30/68	38/55	48/48
Number of Roll Calls	133	379	226	158	125	53	54

Source: Derived from *Congressional Roll Call, 1973,* and *Congressional Roll Call, 1975.*

Explanation:

Conservative coalition support/opposition: Percent of votes on which the representative supported or opposed a coalition of Republicans and Southern Democrats on those votes where a majority of Republicans and Southern Democrats opposed a majority of Northern and Western Democrats.

Party unity support/opposition: Percent of votes on which a representative voted with or against a majority of his party, on those votes where a majority of Republicans opposed a majority of Democrats.

Presidential support/opposition: Percent of votes on which a representative supported or opposed the President's position, on those votes where the President took a position.

This supposition is confirmed when we look at the six chairmen's ratings by interest groups concerned specifically with agriculture, military affairs, and business and finance (Table 5-3). In each case, the old and new chairmen were closer together on the issues relevant to their committee than on other issues. [Poage's relatively low National Farmers Union (NFU) rating probably reflects the NFU's liberal stance rather than its backing of price supports; unlike the other two interest groups, the NFU includes general legislation in its index.]

If the relevant ideological differences between old and new chairmen were small, there were marked differences in age and length of service (Table 5-1). Only on Armed Services were these small. These data suggest that, in two cases at least, the reformers may have been less interested in the chairmen's ideology than in how they ran their committees (Barone et al. 1976). The third case, Armed Services, is less clear-cut and will be discussed below.

Effects on Committee Performance

Did the changes affect committee performance? We can answer this question only if we can find a way of measuring that performance. There are two basic approaches to doing so: (1) quantitative measures, which make it possible to compress large amounts of data and reduce reliance on the subjective judgment of the researcher, but which may require the omission of relevant information;

Table 5-3
Issue-Specific Voting Indices for Old and New Chairmen, 1973 and 1974

House Member	Economic Conservatism 1973-1974	Support for Strong Military 1973-1974	Support for Farmers		General Liberalism	
			1973	1974	1973	1974
Poage	58	88	70	55	21	0
Foley	33	25	95	100	84	86
Hebert	67	100	63	25	6	6
Price	0	80	100	93	72	43
Patman	0	71	100	78	46	38
Reuss	17	10	100	63	88	96

Source: Derived from J. Barone et al., *The Almanac of American Politics* (Boston: Gambit, 1976).

Explanation:
Economic conservatism: rating by National Association of Businessmen, Inc.
Support for strong military: National Security index of the American Security Council.
Support for farmers: rating by National Farmers Union; this covers votes on both farm and nonfarm issues on which the NFU took a position.
General liberalism: rating by Americans for Democratic Action.

and (2) subjective evaluation of a committee's activity, which is susceptible to bias but can include information not quantifiable. The following will use both approaches, as they seem appropriate, in the hope that each may compensate for the weaknesses of the other.

One measure of a committee's power is its ability to get its bills passed. Fenno (1973) found that members took pride in their committees' batting averages on their bills. If chairpersons make a difference, then better chairpersons should get more of their committees' bills passed by the House. Perhaps they should also get more of them enacted into law, but here outside factors enter in. Table 5-4 compares the success rates of the three committees in the 93d and 94th Congresses, before and after the chair changes. In Table 5-5 the three committees whose chairmen were ousted are compared with six others having roughly similar jurisdictional scope and importance. Five of these six had the same chairmen in both Congresses, while the sixth, Public Works, underwent a normal change with the retirement of Chairman Blatnik (D-Minn.) at the end of the 93d. There are neither any large changes in the success rates of the three committees with ousted chairmen nor any systematic differences between these committees and the other six. If the changes did affect committee performance, this measure is too crude to detect it. The most that can be said is that the high success rates of Armed Services and Banking and Currency before the changes do not support the notion that the changes were a response to committee failure.

Table 5-4
Success of Three House Committees under Old and New Chairmen

Committee and Congress	Number of Bills and Joint Resolutions				
	Reported Favorably by Committee	Passed by House		Enacted	
		Number	Percent	Number	Percent
Agriculture					
93d	49	37	76	26	53
94th	51	42	82	34	67
Armed Services					
93d	51	50	98	45	88
94th	32	28	88	19	59
Banking and Currency[a]					
93d	51	50	98	48	94
94th	45	39	87	30	67

Source: Derived from biennial reports of the committees, committee calendars, and the *Congressional Record*.

[a]Renamed Banking, Currency and Housing at the beginning of the 94th Congress.

Table 5-5
Floor Success of Nine House Committees, 93d and 94th Congresses

| | Bills Reported Favorably by Committee that Passed on the House Floor | | | | | | |
| | 93d Congress | | | 94th Congress | | | |
Committee	Passed/Reported	Percent	Rank	Passed/Reported	Percent	Rank	Change
Agriculture	37/49	76	9	42/51	82	7	+2
Armed Services	50/51	98	2.5	28/32	88	3	−0.5
Banking and Currency	50/51	98	2.5	39/45	87	4	−1.5
Total, committees that ousted chairmen	137/151	91		109/128	85		
Education and Labor	36/41	88	6.5	27/30	90	2	+4.5
Interior and Insular Affairs	91/105	87	8	91/113	81	9	−1
Interstate and Foreign Commerce	62/66	94	4	54/64	86	8	−4
Judiciary	7/7	100	1	55/64	86	5.5	−4.5
Public Works	51/58	88	6.5	54/56	96	1	+5.5
Science and Technology	8/9	89	5	19/22	86	5.5	−0.5
Total, committees whose chairmen were not ousted	255/286	89		300/349	86		

Source: Derived from biennial reports of the committees, committee calendars, and the *Congressional Record*.

Perhaps a closer look at each of our three committees will tell us more. Ornstein and Rohde (1977, p. 234), who studied the Agriculture Committee for the period from 1970 to 1975, concluded that

congressional change has had little impact on the Agriculture Committee. The jurisdiction of the committee was confined to a narrow range of matters, and the committee attracted members who had constituencies which could be served within this range. . . . Even though the committee's structure and leadership changed in the Ninety-Fourth Congress, the nature of the membership and their goals did not, and thus the character of activity and policy outcomes did not change.

This conclusion is supported by events in the rest of the 94th Congress as well.

The Agriculture Committee had faced considerable difficulty in the 93d Congress. On July 11, 1973, an omnibus farm bill was withdrawn from consideration on the House floor when Poage was unable to hold together his coalition. He brought the bill up again eight days later, having agreed to eliminate a ban on food stamps for strikers if organized labor would support an exemption for cotton growers from a $20,000 annual limit on federal support payments; this compromise collapsed when Poage was unable to implement his part of the bargain—the food stamp ban was included over his opposition. The bill was finally passed, but it was hardly a demonstration of Poage's strength. The next year was even worse for the committee, with two major bills—an extension of the Sugar Act and an end to limitations on rice production—killed on the House floor.

These are more failures on important bills than any committee likes to have, and they may have contributed to the sentiment for ousting Poage (Barone et al. 1976; but see Hinckley 1977 for a different interpretation). But the committee continued to face difficulties under its new chairman. In 1975 the House recommitted the conference report on a bill to create a beef promotion board (although the bill was eventually enacted in 1976). An attempt to raise price supports for wheat, cotton, corn, feed grains, and milk was passed but then vetoed, as was a later bill to adjust milk price supports on a quarterly basis. These last were defeats outside the House, but they help to show that the committee faced and faces a generally difficult environment, in which nonfarm interests are increasingly powerful, so that any chairperson is likely to find consistent floor success difficult.

Ornstein and Rohde found one change in the committee's success. The percentage of Northern Democrats voting for major farm bills on the floor increased markedly in the 94th Congress, a change they attribute to a greater willingness of the committee to bargain with urban and labor interests. At the same time, there was an equivalent *decrease* in Republican support. While the available data do not sustain a firm conclusion, they suggest that the content of farm bills is becoming more consumer-oriented. If so, the change in content and the change in chairperson may reflect changes in the voting balance of the House (Ornstein and Rohde 1977, p. 235).

Although the Armed Services Committee processes numerous bills each year, the major controversies it deals with are usually included in the annual authorization for military procurement, research, and development. (A few years ago, when construction of sites for antiballistic missiles—then included in the military construction authorization—became controversial, this item was shifted into the procurement bill.) This bill is conveniently susceptible to quantitative study because the authorizations are in dollars. Moreover, there is a ready comparison available between the authorization and the appropriation; the latter is handled by a committee which did not change chairmen. Table 5-6 compares the handling of these two bills for each calendar year from 1973 to 1976. Three points stand out. First, only one committee bill was seriously cut on the floor—the authorization bill in 1973. This was a defeat for Hebert, but scarcely typical of his long career—and he recovered well in 1974, when the committee's bill was unchanged on the floor.

Second, 1975 saw both bills cut in committee substantially below the President's request. Since both committees cut deeply, the reduction cannot be attributed to the Armed Services chair change. Moreover, the absolute size of each bill was substantially higher than that of the preceding year, even allowing for the extra three-month period covered by the 1975 bill.

Third, 1976 saw not only small cuts in the President's requests, but also substantially bigger increases over the year before than in any other year. Price certainly succeeded in getting bigger military budgets passed—but so did Chairman Mahon of Appropriations, an advanced septuagenarian and a conservative Texan, who in 1975 was beginning his 41st year in the House and his 11th as Appropriations chairman. In any case, successful promotion of military spending is not the sort of effectiveness that most congressional reformers have had in mind.

Of the three new chairmen, only Henry Reuss of Banking, Currency, and Housing actively sought the job. While the committee had a high success rate under Patman in the 93d Congress, Reuss felt it was not being effective, given the magnitude of the country's problems. After becoming chairman, he launched a major study of financial institutions and their regulation and declared his intention to bring the Federal Reserve Board and its Open Market Committee under greater congressional influence. However, his record in the 94th Congress was mixed. Action on financial reform was not completed by the committee. Since this was a major task, it might reasonably be argued that this would take more than one Congress. However, Reuss was also defeated directly on some occasions. For example, the committee refused to support his attempt to order an annual percentage increase in the money supply, and the House failed to override President Ford's veto of a housing bill when Thomas Ashley (D-Ohio),

Table 5-6
Defense Budget Legislation, 1973 to 1976, as Handled by Two House Committees

Committee and Calendar Year	President's Request	Committee Recommendation		Passed by House		
		Amount	Percent below Request	Amount	Percent below Request	Percent above Previous Year
Armed Services						
1973	21,959	21,395	2.6	20,445	6.9	
1974	23,130[b]	22,642	2.1	22,642	2.1	11
1975[a]	34,126[b]	32,022	6.2	32,022	6.2	13
1976	34,219	33,400	2.3	33,300	2.7	30
Appropriations						
1973	77,251	74,494	3.6	74,489	3.6	
1974	87,057	83,700	3.9	83,394	4.2	13
1975[a]	120,976	111,894	7.5	111,894	7.5	6.7
1976	107,964	105,948	1.9	105,594	2.2	18

Source: Derived from *Congressional Quarterly Almanac*, various years. All amounts are times $1 million.
[a]Covers a 15-month period from July 1, 1975, to September 30, 1976, because of the change of the beginning date of the fiscal year.
[b]Does not include $1,300,000 requested for aid to the government of South Vietnam, which no longer existed by the time the bill was considered.

a dissident committee member, led a drive to uphold it. Table 5-7 lists the committee bills that failed of floor passage.

This is certainly not a picture of overwhelming success. However, given the scope of Reuss's plans, it is still too soon to form a judgment here. The committee was often bitterly divided under Patman, as well; this may be inherent in the subject matter (Fenno 1973 suggests this). Part of Reuss's claim was that he could work to bring it together, but he may well need at least another Congress to accomplish this.

Ultimately, our judgment of legislative reform must be rooted in some notion of the legislature's proper function in society. For the United States, at least, as Jones (1976, p. 4) puts it, "While the specific terms used may differ among scholars, there seems to be general agreement that Congress is the most critical institution for translating and aggregating the needs of people so that public policies can be developed and implemented." The evidence to date is that there has been little, if any, immediate change in the performance of these functions by the three committees in question; their translation and aggregation of popular needs in the 94th Congress was similar to that in the 93d.

However, there may well be less immediate effects. Directly, Reuss may succeed in the future in bringing more unity to the Banking, Currency, and Housing Committee; if he does so, we can expect changes in the ways policy is made. Indirectly, all chairpersons are now aware, as they were not before, that

Table 5-7
Bills Reported by Committee on Banking, Currency, and Housing
which Failed to Pass House—94th Congress

Bill Number	Brief Description	Where Defeated
H.R. 6676	To maximize the availability of credit for national priority uses.	Floor
H.R. 7590	Authorize and direct the General Accounting Office to audit the Federal Reserve.	Rules committee
S. 3013	Provide for increased participation by United States in Asian Development Fund.	Rules committee
H.R. 12112	Assistance to ERDA for nonnuclear research and development.	Floor
H.R. 14829	Develop special credit sources and technical help for self-help, not-for-profit cooperatives.	Rules committee
H.R. 14756	Create a National Commission on Neighborhoods.	Suspension calendar

Source: Derived from committee calendar.

they can be deposed. This will constrain their activities and continue the recent flow of power from committee chairpersons to party leaders, on the one hand, and to subcommittee chairpersons, on the other.

Finally, we should be aware that Congress has another function—*legitimation*, securing the consent of the people for the government and its policies. This function is aided by successful translation and aggregation of people's needs into policy, of course, but the two concepts are analytically distinct. It is quite possible to think of a reform which increases the government's legitimacy without actually improving the quality of governance. Hinckley (1977) argues that the three chairmen were deposed because they were old and Southern and had Northern replacements available, not because they were conservative, tyrannical, or incompetent. If so, this may be a case of such a reform.

Congressional Change and Foreign Policy: The House Committee on International Relations

Fred M. Kaiser

Athenian: You realize that some people maintain that there are as many different kinds of laws as there are political systems? . . . Don't think the question at issue is a triviality: it's supremely important, because in effect we've got back to arguing about the criteria of justice and injustice.

Plato, *The Laws*, Book IV.

Twenty-three centuries ago, Plato advanced the proposition that political structure affects political behavior, despite his interpretation in *The Laws* that there is only one (ideal) kind of law, the others being "bogus," approved by "unjust" systems. That classic proposition has translated well, and contemporary political scientists have questioned whether congressional reforms and reorganizations influence congressional behavior, especially public policy and relations with the executive (see, among others, Orfield 1975; Ornstein 1975b; and Rieselbach 1977a).

One method to assess many of the multiple and varied structural changes affecting Congress is to focus on a committee that has undergone major transformations in its authority, jurisdiction, and internal structure. One such unit is the House Committee on International Relations, whose name change from Foreign Affairs in 1975, symbolically reflected its metamorphosis. Moreover, the Committee's jurisdiction has been especially controversial and volatile, epitomized by the war in Indochina. Finally, foreign policy has been one area in which Congress and the relevant committees have adopted innovative and independent policy positions (Frye 1975; Orfield 1975, p. 260). Thus, the coincidental transformations, in structure and behavior, on International Relations permit an examination of the relationships between two factors—both the impact of structure on behavior and their common dependency on other independent variables. This examination focuses on three dimensions of structural change: committee authority, jurisdiction, and internal organization.

The views expressed in this article are the author's and are not attributable to any other source.

Committee Authority

The House of Representatives has remained secondary to the Senate in foreign policy formulation because of constitutional constraints, the interests and attitudes of the respective memberships, and certain institutional characteristics (Carroll 1966). Changing conditions since World War II, however, have permitted the House to improve its position in that policy arena, a situation which has benefited its principal foreign policy committee and its authority.

Of Rieselbach's (1977a) three criteria for evaluating congressional reform—responsibility, responsiveness, and accountability—responsibility refers to congressional attempts to improve its policy-making position, efforts which have been especially noticeable in foreign affairs in the 1970s. Such reform efforts transform committee authority incrementally but with substantial cumulative impact, and affect committees both as developers of relevant legislation and as beneficiaries of specific provisions in those laws. Three types of authority that have acquired added prominence—statutory reporting requirements, congressional veto, and frequent reauthorizations—have measurably increased in the field of foreign affairs. International Relations has experienced, consequently, quantitative and qualitative alterations in its authority, leading to evident changes in behavior.

Reporting requirements imposed on the executive have expanded measurably in foreign affairs (Johannes 1974, p. 13); approximately 150 such statutory obligations affect International Relations jurisdiction (U.S. House of Representatives 1976a). Required reports are especially valuable for Committee oversight, especially in a controversial policy domain, to protect and promote Committee jurisdiction (Ogul 1976, p. 179) against numerous potential rivals (Carroll 1966, p. 92).

Required reports appear relatively well used by International Relations, despite the common assumption of neglect. The only major analyses of reporting requirements were commissioned jointly by House International Relations and Senate Foreign Relations; both Committees used the Congressional Research Service to evaluate and monitor executive branch reports in foreign affairs (U.S. Senate 1976a, pp. 94–104).

The policy impact of reporting requirements is generally indirect and gradual, although under unusual circumstances it may be dramatic and immediate. One such case involved House International Relations, among other committees, and reporting obligations for covert foreign operations of the CIA. A unique reporting requirement in the 1974 Foreign Assistance Act (P.L. 93-559) requires the President to report to appropriate committees, including International Relations, on funds expended for CIA covert, nonintelligence operations in foreign countries.[1] This provision permitted appropriate committees to investigate CIA involvement in Angola in 1975, subsequent to which the activity was halted and Congress voted to terminate further United States funds.

The reporting requirement itself, the Hughes-Ryan Amendment, was added by floor amendment in the waning hours of the 93d Congress on December 30, 1974, and followed in the immediate aftermath of public allegations of improper, unethical, and illegal activities by the CIA and other intelligence agencies.

Congressional veto provisions allow deferring or disapproving executive action, by committee, chamber, or congressional resolution. Although such provisions have been adopted since at least 1932, they have experienced a "steady increase during the last fifteen years . . . especially since 1970, in both number and complexity of such legislative review and consent requirements" (Norton 1976, p. 1). Foreign affairs legislation, including foreign trade, war powers, and foreign assistance, has incorporated the congressional veto or prior review provision in 22 acts, fourth in volume among 18 different subject-matter areas (Norton 1976, pp. 117-27).

Congressional veto provisions in international relations legislation have engendered Presidential vetoes, attesting to their perceived significance to the executive. Most recently, the 1976 Foreign Assistance bill (S. 2662) was rejected by President Ford in part because it incorporated a congressional veto over foreign military arms transfers. The most prominent Presidential rejection of a congressional veto provision was Richard Nixon's veto of the War Powers resolution (P.L. 93-148), which was subsequently overriden. The War Powers resolution, affecting United States military involvement abroad, requires Presidential consultation with and reporting to Congress and certain committees, including International Relations. It also permits Congress to terminate such involvement through two mechanisms: indirectly by failing to sanction the involvement within a specified period of time, or directly by passing a concurrent resolution. After years of Senate Foreign Relations and House International Relations hearings, final congressional agreement included concessions to both the House and Senate models. Frye (1975, pp. 177-215) emphasizes the role of International Relations and the House conferees in determining the initial agenda for such a resolution as well as certain key provisions of the final conference product. Committee deliberations surrounding the War Powers resolution produced ample criticism of executive action in Indochina in addition to preparing the authority intended to prevent similar wars.

Some supporters of the resolution have concluded that it has resulted in executive branch compliance with the reporting requirements, although not with the consultation provision (U.S. House of Representatives 1975, p. VI). Yet determining whether the War Powers resolution veto provisions have discouraged extended United States military involvement is analogous to determining influentials in "nondecisions" (Bachrach and Baratz 1962). It is virtually axiomatic that numerous factors enter Presidential decisions in crisis situations, and the weight of the resolution, symptomatic of congressional antagonism to new, protracted military ventures, is impossible to assess.

Nonetheless, there is reason to suggest that the existence of congressional veto provisions encourages a type of "anticipated reaction" on the part of the administration, that is, to comply with legislatively defined conditions to avoid activating the veto sanction. At least in certain areas, as with foreign military arms sales, congressional veto provisions appear to have induced administrative compliance and even prior "clearance," according to one staffer (personal interview).

Frequent reauthorizations of programs and agency budgets seem to appear more often within International Relations' jurisdiction than in that of any other committee except Armed Services. All the major reauthorizations for programs and agencies occur either annually (for example, State Department, Board for International Broadcasting, Peace Corps, USIA, foreign military sales, international security assistance, and grant military assistance) or biennially (for example, foreign economic assistance, educational exchange program, and Arms Control and Disarmament Agency). These regular reauthorizations have gradually replaced long-term or permanent authorizations of previous decades and present expanded opportunities for policy influence. As one example, annual reauthorization for ACDA was required for 1975 expressly to provide a more intensive and comprehensive evaluation of the agency and its policies. In another instance, the Foreign Assistance Act of 1971 served to restrict CIA expenditures and transfer authority in Cambodia by imposing a ceiling on total United States expenditures in that country (Fisher 1975, p. 219).

Frequent reauthorizations have ramifications within the chamber, since the process tends to undermine the influence of the Appropriations Committee (Shick 1975). The more frequent authorizations and lengthy process limit Appropriations' time for deliberation, require use of continuing resolutions, and provide more immediate and clear signals from the authorizing committee and Congress. The resulting delay in appropriating funds is especially pronounced in foreign affairs, where for five of the past six years no foreign aid appropriation has been signed into law before the middle of the fiscal year. This suggests that the traditional conflict between International Relations and Appropriations (Fenno 1973, pp. 223-24) may have reversed, giving the advantage to the former.

Committee Jurisdiction

Committee jurisdiction has been one of the more stable elements in Congress since the Legislative Reorganization Act of 1946. However, evolutionary developments and specific alterations in formal jurisdiction, especially the House Committee Reform Amendments of 1974 (H.Res. 988), have changed the status quo, although not as appreciably as the reformers proposed. (See Davidson and Oleszek 1976 for an insightful review of this reform process.)

The alterations that resulted from H.Res. 988 affected nearly all the standing committees, but International Relations was perhaps the most substantially transformed. The Committee acquired new legislative jurisdiction over export controls (from Ways and Means, and Banking), international education (Education and Labor), international aspects of the Food for Peace program (Agriculture), trading with the enemy (Interstate and Foreign Commerce), international commodity and international trade agreements (Banking), and measures relating to international economic policy (Banking), as well as "special oversight" jurisdiction over international financial organizations (Banking) and intelligence activities related to foreign policy (Armed Services), among other areas.

This final change—oversight of foreign intelligence activities, formerly the exclusive domain of Armed Services and Appropriations—occurred in the aftermath of revelations of CIA involvement in the internal politics of Chile during the Allende administration. The realignment served as a precursor to later changes in congressional oversight of the CIA, namely, the reporting requirements included in the 1974 Foreign Assistance Act and the House and Senate select committees on intelligence in the succeeding Congress. This particular addition to International Relations jurisdiction, formally included in a floor amendment, revealed a quid pro quo quality in jurisdictional realignments between committees of roughly equivalent status. The amendment's sponsor, Clement Zablocki of International Relations, cited an "arrangement" in the original recommendations by the House Select Committee, later omitted, that prescribed a reciprocal exchange between International Relations (special oversight of foreign intelligence) and Armed Services (similar authority for arms control and disarmament) (*Congressional Record*, October 8, 1974, H 10108).

Other jurisdictional realignments profited International Relations at the expense of committees of declining or lower rankings, that is, Agriculture, Banking and Currency, Education and Labor, Interstate and Foreign Commerce, and Ways and Means. (For committee rankings during this period, see Jewell and Chi-Hung 1974; Westefield 1974; and Rohde and Shepsle 1973). International Relations also benefited from the already broader jurisdiction of its Senate counterpart, Foreign Relations, which had gained jurisdiction over similar topics when Senator Fulbright transferred chairmanships from Banking and Currency in 1959 (Bibby 1966). This suggests that representatives desired to improve the position of the House and, consequently, its principal foreign policy committee vis-à-vis the Senate and the executive. Davidson and Oleszek (1976, p. 52) developed a similar theme, emphasizing the need to reduce International Relations "dependency on State Department initiatives" and summarizing the realignments as responses to external strain as well as internal demands.

The effect of the new jurisdictional alignments on policy is seen in the 1977 International Relations Committee modification of the 1917 Trading with the Enemy Act (P.L. 65-91), legislation that had remained with Interstate and Foreign Commerce until the House Committee Reform Amendments. The

International Relations Committee approved legislation to curb the President's emergency powers, perceived as an "unlimited grant of authority" to effect import surcharges, consumer credit and banking system restrictions, foreign investment limitations on United States investors, and export regulations (House Report 95-459). As approved by the Committee and the House (H.R. 7738), the bill removes a "state of emergency" as a basis for the President's imposition of controls, establishes a new and less comprehensive set of economic controls that could be implemented during crises, requires reports to the Congress on actions taken under an emergency declaration, and provides for a congressional veto over such actions.

Internal Committee Structure

Some of the most significant structural changes on House International Relations have altered the Committee's internal organization, jurisdictional alignments among subcommittees, leadership patterns, and membership characteristics. To a certain degree, these alterations have produced related behavioral and policy transformations. The structural changes and the formal agent and date are outlined in Table 6-1.

The changes in committee structure during the 1970s reflect the variety of primary agents, including party groupings, to which congressional committees are exposed, despite the occasional implication that they are autonomous entities. These internal committee reorganizations are too numerous to elaborate in detail, but some of the more important ones and their behavioral consequences can be noted.

The House Democratic Caucus rulings in 1971 and 1973 produced the "Subcommittee Bill of Rights" (Rohde 1974), and, more importantly, their "Declaration of Independence." These changes limited each member to one subcommittee chairmanship, and had a greater impact on International Relations than on any other House committee. The large number of subcommittees on International Relations (10) and the dual chairmanships of several members produced three vacancies, which were filled by individuals who became active and autonomous leaders (Ornstein 1975a, p. 104; Maffre 1971). These three subcommittee chairmen—Benjamin Rosenthal, Lee Hamilton, and John Culver—and Donald Fraser, another new subcommittee chairman, hired their own staff and received protected jurisdictions and budgets, provisions of the "Subcommittee Bill of Rights" that were not enforced on some other committees until 1973.

The staff that these chairmen hired tended to be selected for their policy predispositions, not on the basis of more traditional criteria (for example, experience in the member's office), to have limited "Hill" experience, to have been "disaffected" members of the foreign policy apparatus (for example,

Table 6-1
Internal Changes on Committee on International Relations, 1970 to 1977

Structural Change	Formal Agent and Date
1. Three new subcommittee chairmen, acquiring authority directly or indirectly because of reforms limiting members of Congress to only one subcommittee leadership post.	1. House Democratic Caucus, 1971.
2. Committee adoption of "Subcommittee Bill of Rights" affecting subcommittee powers and authority and, in consequence, full committee chairperson's authority.	2. House Democratic Caucus, 1971; universal enforcement in 1973.
3. Expansion of total staff from 21 in 91st Congress, to 36 in 93d Congress, to 74 in 95th Congress.	3. Congress (Legislative Reorganization Act of 1970), 1970, initially. House resolution, specifically in each subsequent Congress.
4. Expansion of staff and specific provision for minority staff, effective in 94th Congress.	4. House of Representatives (H.Res. 988), 1974.
5. Change in membership size: increase in 91st and 93d Congresses and decrease in 94th Congress.	5. House of Representatives, vote at commencement of appropriate Congresses.
6. Alterations in party ratio on Committee in 90th, 91st, and 94th Congresses.	6. House of Representatives, vote at beginning of appropriate Congresses.
7. Realignment of jurisdiction between Subcommittee on Asian and Pacific Affairs and on the Near East.	7. Committee, 1971.
8. Creation of ad hoc subcommittee to investigate international drug trafficking in 93d Congress.	8. Committee, 1973.
9. Major jurisdictional realignments among subcommittees, termination of regional subcommittees, and replacement by functional subject-matter subcommittees.	9. Committee, 1975.
10. Major jurisdictional realignments among subcommittees, returning to the pre-1975 alignment, for the most part, of regional and functional subcommittees.	10. Committee, 1977.

Foreign Service, AID), to have sought a policy-influencing position, and/or to have a stronger "partisan" orientation (that is, to serve directly and exclusively the subcommittee chairman) than their predecessors and counterparts on the full committee and on most other subcommittees during the 1970s (Maffre 1971; Poole 1975, p. 32). They reflected a greater "entrepreneurial" than "professional" orientation (Price 1971).

Several noticeable differences in behavior resulted from the elevation of new chairmen and their acquisition of staff on International Relations. In quantitative terms, the number of subcommittee hearings more than doubled from the 90th Congress through the 93d Congress (U.S. House of Representatives 1976b, p. 86), an increase largely attributable to these transformations (Ornstein, 1975a, p. 104). The oversight activity rate of these same subcommittees was greater than any others on International Relations during the 93d Congress (Kaiser 1977). This indicates that both "conversion" and "opportunity" factors (Ogul 1976, p. 22) were affected, placing members predisposed to conduct oversight in positions of authority and supplementing that commitment with basic resources at the chairperson's immediate disposal. Consequently, when the exigencies of international events warranted, as during the 1973 Middle East war and subsequent Arab oil embargo, an assertive subcommittee leader (Hamilton in this case) was in a position of authority to respond.

Other new chairpersons used their posts to develop "critical alternatives," as one phrased it, to basic foreign policy assumptions and directions. Donald Fraser's subcommittee on International Organizations, for instance, conducted extensive hearings on human rights during the past three Congresses, focusing on the abusive and authoritarian aspects of regimes supported by the United States, including those in Chile, Indonesia, and South Korea. An outgrowth of these hearings, reinforced by other complementary pressures, has been the creation of an Office of Human Rights in the State Department, new policy guidelines for the United States Delegation to the UN Commission on Human Rights, and innovative policy positions regarding foreign aid, for example, legislation reducing foreign assistance to countries that systematically violate human rights. Fraser's subcommittee, with additional staff, has continued to investigate South Korean CIA influence within the United States, an inquiry that has potential ramifications for United States-Korean relations; the influence of foreign governments on United States public officials and, by extrapolation, United States policy; the connection of foreign governments to international organizations operating within the United States; and the operations of foreign intelligence agencies within the United States as a possible quid pro quo for United States CIA operations in those countries.

Other policy innovations, in consequence of the increased activism of various subcommittees, include the readoption of UN economic sanctions against Rhodesia; House termination of foreign aid to Greece in 1971; passage of the War Powers resolution; and transformation of a "transition" fund, originally intended for Rhodesia, to aid black-ruled African countries.

Jurisdictional realignments among the ten subcommittees on International Relations had been modest until 1975. The major realignments in the 94th Congress, reversed in the 95th, included four major aspects: termination of the five geographic or regional subcommittees, dating from the mid-1940s, but which were reestablished in 1977; creation of five functional subcommittees in their stead for the two-year period; modest alterations and restatements of the remaining subcommittees' jurisdictions; and creation of a Subcommittee on Oversight to replace the Special Review subcommittee. The Oversight subcommittee did not survive into the 95th Congress, leaving nine subcommittees at present.

The major realignments and reversals within a two-year period reflect both substantive and procedural disputes among the members. The rationale behind the initial realignments in 1975 had several components: to accommodate the committee's expanded jurisdictional and oversight responsibilities, to provide for more flexible and comprehensive subcommittee coverage while ending the overlap and possible competition between regional and functional entities, and to distribute subcommittee assignments and workload more equitably. There were additional reasons for transforming the subcommittee system. The changes would preclude any particular subcommittee and its members from being confined to a geographic region, despite its priority for the member, the Congress, or the administration. Ending the regional subcommittees would prevent such units from monopolizing and dominating particular issues, such as the war in Indochina. Such primary jurisdiction, on a committee such as International Relations with relatively well-defined jurisdictions, led to exclusive control of some issues. Consequently, policy considerations were important factors in the realignments.

By 1977, conditions both within and outside International Relations had changed measurably. The new Committee chairman, Clement Zablocki, retained control of his active subcommittee on International Security rather than transferring to the moribund Oversight subcommittee that his predecessor, Thomas Morgan, had chaired. In a more general sense, the intense feelings about the Vietnam war had moderated, and similar ventures appeared remote enough to allay anxieties that a return of the regional subcommittees would recreate monopolies over critical issues.

According to regional subcommittee proponents, the experiment with exclusive reliance on functional subcommittees reduced the effectiveness of particular members and interests on the Committee without producing the flexibility and balanced workload that was anticipated in 1975. The demise of regional subcommittees, it was maintained, meant the loss of hegemony in the Committee and a divided locus of activity for geographic or country-oriented issues, in turn reducing the policy leadership of individual committee members by eliminating their institutional base. For instance, the subcommittee on Europe and the subcommittee on Africa had developed some independent, innovative policy positions, reflecting, in part, the interests of domestic constituencies and international clientele. Terminating regional subcommittees would have undermined the mutually reinforcing relationship that may have been critical in advancing policies in opposition to those of the administration.

Conclusions

Two critical difficulties in assessing the impact of structural change on policy developments involve (1) comprehensively and systematically identifying innovations in policy that is often replete with nuances and complexities, and (2) weighing structural factors which, although analytically distinct, are intimately intertwined with other variables. Nonetheless, this selective examination of International Relations revealed instances in which numerous and varied reorganizations, reforms, and restructurings produced changes in both policy and relations with the executive. The policy alterations may be subtle and gradual because of the normally lengthy policy process, the multiple functions policy making serves, and the dispersion of policy influence among multiple agents. On some occasions, dramatic or immediate policy transformations were associated with specific structural changes, as with termination of CIA activities in Angola, alterations in human rights policy, restrictions on foreign assistance to particular nations, and certain provisions in the War Powers resolution.

The dependency of both structure and behavior on other common variables—environmental factors and individual actors' attributes—is evident. Administrative responses to international developments that reflected a "performance gap" (Walker 1974), such as the war in Indochina and CIA abuses, elicited both policy and structural innovations on International Relations. Moreover, the Committee was affected by the expanded ability of other organizations in the House, especially the Democratic Caucus, to stimulate policy actions and to disperse influence within the House committees.

Any calculations of political behavior, or its transformation, must account for the determining role of individual actors in the ultimate equation. In the case of International Relations, the subcommittee chairmen who benefited from the diffusion of authority, improved resources, and greater autonomy tended to be assertive leaders who converted the new powers into innovative policy and/or increased independence from the executive. In this situation, structural change served as an intervening variable and as a necessary, but not sufficient, condition that helped to define the opportunities for innovative behavior.

Note

1. The recent establishment of the House Select Committee on Intelligence, (H.Res. 658, approved July 14, 1977) does not affect the statutory requirement

to submit reports to International Relations, despite the intention of some advocates to reduce the number of committees with access to intelligence information.

7

The Policy Impact of Reform of the Committee on Ways and Means

Catherine Rudder

The Old Ways and Means Committee and Its Transformation

The 94th Congress will be recorded as a "reform Congress" that altered rules, procedures, and consequently power relationships in the House. A major target of House reform was the Ways and Means Committee and its chairman, Wilbur Mills (D-Ark.), often cited as the single most powerful person in the House. Constitutionally empowered to originate tax legislation, the House delegated that duty to the Committee on Ways and Means whose jurisdictional vortex has drawn in numerous matters of national concern: foreign trade, social security, unemployment compensation, national health insurance, and public assistance. Mills could prevent congressional action in these areas. For example, with his committee support assiduously maintained, he set the terms for Medicare, the 1968 tax surcharge, the 1969 tax reform act, and revenue sharing in 1972 (Manley 1970; Orfield 1975; Pierce 1971, pp. 135-78).[1] Mills was an expert substantively in Ways and Means legislation and politically in maintaining his preeminent position in the committee and Congress.[2]

Ways and Means members claimed that the complexity and national significance of the committee's subject matter required insulation from short-term electoral forces and district concerns. The committee needed to be free to forge bills that could take into account various philosophies and interests. This delicate balance could not withstand floor amendments, any one of which could undo a compromise or cost the Treasury millions of dollars. Thus, freedom was given to the committee because it did what the House wanted it to do: it produced tax bills widely acceptable to House members. Manley (1970) and Fenno (1973) both maintain that these bills were widely acceptable because members of the House approved the committee's decisions rather than because individual members lacked the expertise, time, energy, procedural ability, organization, or willingness to risk reprisals.

The author gratefully acknowledges the American Political Science Association Congressional Fellowship that provided me with first-hand experience in Congress. Representative Abner Mikva graciously assisted me in gaining the interviews with the members, and he and his staff shared their congressional "home" with me during my stay on the House side. Genie Irmoyan, Jacques DePuy, and Zoe Gratzias deserve special mention. I would not have been able to accept the Congressional Fellowship without the support of the University of Georgia. Finally, Joyce Murdoch provided valuable assistance in the preparation of this chapter.

In the 94th Congress, with 75 freshman Democrats to provide the votes, the Ways and Means Committee became the major target of congressional reform. While previous challenges to Mills and the committee demonstrated that neither the committee nor its chairman was inviolable, an unfortunate series of publicized incidents involving the chairman and a striptease dancer made the committee more vulnerable to reform (*Congressional Quarterly Almanac* 1974, p. 36).

Several changes actually occurred before the organizational meetings of the 94th Congress in December 1975. The Democrats in the 93d Congress had adopted three particularly relevant procedural reforms—one directed in general at committees operating in secret, a second designed to curtail the automatic use of the seniority system to select committee chairpersons, and a third aimed specifically at Ways and Means' ability to prevent floor amendments to its bills (*Congressional Quarterly Almanac* 1974, pp. 31, 718; *Wall Street Journal* February 22, 1973, p. 2).

The Democratic Caucus of the 94th Congress met from December 2 to December 5, 1974, immediately after Chairman Mills' widely publicized erratic behavior. After a year of his frequent absences from the committee, his defiance of the Caucus, and little legislative productivity in the areas of tax revision and health insurance, the Caucus possessed the freshman votes to dismantle the power of Chairman Mills and the committee.[3]

First, the Caucus stripped the power of the Democratic members of Ways and Means to make Democratic committee appointments, a duty they had performed since 1911 when a "reform" gave them the committee-on-committees function. In addition, the committee was enlarged, not by two members, as was the Rules Committee in 1961 in an effort to liberalize it,[4] but by almost 50 percent, from 25 to 37 members. Moreover, the previously permanent Democratic-Republican ratio of 3:2 was increased to 2:1, to reflect the overwhelmingly Democratic Congress. The large influx of new participants and the increase in size were bound to affect the committee's operations, but the method of recruitment to the Ways and Means Committee also changed and in turn affected its membership. The composition of the committee was also affected by a promise the freshman Caucus extracted from the Steering and Policy Committee to appoint at least two freshmen to Ways and Means (*Washington Post*, December 12, 1974, p. B14). Finally, strengthening the requirements of a 1974 House resolution on committees, the Caucus required that Ways and Means establish five subcommittees; previously, all business was conducted in full committee.

In the midst of the Caucus-mandated changes, Chairman Mills was hospitalized, in December 1974, and resigned as chairman of the committee, a post to which he probably could not have been reelected. He was not well. The Caucus was obviously in a "reform mood," and Mills would have had to face nomination by the Steering and Policy Committee and secret ballot election by the restive Caucus. Mills was replaced as chairman by Al Ullman (D-Ore.), the next most senior Democrat on the committee.

The changes in the Ways and Means Committee since 1973 have been considerable, and the Caucus actions of the 94th Congress have resulted in a radical restructuring of the committee. That the operation of the committee would be fundamentally affected by these changes seems apparent. However, the most interesting question raised by the reforms is whether they have altered the substance of Ways and Means legislation. Has taxation policy been affected? Whom will the reforms benefit and who will lose? To what extent have the reforms produced a more "liberal" committee, as some reformers apparently had hoped?[5]

The answers to these questions cannot be conclusive. It is impossible to isolate any reform and to study its effect separate from the other changes the committee has undergone. Moreover, the entire Congress has been altered, by changed membership and new procedures and practices, such as the Budget and Impoundment Control Act of 1974, that necessarily affect the work of Ways and Means.

Still, it is possible both to assess the changes in light of whether committee members themselves perceive differences in the legislation they produce and to examine major legislation produced by the committee since its restructuring. Two reforms, in particular, are considered here: the expansion of the committee and the reform of the closed rule.

In addition to secondary sources, I use primary sources of data and examine the impact of these reforms. First, I was a participant observer of the meetings of the Ways and Means Committee and its subcommittees on trade and social security from April to August 1975. As a staff assistant to Representative Abner Mikva (D-Ill.), a new member of the committee, I was specifically assigned to cover Ways and Means. This assignment provided contextual knowledge of, and first-hand experience with, the committee and two of its subcommittees. The second source of original data derives from personal interviews with 27 members of the committee in July 1975. A fair representation of old and new members, Republicans and Democrats, Southerners and non-Southerners, and conservatives and liberals were interviewed.[6] The interviews ranged from 13 to 45 minutes each; a common core of questions was asked each member.

The Expansion of the Committee

Enlarging the committee by 50 percent altered the committee membership, and in particular its philosophical predilections, substantially. The committee is considerably different from previous years: for the first time in this century there is a black, Charles Rangel (D-N.Y.), on the committee; for the first time, a woman, Martha Keys (D-Kans.), serves on it. In the past, prerequisites for membership on the committee included considerable prior service in the House and a moderate style.[7] But the average length of prior House service for Ways and Means Democrats has dropped from 7.4 to 4.5 years. Four freshman Democrats, two of whom had served in the House previously, were unprecedently appointed to the committee in 1975. Moreover, the new members, including the freshmen, are more outspoken and more integral to the committee than new members had been in the past. For example, in 1975 Pete Stark (D-Calif.) led a floor fight against the committee's proposed 23-cent gasoline tax, Mikva led in developing the rebate schedule in the Tax Reduction Act of 1975, and Ullman often relied on Joseph Fisher (D-Va.) to assist on the 1975 energy tax bill. Fisher, in fact, commanded the floor for six hours when the energy tax bill was considered in the Committee of the Whole (*Washington Post*, June 13, 1975, p. A2). New assignments to Ways and Means in 1977 continued the trend. Four of the six new Democratic members were freshmen. The average length of prior House service for these new Democratic members is less than one year (0.67 year); and the two new Republican members, while not freshmen, were only beginning their second terms in Congress. Thus, with the new assignments of 1975 and 1977, almost one-half (44 percent) of the Democratic members were from the class of 1975 or 1977.

Members of the committee disagree about whether the substance of legislation has, in fact, changed as a result of the committee's expansion and concomitant change in composition. Although there is general agreement among those interviewed that the committee is "slightly more liberal," there is little agreement about whether this increased liberalism can be translated into legislation different from that which the old committee might have produced.

One veteran Democrat, for example, argued that the committee's deliberations are more cumbersome but that the final legislative product is not necessarily any different from that which the unreconstructed committee might have reported. He observed, "The difference in trying to get a consensus of 37 members as opposed to 25 is tremendous, and it's more than the numbers would indicate. . . . Ultimately, it's the same legislation. It just takes much longer." Said another, "It's harder to reach agreement."

Nevertheless, several specific interests such as oil, big business, and the American Medical Association are perceived, especially by senior members, Republicans and Southern Democrats, to have lost support on the committee. For example, a long-time committee member said the new members "are suspicious, more so than I've ever seen before. They go to the Caucus and challenge on the floor. I feel sorry for business. Every proposal is seen as a rip-off, even though it may provide jobs." An oil-state Democrat similarly characterizes the new members as "more liberal on fiscal policies, in favor of distributing the wealth. Before there was a balance with no preponderance of any one side."

The perceived difference in substantive outcomes is illustrated by a veteran Republican who felt "The Tax Reduction Act [of 1975] would have been different. For capital recovery we would have gotten one-fourth rather than the one-sixth we got. And there wouldn't have been a negative income tax where people got rebates for taxes they never even paid. That never would have happened in the old committee."

Some members perceive that a new kind of person is being assigned to Ways and Means—more brash, less agreeable, more irritating to the old members. Said one veteran Republican,

Take Stark [a new member] and Corman [an old member]. There's not so much difference in their philosophy but in their approach. Mills would try to build a consensus . . . and Corman would help to work toward a consensus. That's not true anymore with the many new faces with strong philosophical views. It's pulling the committee apart. We must search to find common ground.

The composition of the new committee has thus changed in that the new members are more diverse, less legislatively experienced, and much more likely to participate in the committee. The committee members are also, on the average, somewhat—but only somewhat—more liberal in their voting patterns on the floor of the House. Committee Democrats and Republicans vote more often with their party than committee members did in the past.

Using conservative coalition and party unity scores, Table 7-1 demonstrates these trends. The mean conservative coalition score for the committee in the 93d Congress was 52; the score dropped slightly to 48 for the first session of the 94th, then rose again to 50 for committee members of the 95th Congress. However, if this measure is seen in the light of an expanded committee and a changed party ratio, the possibilities for more liberal legislation, as several veteran and Republican members have complained, do become manifest. In cases of full attendance, 19 votes are needed for a majority in the committee. In the 94th Congress, 19 of the Ways and Means Democrats had conservative coalition scores below 55, suggesting that a winning coalition could be built exclusively from the moderate and liberal Democratic members. For the 95th Congress, the prospects of such a coalition look equally likely, depending on the voting records of the new freshman members.

As Table 7-1 shows, expansion of the committee has had a negligible impact on the Republican side. The conservative coalition and party unit mean scores are similar for old and new members. It is on the Democratic side that enlarging the committee has affected its composition. New Democrats, especially those added in 1975, are more liberal, but not sufficiently to lower the mean Democratic score significantly. However, the 1975 new Democratic members do increase party unity for committee Democrats. New Democrats are more likely to vote with their party on floor votes (on which there is a party division). The party unity score for new Democrats of the 94th Congress is 77; the mean score for veteran Democrats is only 61. This suggests that the committee, because of the additional Democratic members, is more likely to reflect the position of House Democrats but that the Democratic side is only slightly more liberal than in the past.

Table 7-1

A Comparison of Ways and Means Members in the 93d Congress with Those in the 94th (1st Session) and 95th Congresses: Party Unity and Conservative Coalition Scores

	93d Congress (1973–1974)	
	Mean Conservative Coalition Score	*Mean Party Unity Score*
Democrats	34	61
Republicans	78	74
Committee	52	—
	94th Congress (1975)	
Democrats	32	69
New Members	28	77
Old Members	44	61
Republicans	81	80
New Members	81	78
Old Members	82	82
Committee	48	—
	95th Congress	
	(1975)[a]	*(1975–1976)*[a]
Democrats	32	69
New Members[b]	30	70
Old Members	33	69
Republicans	82	78
New Members	81	80
Old Members	82	76
Committee	50	—

Source: *Congressional Quarterly Weekly Report*, January 25, 1975, pp. 189–194, 199–203; January 24, 1976, pp. 169–173, 179–183.

[a]Scores for the 95th Congress are based on 1975 and 1976 ratings because 1977 ratings were not available.

[b]Four of the six new Democratic members are freshmen and, because they had cast no votes, are excluded from the calculations.

The new Democrats added in 1977 continue the trend begun in 1975. There is, however, one interesting difference between the new members of 1975 and those of 1977. The former are more electorally vulnerable than the latter. In the 1976 congressional races, four of the nine (44 percent) new 1975 members encountered stiff opposition in their general election races; only one of the six new members (17 percent) in 1977 faced serious competition (using 55 percent or less of the vote to indicate a competitive election).

Despite the increased number of liberals on the committee, there is not a dependable liberal majority. A useful comparison of the old and new committee is provided by the proposal to end the oil depletion allowance, which gave the oil industry a lucrative tax reduction. This proposal was considered by the old committee in 1974 and again by the new committee in 1975. In both years the proposal lost, but on the second vote oil-industry opponents almost doubled their strength. In 1974 the proposal lost 19 (75 percent) to 6 (25 percent); in 1975 it gained ground in a 22 (60 percent) to 14 (40 percent) vote. Thus, the increased proportion of liberals on the committee has not always been sufficient to constitute a majority in the new committee. One reason liberal positions often lost in committee votes, according to a new Democrat, is that liberals "tend to be fragmented. They tend to be doctrinaire. They insist on principle regardless of results. There are certain causes which members have fought for years; other matters become secondary."

There is also the problem of time. During the energy bill markup, for example, the committee and subcommittee meetings literally consumed the entire day from 8 a.m. to 8 p.m. As a consequence, there has been little time to reflect, coalesce, or plan strategy. Moreover, personality conflicts and rivalries between old and new members and among old members have apparently lessened, but not prevented, cooperation.

A more important reason for the unstable support of "liberal issues," as conceived by the members, is the need for the new members, especially those from unsafe districts, to respond to interest group and district demands (*Congressional Quarterly Weekly Report* 1976, p. 43). A representative dependent upon the United Auto Workers for support will tend to vote with the union even though its position on automobile efficiency taxes, for example, may not be the "liberal" one. Or if a number of multinational corporations have home offices in a representative's district, it is difficult for that member to vote to eliminate an important tax advantage, such as the Domestic International Sales Corporations (DISCs), even though DISCs may constitute a substantial tax loophole. With regard to the substance of the legislation the committee has produced, one liberal veteran member expressed it this way: "The expansion of the committee has not had as much impact as reformers thought it would. The committee is only slightly more liberal."

A comparison of the two tax reduction acts of 1975 is instructive on this point. In February 1975, the Ways and Means Committee reported a tax rebate bill of $2.3 billion. Although the committee persistently rejected two attempts to remove the oil depletion allowance, the bill did include provisions that redistributed the tax burden. The tax burden of low-income persons had increased more than that of any other group over the last twenty years. But the 1975 tax cut designed by the new Ways and Means Committee was proportionately greater for those with low incomes—in effect, reversing the regressive 20-year trend (*The New York Times*, September 28, 1975, p. A37).

In the fall of 1975, the Ways and Means Committee considered extending the tax reduction act and revising the tax code, popularly referred to as "tax reform." Two demands had been made on the committee, one by the Budget Committee and the other by the President. In its May budget resolution, the Budget Committee instructed the Ways and Means Committee to increase revenues in fiscal year 1976 by $1 billion; President Ford demanded that any tax cuts be linked with spending reductions, a proposal usually interpreted as supporting a conservative fiscal policy of reducing the federal deficit (*Congressional Quarterly Weekly Report* 1975, pp. 2251, 2596-7). By a 21-16 vote, the committee rejected Ford's idea outright and accepted Chairman Ullman's plan to exclude spending reductions from the bill (*Congressional Quarterly Weekly Report* 1975, p. 2251).

Meeting the Budget Committee's goal of increasing revenues by reducing tax expenditures or loopholes (considered a "liberal" position by committee members) proved difficult. At first it looked as though tax expenditures, which enabled affluent people to pay fewer taxes, might be reduced. A tentative decision to limit the tax shelter in oil and drilling investment was made. At the time *Congressional Quarterly Weekly Report* (1975, p. 2221) reported: "By accepting a proposal that it had turned down in 1974, the Ways and Means panel underscored the oil industry's diminishing power to protect its interests in a hostile 94th Congress." In addition, the committee refused to include costly provisions to encourage capital formation despite heavy pressure from the administration and industry (*Congressional Quarterly Weekly Report* 1975, p. 1495).

However, three days before reporting the bill, the committee reversed itself and trimmed the $2.6 billion in additional revenues tentatively proposed to $752 million (*Congressional Quarterly Weekly Report* 1976, p. 41). Chairman Ullman faced solid Republican opposition (12 votes) because the Republicans refused to support the bill without spending ceilings, as requested by the Republican President. Since the committee had rejected such ceilings, seven Democrats could block the passage of the bill. To be able to report a bill at all, the bill had to be weakened to pick up support from wavering Democrats. In some cases, lobbyists actually provided the weakening language (*Congressional Quarterly Weekly Report* 1975, pp. 2608-2609). Members, especially new ones not impervious to district demands, responded to lobbying from those industries in their districts (*Congressional Quarterly Weekly Report* 1976, p. 43).[8]

Looking at these two tax bills reveals some patterns. The committee is probably more liberal than the old committee in fiscal policy.[9] Further, the redistribution of the tax burden in the Tax Reduction Act suggests that the committee is willing to support a more progressive income tax system. Observers are probably thrown off, however, by the tax revision bill in which the committee retreated from a tax reform position. The votes simply were not there, and the reason probably reflects the characteristics of the committee's new members. A majority of the new members are liberal in fiscal policy and in supporting a fairer distribution of the tax burden; but many are not from safe districts, are not guaranteed reelection, and must listen and respond to interest-group demands. Reese (1975a, p. 4), using 16 roll call votes on tax advantages during markup of the tax reduction and energy bills, demonstrated that the new committee showed no predilection to reduce tax preferences or loopholes during its first six months in operation. On only five roll calls did the tax reform position win. Only ten members supported reducing tax preferences on more than half the votes, and five of those members were veteran, not new, committee members. Most of the new members, Republicans and Democrats, voted against the tax reform position on the majority of the votes.

Thus, the committee reform was double-edged: new members were selected to end Ways and Means' insulation from the Democratic Caucus, the Congress, and national forces, but this receptiveness is by definition not selective. As a result, the committee is as little able now to reduce tax expenditures or plug loopholes as the old committee was. However, some substantive changes have resulted from the enlargement of the committee.

The change in the composition of the committee has led to a more diverse, more "representative" committee, at least in one sense. On the basis of conservative coalition scores, the committee is slightly more liberal than in the past, but this new liberalism has not necessarily translated into reporting liberal legislation. The committee has supported a liberal fiscal policy and a more progressive taxation system, but it is open to the pleas of special economic interests. This susceptibility to interest-group demands is, in part, a result of the committee reform that placed members from less safe districts on the committee. The reform removed the insulation of the committee from "liberal" economic impulses and from "conservative" ones as well.

Closed-Rule Reform

Even more than the expansion of the committee, the reform of the use of the closed rule appears to have had a substantial impact on legislative outcomes. *Closed-rule reform* actually refers to two changes. First, in 1973, the Democratic Caucus of the 93d Congress approved a procedure to amend Ways and Means bills. Any 50 Democrats can now propose an amendment to the Caucus; if a majority approves, the Democratic members of the Rules Committee are instructed to write a rule to permit the amendment to reach the floor. Second, the reform refers to the general, since January 1975, decreasing use of the strict closed rule for Ways and Means legislation.

In the past, it was argued that a closed rule was necessary because Ways and Means legislation was complex and because a delicate compromise constructed in committee could be destroyed by modifying amendments on the floor. At the same time, closed rules gave the Ways and Means Committee considerable power to determine the shape of the tax law and gave members who disagreed with sections of Ways and Means bills little recourse other than voting against the entire bill. Until the closed-rule reform, for example, opponents of the oil depletion allowance had had no chance to remove that preference from the tax code. Since the majority of Ways and Means members supported the allowance, it was retained.

Interestingly, dissident committee members, not noncommittee Democrats, have used the 1973 procedural change. In 1974 Charles Vanik (D-Ohio) and William Green (D-Pa.) each proposed an amendment to a tax revision bill. The Caucus instructed the Rules Committee to permit a floor vote on these two amendments—one to change the foreign tax credit for businesses to a foreign tax deduction and the other to eliminate the oil depletion allowance. Both amendments reduced tax preferences of businesses. This defiance of Wilbur Mills and the majority of the Ways and Means Committee was met, in turn, with defiance. Mills refused to bring the bill before the Rules Committee, claiming he had been given contradictory instructions: for a closed rule by Ways and Means and for a modified closed rule by the Caucus. The bill died. The closed-rule reform had ended in deadlock (*Congressional Quarterly Almanac* 1974, pp. 188–89).

In 1975, however, there was another challenge, on the 1975 Tax Reduction Act, and the outcome was quite different. Again Ways and Means refused to remove the oil depletion allowance. Chairman Ullman supported this position, suggesting that the matter be taken up in a subsequent bill, but Green and Sam Gibbons (D-Fla.), along with five new members of the Ways and Means Committee, gathered the required 50 signatures and petitioned for a Caucus vote. Their amendment and another to retain the allowance for independent oil producers were allowed. Green and his allies won the day on the floor and removed the allowance. (The special provision for independents, however, was added to the bill in conference.) (See *Congressional Quarterly Weekly Report* 1975, p. 351.)

Having lost that battle, Ullman began to realize his subservient position vis-à-vis the Caucus. In short, the Ways and Means Committee had been, and would probably continue to be, overruled on certain matters, given the current Caucus predilections. As a consequence of this realization and of his political situation in the committee, which often required 19 Democratic votes to form a majority in the face of unified Republican opposition, Ullman began to help the dissidents short-circuit the Caucus procedure to add amendments to Ways and Means bills. On the tax revision and extension bill, to form a majority, Ullman agreed to request a modified closed rule to permit six strengthening amendments. Hence, Ullman gained the Democratic votes needed to report the bill, and the dissidents were spared the choice of no tax reform or of appealing to the Caucus (*Congressional Quarterly Weekly Report* 1975, p. 2521).

Thus, the new procedure to modify closed rules on Ways and Means bills, first tried in 1974, was successful first in 1975. Also, since 1975, rules on most major Ways and Means legislation have not been strictly closed, permitting more House discretion than ever before on the particulars of Ways and Means bills.[10]

It should be noted that the new procedure to allow floor votes on specific amendments is available only to Democrats. Thus, if the Democrats are satisfied with a closed rule, the Republicans have no recourse other than the hope that the Rules Committee will continue to grant fewer and fewer closed rules.

The impact of the 1975 changes in the use of the closed rule can be evaluated in terms of the substance of the bills the House produced. Because of the new Caucus procedure to force floor votes on specific amendments, both the tax reduction act and the tax extension and revision bill are somewhat more liberal than they would have been without it (in the sense that tax preferences for businesses were reduced to some extent from those in the Ways and Means bills).

The reason liberal positions have benefited from the new procedure is situational, not a logical necessity.[11] The Democratic Caucus has tended to be less tolerant of tax preferences for large businesses than Ways and Means. Should the philosophical composition of the Caucus change, the success of liberal positions would also presumably change. The new procedure could work to benefit other interests, groups, or philosophical positions. In effect, the new procedure has provided an appeal process for disgruntled Ways and Means Democrats and thus has paved an avenue of greater accountability of the Ways and Means Committee to the Caucus. The procedure by no means ensures the success of a proposal on the floor of the House, especially in the face of opposition from unified Republicans and defecting Democrats. It simply lets Democrats decide whether a proposal has sufficient merit to warrant floor consideration. Nor has the procedure invited uninformed attacks on Ways and Means decisions; to date, the procedure has been initiated only by Ways and Means members.

In contrast to the new "appeal" procedure, the gradual use of modified-open and open rules is less demonstrably salutary. There is general agreement that the energy tax bill, reported under an ironically entitled "orderly open rule," was completely gutted on the floor of the House, with over 200 amendments proposed (though all were not actually considered on the floor).[12] Many people have argued that the open rule prevented the House from producing a coherent, tough bill. And that experience probably led the Ways and Means Committee, later in the year, to shy away from requesting open rules on, for example, the unemployment compensation system revision (*Congressional Quarterly Weekly Report* 1976, p. 63). It is clear that open rules have given the tax committee's opponents an opportunity to challenge Ways and Means decisions. For example, under the open rule, every title in the original energy tax bill was substantially amended. In several cases, Ways and Means members led the fight against sections of their own bill (*Congressional Quarterly Weekly Report* 1975, pp. 1275-76). Moreover, House freshmen, in contrast to previous years, displayed little reverence for norms of apprenticeship, silence, or specialization. For example, a noncommittee freshman, Philip Sharp (D-Ind.), successfully substituted the Commerce Committee's proposal on fuel efficiency for the Ways and Means plan.

Table 7-2 illustrates the extent to which Ullman could not even rely on his own committee to support the energy tax bill on the floor.[13] On half of six major votes on sections of the bill, the chairman failed to rouse a majority of his own committee. Committee members actually took different positions on some floor votes from the position they had taken in committee (Reese 1975b, p. 3). Obviously, the committee no longer evidenced the integration and loyalty that had been its hallmark.

The bill was substantially weakened on the House floor, which never would have happened in the old committee. In the past, there would have been no open rule, nor would have Mills reported a bill on a close 19-16 margin, as Ullman

Table 7-2
Ways and Means Committee Members' Support of H.R. 6860
on House Floor, on Six Major Votes

Vote		Supporting Ways and Means Position	
1.	To weaken import quotas	Democrats	72% (18)
		Republicans	0 (0)
		All committee members	49 (18)
2.	To strike the gasoline tax	Democrats	40 (10)
		Republicans	0 (0)
		All committee members	27 (10)
3.	To strike Title II	Democrats	80 (20)
		Republicans	17 (2)
		All committee members	59 (22)
4.	To strengthen the automobile efficiency tax	Democrats	48 (12)
		Republicans	92 (11)
		All committee members	62 (23)
5.	To substitute civil penalties for the automobile efficiency tax	Democrats	32 (8)
		Republicans	83 (10)
		All committee members	49 (18)
6.	To recommit the bill	Democrats	84 (21)
		Republicans	0 (0)
		All committee members	57 (21)

Source: *Congressional Record*, June 11, 1975, pp. H5277, H5306-7, H5325; June 12, 1975, pp. H5376-7, H5390; June 19, 1975, p. H5749.

did. Said one veteran Democrat, "Mills would have produced a different bill. It would have come out on a closed rule in the old days. That's maybe no longer possible. Al [Ullman] took a tougher route, and it showed with the difficulties he had on the floor."

To indicate exactly the extent to which Ullman and Ways and Means miscalculated House sentiment, the vote on the proposed 20-cent/gallon additional gasoline tax should be reviewed. This proposal was a key element in the bill (considered separately from another 3-cent tax), but it lost almost 4:1 (345-92) (*Congressional Record* 1975, pp. 5306-5307). A majority of the committee voted to strike its own provision. Of the new Democrats on the committee, only one maintained support of the gas tax to vote with the committee position. This mass desertion of the chairman on the floor was unprecedented. One senior Democrat on Ways and Means explained the vote this way: "It [the energy bill] was a fiasco. It should have been obvious to anyone that the country wouldn't accept a 23-cent gas tax. It should have been equally obvious that gasoline shouldn't bear the burden of all energy conservation. What was passed was an innocuous piece of paper."

It can be argued that the House's performance on the energy bill was less an indication that Ways and Means bills should not be reported on an open rule than that the House and the country were not politically ready for a strong energy policy. The open rule simply allowed the House to work its will.[14] The open rule did let individual members of Congress express their positions on parts of the bill and allowed Congress to produce an energy bill, albeit in weakened form.

Even though the energy bill may not have been typical of Ways and Means legislation, the committee members apparently learned some lessons from the experience. The limited success of the bill—every important section was weakened—stands in stark contrast to the committee's past success on the floor. As a strident senior Democrat commented, "I'd love to get out a tax reform bill and ram it down their throats under a closed rule."

Ullman's distaste for the open rule on complex taxation legislation was demonstrated in 1976 when a coalition of House Republicans and conservative Democrats managed, in effect, to obtain an open rule for the estate and gift tax bill (H.R. 14,844) rather than the modified closed rule the Rules Committee had granted. Rather than risk disintegration of the bill, the House Democratic leadership withdrew the measure (*Congressional Quarterly Weekly Report* 1975, p. 2417).

The reform of the closed rule has lessened the ability of Ways and Means to determine taxation policy univocally. For the first time, the House has been given an opportunity to vote on specific provisions in tax legislation, but the long-run effect of the new procedure for allowing amendments on tax bills will be determined by the composition of the Democratic majority and the Congress. Thus far, the procedure has worked to benefit disgruntled Ways and Means

Democrats and those who have desired to reduce tax advantages for certain business operations.

The effect of the use of an open rule on Ways and Means legislation has been examined in light of one particular bill, the energy tax bill of 1975. Norms such as apprenticeship, freshman silence, and specialization were not followed on the floor. House members' perfunctory support of Ways and Means positions was no longer evident. Floor success was no longer ensured. The Ways and Means chairperson can no longer expect automatic support from the House as a whole or from his/her own committee. The bill that the House did produce was generally considered weak.

An open rule gave individual House members greater voice in Ways and Means legislation and reduced the committee's exclusive claim on tax bills. At the same time, the open rule permitted such significant weakening of the energy tax bill that it was dubbed a "nonpolicy." Complained one veteran Democrat, "Now we have 435 independent Democrats and Republicans. . . . The modified rules have destroyed the opportunity for strong leadership and will potentially destroy the institution." There are already suggestions to "reform the reform." For example, one proreform observer of the energy debacle declared, "The 'orderly open rule' proved to be a near disaster. . . . It seems obvious that a more restrictive rule is needed" (Reese 1975b, p. 8).

Summary and Conclusion

The overall effects of expanding Ways and Means and of loosening the closed rule have been to widen the number and kind of influences on committee legislation and, as a consequence, to alter the substance of tax legislation.

The fact that new committee members disproportionately come from unsafe seats has affected the committee. While including these new members has led to more diversity and more responsiveness to district opinion, it has also lessened the ability of Ways and Means to make tax decisions from a national viewpoint. If individual members' first goal is reelection, then those from competitive districts must vote with reference to how those votes will affect their reelection prospects. Thus, the process has been altered to make members more accountable to consituents who pay attention, particularly interest groups.

One might argue that congressional reform, if anything, has been too successful, that democratization has been too complete. Ways and Means, for example, has been stripped of its power to make binding decisions. In the reformed committee, no decision is final; each is subject to reversal in the Caucus and on the floor of the House. What this means, beyond the obvious point that more people are able to participate in taxation decisions, is that a legislative package cannot be developed in the committee with any assurance that it will pass intact on the floor.

Democratization of the Congress has coincided with a national realization that resources are finite, that legislative solutions cannot be found in relatively painless distributive policies. The new "politics of scarce resources" requires redistributive and regulative policies. One example of this kind of politics is the energy tax bill. The Ways and Means Committee "bit the bullet," as some members like to express it, and reported a tough peice of legislation that included a 23-cents/gallon gasoline tax and incentives to save gasoline. When the bill went to the floor, the incentives were retained, while every stringent section of the bill, including the gasoline tax, was either eliminated or weakened substantially. Many Ways and Means members voted against their own bill, as it was considered title by title on the floor. Though the energy tax bill might have failed had it been voted upon as an entire package, in general, logrolled bills that call for sacrifice or redistribution will have a better chance to pass without being gutted if coalitions can be built and maintained around an indivisible legislative package.

Finally, democratization emphasizes only one facet of representative democracy, one that stresses the need for governmental responsiveness. However, there is another aspect of representation that has been slighted by the zeal to break down unaccountable structures of power: the obligation to govern and to govern responsibly. For Congress to function, to produce coherent, responsible legislation, structures of power are needed. In the case of taxation legislation, for instance, some group (presumably Ways and Means) has to have the ability to aggregate interests and to maintain the coalition that it develops.

Notes

1. Both popular and more serious reports have noted Mills's power. For example, Don Riegle (1972, p. 84) observes, "The man whose power within the Congress probably counts more than all the other members put together is Wilbur Mills of Arkansas. . . . His power is enormous."

2. This account of the Committee on Ways and Means prior to 1975 relies heavily on Manley (1970) and Fenno (1973, pp. 2-9, 15-26, 51-57, 83-89, 105-107, 114-18, 123-24, 137-38, 152-54, 183, 200-212, 222, 226, 229, 234-39, 256, 260, 276-77). Also see *Los Angeles Times*, December 4, 1974, pp. 1, 24; *Business Week*, May 8, 1971, pp. 72-75; and Broder 1971.

3. For background information on past challenges to Ways and Means and to Chairman Mills, see *Congressional Quarterly Weekly Report*, March 4, 1972, pp. 474-75; July 13, 1973, pp. 1892-93; *Chicago Tribune*, April 10, 1974, p. 18; *Washington Star-News*, July 7, 1974, p. A15; and *Wall Street Journal*, July 10, 1973, pp. 1, 19. For additional information on the 1974 Caucus changes, see *Washington Post*, December 4, 1974, pp. A1, 12; and *The New York Times*, December 4, 1974, pp. 1, 33.

4. On the expansion of the Rules Committee, see Robinson (1963).

5. As employed in the chapter, the word *reform* is used for convenience, without approval or disapproval.

6. Members interviewed include Al Ullman (Ore.), James A. Burke (Mass.), Dan Rostenkowski (Ill.), Phil M. Landrum (Ga.), Charles A Vanik (Ohio), Omar Burleson (Tex.), James C. Corman (Calif.), William J. Green (Pa.), Sam M. Gibbons (Fla.), and Joseph E. Karth (Minn.)—veteran Democrats; Herman T. Schneebeli (Pa.), Barber Conable (N.Y.), John J. Duncan (Tenn.), Donald B. Clancy (Ohio), Bill Archer (Tex.)—veteran Republicans; Richard Vanderveen (Mich.), Henry Helstoski (N.J.), William Cotter (Conn.), Fortney H. Stark (Calif.), James R. Jones (Okla.), Andy Jacobs, Jr. (Ind.), and Abner Mikva (Ill.)— new Democrats; Philip M. Crane (Ill.), Bill Frenzel (Minn.), James G. Martin (N.C.), L.A. "Skip" Bafalis (Fla.), and William M. Ketchum (Calif.)—new Republicans.

7. Manley (1970, p. 295) describes the kind of person who had been recruited for Ways and Means: "The recruitment criteria for the Ways and Means Committee are likely to turn up pragmatic men, moderate in style, with a conspicuous absence of any tendency to launch a crusade against alleged tax inequities."

8. To illustrate the extent to which district demands may be more salient for new members than in the past, it is instructive to compare the "new" Ways and Means with the "old" one. Manley (1970, p. 51) reports that of the 28 Democrats and 24 Republicans appointed to Ways and Means between 1947 and 1966, only 4 and 5, respectively, have come from unsafe districts—that is, the member received less than 55 percent of the vote in the election immediately prior to appointment to Ways and Means. In contrast, of the 1975 appointees, 5 of the 13 Democrats (including Harold Ford, who replaced Fulton in October 1975) and 2 of the 7 Republicans received less than 55 percent of the vote.

9. As a condition for reporting a tax increase, in 1968 Mills demanded and received a spending reduction coupled with a tax surcharge despite the fact that the administration (of his own party) desired the surcharge without the spending reduction (Pierce 1971). In a somewhat similar situation, the new committee in 1975 *rejected* the Republican President's request that reductions in taxes and spending be linked. In other words, there has apparently been a reversal on fiscal policy by the Ways and Means Committee.

10. However, in 1976 the Ways and Means Committee retrenched somewhat, requesting a closed rule for H.R. 10210 to revise the federal-state unemployment compensation system (*Congressional Quarterly Weekly Report* 1976, p. 63). In 1975, Republicans chided Democrats that the closed rule had not been reformed. Said Frenzel, "A glacier also makes progress" (*Congressional Quarterly Weekly Report* 1975, p. 257).

11. On this point, see, for example, Orfield (1975).

12. The rule is noted on the "Daily Digest" of the *Congressional Record*, June 3, 1975.

13. For an excellent analysis of the congressional action on the energy tax bill, see Drew (1975).

14. Editorially, the *Washington Post* (June 23, 1975, p. A18) asked:

Why did the House behave so badly when the energy bill came to the floor? The common explanation was a lack of nerve, but, in fact, the reason is much more substantial. Energy policy is now the most divisive regional issue to afflict this country since civil rights. Even the civil rights bill became manageable for both parties in Congress as early as the middle 1950s. . . . People organizing nation-wide campaigns know that there is no way to take strong positions on energy conservation without losing blocks of support in one part of the country or another.

For accounts of the energy bill on the House floor, see the *Washington Post*, June 13, 1975, p. A2; June 11, 1975, p. A2; June 12, 1975, pp. A1, A6; June 20, 1975, pp. A1, A6.

8 Policy Implications of Rules Committee Reforms

Bruce I. Oppenheimer

The major task of the House Rules Committee has been to provide the rules for the consideration of legislation on the House floor. Until recently, the Committee has only occasionally dealt with legislation over which it has had direct, substantive responsibility. Despite this condition, Rules has maintained an important policy-making role in the House of Representatives. In part, this reflects the fact that concern with process and concern with policy are rarely, if ever, mutually exclusive. In part, it reflects the strategic position of the Rules Committee in having the opportunity to review nearly all legislation before it can be called up for debate on the House floor. And in part it results because the members of the committee have definite policy interests and preferences, although their reason for membership may derive from desires to be influential within the House (Fenno 1973).

The legislative politics and public policy literature provides numerous examples of the effects the Rules Committee has had on policy (see, for example, Bolling 1966, chap. 19; Robinson 1963; Munger and Fenno 1962; Sundquist 1968; Eidenberg and Morey 1969). In particular, the period from 1955 to 1966, during which Judge Howard Smith (D-Va.) chaired the committee, has received extensive attention. Major legislative proposals involving economic policy, civil rights, and aid to education were delayed or defeated by the conservative coalition on the Rules Committee. The expansion of the committee from 12 to 15 members in 1961 and the adoption of a 21-day rule in 1965 were major efforts to undercut the committee's conservative policy influence.[1] With rare exception, the Rules Committee's power to affect policy came from its ability to operate as a veto point and from Judge Smith's capacity to use that sanction to bargain for policy concessions.

Since 1967, and more significantly coinciding with the period of House reform in the 1970s, the Rules Committee has undergone considerable change. Although its activities receive substantially less publicity and editorial comment than in the 1950s and 1960s and it no longer relies solely on its capacity to delay or defend legislation to influence policy, the committee continues to have an important policy role in the House.

In this chapter I examine three ways in which the Rules Committee now influences policy that are substantially different from its policy role during Judge Smith's chairmanship.[2] The three are as follows: (1) the development of a Rules Committee that is strongly oriented to national Democratic party policy and works as an arm of the party leadership; (2) committee efforts to use the rule writing and granting process to overcome the fragmented approach to legislation in a highly decentralized House; and (3) the growth of the committee's attention to matters of original jurisdiction.

These changes in the policy role of the Rules Committee are more directly a result of the committee's response to the reforms of the 1970s that decentralized, democratized, and fragmented the decision-making processes in the House than of specific reforms of the Rules Committee.[3] Nevertheless, certain changes in the Rules Committee were necessary prerequisites to assuming this new policy role. First, following Judge Smith's defeat in 1966, the senior Rules Democrat William Colmer (Miss.), in a successful effort to undercut a potential challenge to his becoming chairman, accepted the first set of committee rules. Among other things, the rules allowed for weekly committee meetings and for the ranking majority member to call meetings to order and preside in the absence of the chairperson. This undercut the ability of a conservative chairperson to act in an arbitrary manner.

Second, there was important turnover in the committee's membership. Smith was replaced by William Anderson, a Tennessee moderate. And when William Colmer retired at the end of the 92d Congress, Speaker Carl Albert chose Gillis Long (La.), another moderate, over Sonny Montgomery (Miss.), a conservative, to fill the vacancy, despite the fact that a coalition of Southern conservatives urged the appointment of Montgomery. When other vacancies occurred, the leadership appointed members on whom it could rely.

Third, at the start of the 94th Congress, the Democratic Caucus voted the Speaker the power to appoint all Democratic members of the Rules Committee. Prior to that time, Rules Democrats were formally appointed by the Democratic Committee on Committees, although informally that body accepted the recommendations of the Speaker and the Majority Leader. Although the change was actually small, it was not without meaning. Aside from formalizing the appointment procedure, it meant that the Majority Leader no longer shared the power with the Speaker. (It had been Majority Leader John McCormack's promise that allowed William Colmer to return to the Rules Committee when the Democrats again took control of the House following the 1948 election.) Moreover, the change meant that the Speaker could technically choose not to reappoint members of the Rules Committee. It is unlikely that this sanction will be used. Nevertheless, as one senior Rules Democrat explained this Speaker's veto, "But inertia is very important around here . . . and you equalize the inertia by giving him this veto. . . ."

Finally, on a couple of occasions the House Democratic Caucus instructed the Rules Committee to make certain provisions in granting rules for particular bills. Although too much can be read into these occurrences, they further reinforce the efforts to make the Rules Committee accountable to party policy. The combined effect of these changes in the Rules Committee has been to create a committee capable of working in harmony with the majority party leadership and of assisting the leadership to structure legislative policy.

Strong Orientation toward Democratic Party Policy

It is not surprising, given the turnover in Democratic membership on Rules and the increased role of the Speaker in the appointment of Rules Democrats, that Rules Democrats are strong party supporters in their floor voting. There has been a steady increase in the difference between the mean party unity score of Rules Democrats and the mean party unity score of all House Democrats, starting in the 92d Congress and continuing through the 94th Congress, 1st session (Table 8-1). This trend would have continued through the entire 94th Congress were it not for the fact that three Rules Democrats missed a substantial number of the floor votes.[4]

More significant, however, is the party unity demonstrated by the Rules Democrats on committee roll calls (Table 8-2). Only two Democrats, James Delaney (N.Y.) and John Young (Tex.), part with the majority of their Democratic colleagues with some frequency.[5] Since the Democrats maintain an 11-5 advantage on the committee,[6] the defections of Delaney and Young are not enough to defeat the majority party's efforts. Moreover, the Democrats receive support from John Anderson (R-Ill.), the lone Republican moderate on Rules, on about 40 percent of the party unity roll calls.

Compared with the pre-1961 committee, when Smith and Colmer would join the four Rules Republicans to deadlock the committee, the difference is enormous. And even after the 1961 enlargement victory, the Democratic leadership possessed only a precarious 8-7 majority (Peabody 1963). As one Rules Democrat described it,

There was never any time when we had the eight that I didn't have a nervous stomach. There was always the opportunity for a pickoff and make an 8-7 win an 8-7 loss. Smith and Colmer together or separately were capable of figuring out who to approach and how, be it in terms of district or personal preference or a tradeoff or whatever. They had eight targets sitting there. If they get one, it turns from a majority to a minority.

The 8-7 margin of 1961 became more comfortable once Anderson replaced Smith in 1967, but was not ensured until Long replaced Colmer at the start of the 93d Congress in 1973.

The impact of this membership change is readily illustrated by data on Rules Committee decisions on rule requests (Table 8-3). Starting with the 91st Congress, in quantitative terms, and with the 93d in qualitative terms, and continuing through the 94th Congress, 1st session, the Rules Committee was extremely lenient in granting rule requests. In the 91st Congress, the number of

Table 8-1
Mean Party Unity Scores for Rules Committee Democrats and All House Democrats

					Congress					
	86th	87th	88th	89th	90th	91st	92d	93d	94th (1st Session)	94th (Entire)
$\overline{X}$ Rules Democrats	70.3	79.8	73.0	69.3[a]	72.1	62.4[a]	62.8[a]	70.8	77.0	73.1
$\overline{X}$ All House Democrats	72.0	76.0	71.0	67.0	63.0	59.0	60.0	66.0	69.0	68.0
Difference between $\overline{X}$ Rules Democrats and $\overline{X}$ House Democrats	−1.7	3.8	2.0	2.3	9.0	3.4	2.8	4.8	8.0	5.1

Figures are based on party unity scores as computed in *Congressional Quarterly*, Voting Studies.
[a]Indicates average was computed only after score for an individual, who missed more than one-third of roll calls used in computing score, was adjusted by using the member's average party unity score from the other Congresses during which he/she was on the Rules Committee.

Table 8-2
Party Unity Scores for Democratic Members of the Rules Committee

| | 93d Congress | | 94th Congress | |
	Roll Calls	Floor Roll Calls	Rules Committee Roll Calls	Floor Roll Calls
Madden	92	91	94	94
Delaney	71	73	66	81
Bolling	84	74	92	91
Sisk	87	80	78	73
J. Young	70	60	49	55
Pepper	85	89	89	88
Matsunaga	92	92	95	91
Murphy	89	86	87	86
Long	84	76	82	70
McSpadden	66	51		
Moakley			90	93
A. Young			96	96

Figures have been adjusted to negate the effect of absences. Unity scores are based only on roll calls on which a yea or nay was recorded by the individual.

bills Rules killed was halved from that of previous Congresses, dropping from 25 or more in the 87th to 90th Congresses to 13. By the 93d Congress, when firm leadership control of the committee was established, rule-granting activities became even more lenient. Nearly 20 percent more rules were granted in the 93d Congress than in any previous Congress. Moreover, of the 13 bills that did not reach the House floor in the 93d Congress because the Rules Committee failed to hear, denied, or deferred the requests, 7 came after the Committee's August deadline (and 4 of the 7 came during the lame duck session following the election), 1 was adversely reported from a standing committee, and 1 was in all likelihood opposed by a majority of House members. This trend continued through the 94th Congress, 1st session. Seen in a policy perspective the Rules Committee which had been a tight squeeze for liberal Democratic legislation had become a sieve.

The consequences of a lenient Rules Committee were not entirely desirable from a variety of perspectives. Predictably Republicans complained that Rules no longer served the purpose for which it was designed. The comment of one is typical:

They say take a bill to the floor to give the members a chance to vote on it. Then, why do you need a Rules Committee? Why not just send everything to the floor? Rules has its own power and its own purpose. I don't think this bill should be here today. We grant too many damn rules.

Table 8-3
Record on Rule Requests, 87th Congress through 94th Congress

	87th	88th	89th	90th	91st	92d	93d	94th (1st Session)	94th (2d Session)
Number of Rules Granted	n.a.	n.a.	n.a.	n.a.	218	204	255	157	143
No Hearing Held[a]	22	19	26	19	8	12	8	1	19
Requests Denied or Deferred	9	7	6	6	5	3	5	2	3
Total Number of Hearings, Denied or Deferred	31	26	32[b]	25	13	15	13	3	22

Source: For the 87th through 90th Congresses, D.M. Fox and C.P. Clapp, "The House Rules Committee and the Programs of the Kennedy and Johnson Administrations," *Midwest Journal of Political Science* 14: 662–72; "The House Rules Committee's Agenda-Setting Function, 1961–1968," *Journal of Politics* 32: 440–44. Data on the 91st and 92d Congresses come from statistical reports compiled by the Rules Committee staff. Data on the complete 93d and 94th Congresses come from calendars of the committee. For the 94th Congress, 1st session, an unofficial count was made by a Rules staff member.

[a]Excludes requests withdrawn, use of consent calendar, 21-day rule, suspension, and legislation superceded.
[b]In addition, eight proposals reached the floor through use of 21-day rule.

But even the most liberal Rules Democrats felt that the committee was not being selective enough in granting rule requests. As one frustrated liberal observed in early 1975,

As it is now, Banking and Currency has sent us about six bills this year. Some of them don't pass. Others are vetoed. A good Rules Committee would send some of their bills back and tell them to build stronger consensus. We sent the energy bill back once and tried to send it back again until the Commerce Committee got its bill together. But the leadership, after President Ford ripped the pages off the calendar, felt it had to act and badgered the Rules Committee into reporting the Ways and Means bill. The leadership made the Rules Committee go against its best judgment.

Because of the lenient rule granting during the 93d Congress and 94th Congress, 1st session, Democrats suffered a series of embarassments on the House floor. In the 93d Congress, 16 rules were defeated on the House floor, a number larger than the combined total for the preceding six Congresses. This problem was avoided during the 94th Congress, 1st session, only because of the overwhelming 2:1 Democratic majority in the House. Nevertheless, the leadership often urged Rules to report legislation that required serious, time-consuming rewriting or was doomed to defeat. The 1975 energy legislation provides a classic example. Although Rules Democrats persuaded the leadership to delay consideration of the Ways and Means bill, H.R. 6860, in hopes that it could be merged with a bill being considered by the Interstate and Foreign Commerce Committee, they were finally obliged to report this energy tax legislation. A substantial effort was needed to get the rule adopted on the floor, and not one Republican voted for the previous question on the rule. Floor debate on the bill then consumed the better part of two weeks, instead of two days as originally planned by the leadership and Ways and Means chairman, Al Ullman (D-Ore.). Twenty roll call votes on amendments were taken. And *Congressional Quarterly Weekly Report* (1975, p. 1275) described the bill that finally passed as "a stripped down energy tax measure that at best was only a start toward a national energy policy."

Led by Richard Bolling (Mo.), who had served as the chief leadership operative on the committee almost continually since 1955, Rules Democrats persuaded the leadership that it was necessary to tighten the rein on granting rules if the House were to function more effectively in making legislative policy decisions. This was possible only because the Rules Committee had become an arm of the majority party leadership and not an opponent as it had been in the 1950s and 1960s.

The effects of this adjustment can be seen in the 94th Congress, 2d session (Table 8-3). Although it is normal for more rule requests to go unheard, be defeated, or be deferred in the 2d session, one has to go back to the 90th Congress to surpass the number of bills that Rules stopped in the 94th Congress, 2d session. The Rules Committee's decision to block consideration of federal strip-mining legislation during the 94th Congress, 2d session, is a good example of the tougher approach. Similar legislation had been vetoed by President Ford in 1974 and 1975. The Interior and Insular Affairs Committee had made certain compromises to remove some administration objections, but Ford continued to oppose the legislation. Further, House Democrats would have more difficulty in obtaining the two-thirds vote necessary to override a veto than they had in their two previous attempts, especially as the 1976 election grew closer. In addition, the bill would tie up the floor for a considerable time. In the 95th Congress, the Rules Committee quickly granted a rule to a new strip-mining bill, knowing that a new President would sign it.[7]

This tougher Rules Committee attitude toward requests, which began midway through the 94th Congress, is very different from the role the Committee played as a tough "traffic cop" in the 1950s and 1960s. This is not a Rules Committee where the majority see its goal as delaying or defeating liberal legislation. This Rules Committee is one where the majority are formally appointed by the Speaker and show high levels of party voting both on the floor and in the committee. It is not a Rules Committee where the powerful chairman and ranking Democrat vote and work more often with the committee's Republican members and the Republican House leadership than with their own party's. The Rules Committee is tougher because it and the Democratic party leadership find that in the reformed House some quality control must be applied to the legislation that a decentralized subcommittee structure produces, if there is to be a chance to enact party programs.

Rule Writing

Because the Rules Committee and the majority party leadership now work in harmony on whether to grant rules, the committee can spend more time designing rules that assist the leadership to develop more orderly and reasoned consideration of complex issues. In this regard, some of the committee's members are trying to overcome the excesses that they perceived have resulted from the House reforms of the 1970s. In particular, they argue that the democratizing and decentralizing reforms have contributed to problems of fragmentation in House decision making. Given that Richard Bolling is the committee's acknowledged leader, it is not surprising that committee efforts have focused on many of the same problems addressed directly and indirectly by the select committee Bolling chaired in the 93d Congress: jurisdictional overlap, duplication of effort, competition for policy turf, isolation of decision-making environments, and lack of integrative approaches to policy problems.

Beginning in the 93d Congress and increasing substantially in the 94th, the Rules Committee has been writing a significant number of "complex rules" to help cope with the problems of fragmentation. Prior to the 93d Congress, most rules that the committee granted specified whether amendments could be offered (open versus closed rules), waived certain points of order, specified the amount of time to be allowed for general debate and who would control that time (usually the chair and ranking minority member of the committee reporting the legislation), provided for a motion to recommit, and/or included a clause to facilitate a conference with the Senate. Rules of this type could generally be called *simple* rules. Only on rare occasions would a rule be more complex and require lengthy explanation on the floor.

The complexities, added with some frequency (Tables 8-4 and 8-5) since the 93d Congress, come in several areas. First, to resolve problems of jurisdictional overlap, the Rules Committee writes rules that divide control of the general debate not just between the majority and minority on one committee but among the majority and minority on several committees.[8] A variant of this procedure gives control of debate time to other members of the reporting committee when they disagree with positions taken jointly by the chair and ranking minority member. Second, the Rules Committee often specifies that a particular amendment be in order as a substitute for a committee bill, or a title of that bill. At times, this is done because the amendment would otherwise be out of order, but more usually the amendment is a substantial alternative to the committee bill or title. By making it specifically in order, the Rules Committee calls attention to the major alternative and uses it to structure floor debate

Table 8-4
Simple and Complex Rules, 92d through 94th Congresses

	92d	*93d*	*94th*
Simple Rules	193	231	265
Complex Rules	9	24	35
Total Rules Granted	204	255	300

Table 8-5
Types of Complex Rules, 92d through 94th Congresses

	92d	*93d*	*94th*
Specific Amendment in Order	9	20	17
Split Control of Debate	2	4	19
Amendments Specified in Rule or Prior Printing in Record	0	2	8
Rule with More than One Form of Complexity	2	2	9

between two significant approaches to the issue. Third, the Rules Committee writes some "modified" rules. This form of complex rule usually specifies conditions under which the legislation will be open to amendment. The conditions might require that amendments be printed in the *Congressional Record* prior to a given date, or that amendments be allowed to certain titles or sections but not to others, or that the only amendments allowed are those the Rules Committee specifies in the rule. A modified rule serves to structure debate, to allow bill managers to know in advance what amendments will be offered, to avoid impulsive amendments and delaying amendments, and to prevent complex legislation from being "unraveled" through a barrage of amendments. Some rules contain more than one of these complex provisions.

The policy implications of using complex rules may not be immediately apparent. One can talk in terms of better-structured floor debates, presentation of competing positions on legislative issues, and freedom from delaying amendments, but only indirectly intimate policy consequences. Some examples more fully convey the policy effects that the use of complex rules has had.

In early 1976, the Rules Committee granted a rule for H.R. 9464, a natural gas bill, providing for three hours of general debate—two hours to be controlled by the member of the Interstate and Foreign Commerce Committee recognized to call up the bill and the ranking minority member on that committee, and one hour by Congressman Robert Krueger (D-Tex.). The rule further allowed an amendment by Krueger in the nature of a substitute as well as an amendment by Congressman Clarence (Bud) Brown (R-Ohio) if the Krueger amendment were defeated. Both the Krueger and Brown amendments dealt with the deregulation of natural gas. What the Rules Committee did in granting this rule by a 12-4 vote was to recognize that the major issue involving natural gas was that of deregulation. The Senate had already included a deregulation provision in its natural gas bill. However, opponents of deregulation on the House Commerce Committee structured H.R. 9464 to include only emergency provisions, thus making the deregulation amendment nongermane. To give the House a chance to vote on the deregulation issue and to focus debate on that issue, Rules made the Krueger and Brown amendments in order and provided Krueger with time during the general debate. Although the merits of the Rules Committee's decision in this case can be debated, it should be noted that from a policy standpoint the way the rule was written was as important as the decision to grant a rule at all.

A second example illustrates the use of a complex rule to limit the amending process. On March 29, 1976, by an 8-7 vote the Rules Committee granted a modified rule for consideration of H.R. 12406, amendment to the Federal Election Campaign Act of 1971. This was during the middle of the Presidential primaries, and passage of the bill was necessary before the contenders could again receive matching federal campaign funds. The rule stated that no amendments to the bill would be in order except the 13 specified in the rule. These included amendments to strike provisions of the bill restricting the proliferation of political action committees and the use of corporate political action committees, to provide for public financing of congressional elections, and to limit congressional veto of FEC advisory opinions. The Rules Committee effectively barred amendments to stop contributions by political action committees and amendments to delay passage by the House and tie up a conference with the Senate. Richard Bolling described the rule as a "compromise between practicality and fairness" (*Congressional Quarterly Weekly Report* 1976, p. 802). The committee desired to have votes on controversial provisions, but recognized the need to restore funds to the contenders as quickly as possible.

During the 94th Congress, only 11 percent of the rules granted were complex. These covered many of the significant pieces of legislation. Aside from the two already mentioned, the committee designed complex rules for legislation to regulate lobbying, to establish a postcard voter registration system, to extend unemployment compensation, to use certain naval petroleum reserves for domestic consumption, to extend and amend revenue sharing, to make meetings of government agencies open to the public, to suspend prohibitions on military assistance to Turkey, to regulate energy supplies and pricing, to amend rules of criminal procedure, and to halt the importation of Rhodesian chrome.

The use of complex rules has continued in the 95th Congress. Nowhere can this be seen more clearly than in the rule for consideration of the National Energy Act of 1977. Recognizing that the rule would be critical to the passage of any broad energy proposal, Speaker O'Neill included Rules as one of the committees to be represented on the Ad Hoc Committee on Energy.[9] Moreover, the activities of the committees and subcommittees to which parts of the Carter energy proposal were referred were monitored by the Rules Committee staff. In presenting the rule on the House floor, Richard Bolling announced, ". . . this is a very complicated rule on a very complicated subject which came to the Committee on Rules in a very complicated way" (*Congressional Record* 1977, p. H8137). The rule limited the amendments to be offered to those specified in the bill, including 20 to be offered en bloc by the Ad Hoc Committee and approximately 12 others to be offered by individual House members. For the most part, the amendments were restricted to major provisions of the legislation, such as deregulation of natural gas and gasoline taxes. Because of the tight design of the rule, opponents of the energy package were prevented from loading it down or delaying it with last-minute amendments. But they were given the opportunity to vote on controversial provisions, to substitute the language of the Republican program, and to recommit the bill with or without instructions.

Compared to the more limited energy proposals of the 94th Congress, which tied up the House floor for weeks and resulted in passage of several heavily amended pieces of legislation (certainly nothing that could come close to being described as an energy program), the House was able to complete action on the 1977 legislation in five legislative days. Naturally, the rule was only one part in the legislative effort, but it was not an insignificant one.

The use of complex rules has become a significant resource of the Democratic party leadership in the House. Not only do carefully designed rules better structure debate, ensure votes and attention to significant features bills, allow the minority an opportunity to offer alternatives, and prevent the piecemeal unraveling of the majority's legislative proposals, but also collectively they make it possible to manage the party's overall legislative program with some planning and efficiency.

Original Jurisdiction

The Rules Committee does more than just decide whether to grant rules to legislation reported by other House committees. It also has a substantial area of original jurisdiction. Among other things, the Committee can produce legislation affecting House rules, altering procedures, and establishing new committees. (In addition, Rules has the rarely used power to hold hearings on and report any legislation it wants.)

During the period of conservative coalition influence on Rules, the committee's original jurisdiction role was not played actively. Much time was spent bargaining over which bills would receive rules and, at times, when Judge Smith chaired the committee, even getting to meet. With Rules acting as a leadership arm since the 93d Congress, there has been the time and willingness to expand the original jurisdiction role into important areas of policy as well as process.

In the 93d Congress, the Rules Committee was responsible for the legislation that established the new congressional budget process. The creation, in 1975, of the House Select Committee on Intelligence, and its abolition and recreation when the first committee proved unworkable, reflected the work of the committee. And in 1977 Rules had jursidiction over the legislation that created the Ad Hoc Committee on Energy. In these cases, Rules members worked closely with the party leadership to seek solutions that would allow the House to deal more effectively with the policy problem. At other times, Rules has held up matters of original jurisdiction until sufficient leadership control of the activity could be ensured. Early in the 95th Congress, after Rules found that it already had "150 proposals before it to create at least 18 different select committees," including ones on national security, abortion, nuclear policy, insurance rates, and nationalization of the oil industry, the committee formed an ad hoc subcommittee chaired by Gillis Long (D-La.) to consider proposals for select committtes (Russell 1977). Rules recommended only the creation of a permanent Select Committee on Intelligence and a Select Committee on Population.

Obviously, the decision to create these select committees has certain policy implications. It gives attention to an issue. House members assigned to the select committees have a stake in the jurisdiction, even if it leads only to further visibility for the issue. Moreover, select committees receive staff support and budgets, can hold hearings, and can produce legislation.

The House leadership has given indications that it is interested in extending the original jurisdiction role of the Rules Committee into a wider range of policy areas. On several occasions, the leadership has considered referring complex legislation that cuts across the jurisdictions of several committees to Rules rather than use a multiple-referral approach. In the 94th Congress, Speaker Albert intended to refer the Humphrey-Hawkins full-employment legislation to Rules for hearings rather than to Education and Labor. Congressman Hawkins (D-Calif.) objected strenuously, and Albert sent the bill to Education and Labor. Although the leadership and most Rules members would like to expand the committee's original jurisdiction role, they will have to proceed cautiously if they are to avoid similar objections from other House members.

Conclusions

In the 1950s and 1960s, scholars and journalists writing about the Rules Committee concentrated on the conservative policy role that the committee played in delaying or defeating liberal legislation. For good reason they focused on the influence that the committee has as a veto in the legislative process. This focus rarely allowed them to ask what policy impact the committee could have if it worked in cooperation with majority party leadership to help steer party programs through the House. Turnover in the Rules membership, tightened leadership control in filling vacancies, and internal Rules Committee reforms in the late 1960s and early 1970s created a situation where a committee majority is now strongly oriented to Democratic party programs and is willing to work as an arm of the leadership to assist in their passage.

The impact of these changes in the Rules Committee can be most clearly seen in those committee activities designed to cope with the problems that developed from reforms which democratized and decentralized House operations. Because of its strong ties with leadership, Rules has been able to use its resources to provide a greater degree of centralized, party control in the House.

But the policy impact of Rules Committee activity is not limited to supporting the leadership, reversing the conservative dominance of the past. In tightening decisions on granting rules, in writing complex rules, and in attending to areas of original jurisdiction, the committee becomes far more important than just a rubber stamp for legislation that the "subcommittee government" of the House produces.

Notes

1. For analysis of the fight to expand the Rules Committee and its consequences, see Cummings and Peabody 1963 and Peabody 1963. On the 21-day rule see Froman 1967.

2. In other work (Oppenheimer 1977a) I discuss a variety of ways in which the Rules Committee has changed and some of the new roles it now performs in the House.

3. For analysis of the various House reforms in the 1970s see Rohde 1974; Ornstein 1975a; Dodd and Oppenheimer 1977a; and Davidson and Oleszek 1977.

4. B.F. (Bernie) Sisk (D-Calif.) and Claude Pepper (D-Fla.) missed a substantial number of votes due to illness, and Spark Matsunaga's (D-Ha.) attendance suffered because of increasing time spent on his successful campaign for the Senate. When the party unity scores are adjusted for absences, the mean for Rules Democrats in the 94th Congress was 83.3 and for all House Democrats 75.5, a difference of 7.8.

5. Committee roll call votes prior to the 93d Congress are not available.

6. In keeping with the committee ratios of 2:1 plus 1 established by the House Democratic Caucus at the start of the 94th Congress, the Rules Committee added a Democratic member, making its composition 11 Democrats and 5 Republicans. This has made the leadership margin even more secure.

7. In another case during the early part of the 95th Congress, the Rules Committee delayed a role on a bill to liberalize black lung benefits to coal miners until it received a promise from Carl Perkins (D-Ky.), chairman of the Education and Labor Committee, that he would offer substitutes for certain provisions of the bill dealing with automatic entitlements to benefits. This move was designed to undercut more restrictive Republican amendments.

8. In part this resulted from the fact that the Speaker was given the power to refer legislation to more than one committee beginning in the 94th Congress. With two or more committees holding hearings and reporting a bill (sometimes in different forms) Rules was forced to provide rules that split the management of such legislation on the floor.

9. The three Rules members on the Ad Hoc Energy Committee were Richard Bolling, John Young, and John Anderson. Bolling served as the ranking majority member, and Anderson as the ranking minority member.

9

Policy Entrepreneurs and Amateur Democrats in the House of Representatives: Toward a More Party-Oriented Congress?

Eric M. Uslaner

A New Breed of Representative

More than half of the members of the 95th House of Representatives (1977–1978) have been elected since 1970; fewer than half of them are lawyers. Since the beginning of this decade, there has been an abundance of "reform" measures passed in the House, in contrast to the fairly staid periods of the preceding decades. How do we account for these reforms, and what are their likely effects?

It is relatively clear that the changes in the House of the 1970s can be traced to the influx of new members. Yet, what is it about these members that has produced some centralizing reforms (aimed at strengthening the congressional parties) and other, often conflicting, decentralizing changes (particularly with respect to subcommittee power)? Bullock (1976) has demonstrated that the newer members tend to be considerably more concerned with the making of public policy, as opposed to seeking reelection or institutional power (compare Fenno 1973, chap. 1), than their predecessors. Yet these changes in House procedure often have conflicting goals, as mentioned above. It thus seems anomalous that the supporters of both centralizing and decentralizing reforms have been concentrated in the same group of newer members. In this chapter I suggest that there is, indeed, a logic behind this apparent contradiction. We should view the new members' support for changes in the structure of House procedures in terms of the representatives' orientations toward party, policy, and procedure.

Specifically, I maintain that the new member can be viewed as a hybrid of Wilson's (1966) "amateur democrat" and an independent "policy entrepreneur."

This is the second (see Uslaner 1977a) in a series of articles that attempts to outline a framework for the analysis of the contemporary House of Representatives in an era in which the role of the political party is decreasing among the electorate but seemingly increasing among elected officials. Future papers will place the constructs of amateur democrats and policy entrepreneurs in a broader theoretical focus and will examine the roles of leaders relative to those of members. Of particular concern is to make sense out of a set of "reforms," advocated by the same people but that seem, by traditional standards, to be contradictory. Leroy N. Rieselbach, Morris P. Fiorina, Oran Young, Russell Hardin, Joe A. Oppenheimer, David E. Price, James A. Thurber, and Joseph Cooper all provided valuable suggestions for this chapter.

The amateur democrat (Wilson 1966, p. 3, emphasis in original)

... finds politics *intrinsically* interesting because it expresses a conception of the public interest. The amateur politician sees the political world more in terms of ideas and principles than in terms of persons. Politics is the determination of public policy, and public policy ought to be set deliberately rather than as the accidental by-product of a struggle for personal and party advantage.

Policy entrepreneurs, on the other hand, are concerned with the formulation of policy, but see themselves as active participants in every stage of policy development.[1] They are egocentric in wanting to be the leading congressional spokesmen on a particular, even if relatively narrow, policy area. They are willing to cooperate with other members, particularly those of their party, but not to repudiate the personal satisfaction and recognition that comes with effective control of a policy area. Less senior members who have made such marks include Mike McCormack (D-Wash) on energy, Bob Krueger (D-Tex.) on natural gas deregulation, Joseph Fisher (D-Va.) on trade, and Bob Carr (D-Mich.) and Thomas Downey (D-N.Y.) on foreign policy.

This new breed of members is marked by both a concern for substantive policy and, like the amateur democrat, support for intraparty democracy (Wilson 1966, chap. 5). They also supported a stronger role for the party leadership in guiding legislation through the Congress. Yet, these concerns may often yield conflicting prescriptions for member action. One cannot merely state that members sometimes support centralizing reforms and sometimes decentralizing ones. How do the same people reconcile these concerns? I suggest that members ask themselves whether the proposed reform is likely to have direct impact upon their capacity to initiate or control policy. If the answer is affirmative, the member will support the change if the proposed reform will increase that capacity. If the answer is no, then the member takes on the role of the amateur democrat rather than policy entrepreneur and poses the further question: Will the proposed reform make the system more equitable (and thus more permeable to junior members' policy aspirations)? The policy entrepreneur role, then, takes precedence over that of the amateur democrat in the decision to support or oppose a particular change. The questions of primary interest to the policy entrepreneur are thus ones dealing with the ability to take action on substantive policy areas; the amateur democrat, on the other hand, is largely concerned with issues of procedure. Thus, the members supporting both centralizing and decentralizing reforms are not necessarily inconsistent. Instead, we must recognize that these goals can often be complementary. Precisely because the policy entrepreneurs realize that a stronger party leadership may be necessary to accomplish their objectives, the potential for support for a stronger party system exists even among such egocentric members. We shall consider some recent reforms in this context.

Reform for What?

By looking at the new member as a hybrid of the amateur democrat and the policy entrepreneurs we can understand why some proposed changes passed and others did not.[2] Because the policy entrepreneurs *see themselves* as formulators of public policy—although this does not imply that Congress is actually "running the country"—it is not surprising that they should concentrate on changing the committee system in Congress. It is through this system that members obtain positions in which they can concentrate on a particular policy area. A strong committee system, marked by powerful chairpersons and a long-standing seniority rule, stood in the way of the younger policy entrepreneurs who were not content to serve an apprenticeship before taking an active role in policy formulation. While this orientation suggests support for decentralizing reforms, note that many newer members had not settled on a particular area of specialization and others who had done so faced recalcitrant chairmen who might block their desired committee appointments. In this context, the members turned to their concern for intraparty democracy in a search for greater equity in legislative procedures.

First, the House Democrats in 1971 limited each member to one subcommittee chairmanship. Thus, there were considerably more opportunities for policy entrepreneurship among the members who could obtain one of the 150 subcommittee leadership slots (as opposed to 21 committee chairmanships) in the 95th House. Yet, this reform did not fully open the policy-making process to the new members. The major concern of the members was to get on the committees they desired. In 1975, the committee assignment power for House Democrats was transferred from Ways and Means to the Steering and Policy Committee, established in 1973; but, more critically, two years earlier the new members had made selection of committee chairmen the task of Steering and Policy and the Caucus.

In 1975, three chairmen were actually deposed, and in one case (Banking, Currency, and Housing) seniority was actually violated in choosing a successor. In the same year, Ways and Means was forced to establish subcommittees, and Appropriations subcommittee chairmen were to be chosen in the same manner as committee leaders. The Democratic Party, with an overwhelming majority in the House, also dictated that each subcommittee (as well as the committees) *overrepresent* the majority party's percentage of the full House membership by one member. These reforms clearly strengthened the power of subcommittee chairpersons at the expense of full committee leaders (Ornstein 1975a, p. 110).

At the same time, the role of the congressional parties was strengthened. A revived Caucus and the Steering and Policy Committee were the key elements in these reforms. The Speaker controlled appointments of half of the Steering and Policy Committee until 1977, when control reverted to the Caucus. On the other hand, the Caucus took away the power of Appropriations and Ways and

Means to nominate five members each to the new Budget Committee and vested this power in Steering and Policy. The 95th Congress also saw the beginning of a close working relationship between Budget Chairman Robert Giaimo (Conn.) and Caucus leader Thomas Foley (Wash.), so that the Democratic Party in the House might move toward some integrated set of national priorities. New Speaker Thomas P. (Tip) O'Neill (Mass.) used the Rules Committee, particularly through Representative Richard Bolling (Mo.)—the *second-ranking* Democrat on the committee and a former candidate for leadership posts—as an arm of the legislative leadership (Oppenheimer 1977b). Rules had long been a major obstacle to party programs, working to frustrate the Speaker rather than to expedite his agenda. The reforms of the 1970s also opened up the assignment process so that junior members, as well as other more ideologically oriented representatives, could attain seats on their most desired committees, including the three "power" panels (Rules, Appropriations, and Ways and Means).

Equity, however, is not ensured by changing the pattern of new assignments. Ways and Means had served as a gatekeeper for chairmen with respect to other committee assignments. Yet, it also has been an obstacle to liberal policy proposals favored by House Democrats. To foster greater conformity with the majority positions within the Democratic party, in 1975 the Caucus increased the size of the committee from 25 to 37, and an attempt was made to stack the committee with liberals. Given the heavy imbalance on the committee in favor of conservatives of both parties, this immediate change was not as effective as newer members had initially hoped (compare Bowler 1976). But Ways and Means was an exception to a more general pattern.

The policy entrepreneurs did find that greater opportunities than ever before were open to them, largely because of their own efforts. The "operating procedures" of the committees changed, as did the assignment process. Ways and Means and Appropriations became more permeable to new members, while Rules became an arm of the leadership. Other committees, such as Interior and Insular Affairs, moved from the realm of the "pork barrel" to concern for issues of energy and the environment. Yet, in the assignment game, members were concerned with their own fortunes. The collective good of the country or of the party was not their immediate concern; first, they had to obtain their own bases to influence policy. In the 1970s, members scrambled with and against one another for desirable committee slots so that they could pursue their policy interest(s) to the greatest extent possible. This concern for policy among the newer members can *perhaps* be traced to the new lure of politics after Vietnam and Watergate. In any event, there appears to be a decline in the number of members who are solely concerned with reelection or with wielding authority, as "power brokers" like Wilbur Mills. Indeed, when Mills refused to report a bill repealing the oil depletion allowance, his power base began to erode. In early 1975 the Caucus directed the Rules Committee to allow floor consideration of two amendments curbing the tax break; the action had the support of both new Ways and Means chairman Al Ullman (D-Ore.) *and* new Rules head Ray Madden (D-Ind.); thus, it did not constitute a threat to the leaders of the relevant substantive or procedural committees. The Caucus motion was partly symbolic; yet it also was offered when many new members still viewed the Caucus as a potential device for mandating party policy.

Caucus decision making on questions of substantive policy is perhaps the most important instance in which the roles of policy entrepreneur and amateur democrat clash. The result is that only when there is overwhelming agreement within the Democratic Party will the Caucus be used as a policy-making organ (such as the Vietnam resolutions of 1971, 1973, and 1975 and the oil depletion allowance in 1975). Even in the case of oil depletion, the question was not entirely one of substance, but also one of procedure. In 1974 it appeared to many members that Mills was no longer the great conciliator (Manley 1970, chap. 4), but was acting more like old-line recalcitrant leaders such as Howard "Judge" Smith or Tom Murray. On questions of policy, members feel intensely personal stakes in their issue area(s), and they recognize that other members are equally ambitious. Too much intraparty democracy could be fratricidal. While some members continued to press for expanded use of the Caucus (and the Steering and Policy Committee) on questions of policy, the prevailing view by the beginning of the 94th Congress was that procedural issues (which, after all, were *instruments* of policy formation) should be the Caucus's primary focus. Paul Simon (D-Ill.), a moderate freshman, summed up the view of the policy entrepreneur: "[I]f policy questions continue to come up at caucuses, you'll find more and more people voting to defer the issue" (*Congressional Quarterly Weekly Report* 1975, p. 912).[3]

Strengthening the parties does not, however, imply increasing the leverage of the party leadership. Indeed, on procedural questions, the commitment to intraparty democracry has often led to reforms that take power away from the leadership and vest it in the full Caucus. After the 1976 elections, when it became clear that the Democrats would enjoy large House majorities for quite some time, the Caucus stripped the Speaker of the power to appoint half the Steering and Policy Committee and made the overwhelming majority of seats elective. Yet, the Speaker retains the power to appoint the Democratic members of Rules. As long as that committee remains largely concerned with procedural issues and equity and conducts its business fairly, there are few reasons to expect further calls for intraparty democracy at the expense of committee member prerogatives.

The situations in which intraparty democracy has been most prominent involve challenges to the committees rather than to the party leadership. The subcommittee bill of rights, the assignment process, and the Steering and Policy Committee nomination of Appropriations subcommittee heads are cases in point. Yet, a proposal to subject Ways and Means subcommittees to the same chairmanship process as those of Appropriations was defeated in caucus at the beginning of the 95th Congress. Some members may have acted with restraint, since only two years earlier Ways and Means quite suddenly had been brought under party control and its new leadership had not been sufficiently "tested" for responsiveness to the party rank and file. Yet, there is also the question of substantive versus procedural issues—and it seems that many members were not ready to dictate how Ways and Means should make policy. As with Rules, the importance of intraparty democracy is a direct function of the responsiveness of the existing committee structure. Procedural reforms become important when policy entrepreneurship is threatened or thwarted.

Thus, the "democratizing" reforms can work toward either centralizing power in the party leadership or further decentralizing power. The critical question is, Will the reform create greater opportunities for policy entrepreneurship? It would, however, be too facile to assume that the commitment to intraparty democracy and a strong legislative party are inconsistent with policy entrepreneurship. As stressed above, some procedural reforms have facilitated individual member initiative on policy. Even more critically, members of the new breed seem distinctly more party-oriented than their predecessors. Generally they have supported a stronger leadership role for the Speaker and Majority Leader, and their ideologies show up in increased cohesion on House roll call votes since the end of the Vietnam war (Uslaner 1977b).[4] The distinction between substantive and procedural questions must be stressed, however. Caucus decisions on procedural questions are not likely to be challenged seriously by party members. In 1974, a close secret ballot in the Caucus killed committee reorganization; yet, a Republican attempt to force Rules to report the reorganization bill drew the votes of only seven House Democrats. The Caucus itself did overturn three 1975 decisions of Steering and Policy on committee heads; the issue in each case was one of the fairness of the chairperson. By 1977, however, no challenges were made to Steering and Policy recommendations.

The policy entrepreneur's support of a stronger role for the legislative party, particularly the Speakership, is also understandable. While the members may not be willing to subject policy making to intraparty democracy, they certainly realize that their own substantive goals are unlikely to be attained in the highly decentralized environment that the subcommittee reforms created. Indeed, one well-placed observer called the current disjointed efforts at policy formation a "Polish parliament." Representatives can formulate policy statements, but not actually make public policy when 435 policy entrepreneurs work independently of one another. The potential for stronger party government thus becomes real if the Speaker aggregates interests, determines which policies get priority at specific times, and works with the policy entrepreneurs to obtain party support for their individual programs. This appears to be what O'Neill is doing, and with some degree of success (Lyons 1977). His first attempt to exert influence did occur on a procedural matter (ethics reform), but he won not only a battle that seemed beyond hope but also the widespread admiration of party members for his leadership role.

Such leadership is not likely to resemble the strong Speakership of a Cannon or a Reed, where members were cajoled into voting for programs they did not support, but it involves considerably more partisanship than existed under Carl Albert or John McCormack. O'Neill does not have an easy task ahead of him, particularly as Congress prepares to deal with controversial legislation such as energy and the economy. Whether O'Neill succeeds depends not only on his own efforts, but also on the realization by policy entrepreneurs that a lack of coordination will lead to failure for many individual members. The first session of the 95th House has been a sobering reminder of the potential for this kind of sustained inaction. O'Neill has attempted to resolve the problem of conflicting jursidictions by appointing select committees to coordinate (or, in some cases, just to study) problems after the standing committees have acted. The ad hoc energy committee, whose members were appointed by the Speaker and reflect the party leadership's position on the President's energy program, is a notable example. If such committees do act to *coordinate* policy in Congress, there is the potential for a stronger role for the party leadership in policy making. Yet, implicit in such a structure is the potential for further decentralizaton of decision making in Congress through the establishment of one more set of policy entrepreneurs. If the ad hoc committees function consistently as an arm of the leadership, then O'Neill may have found the appropriate device for coordination. The entire procedure is fraught with the danger of some independent entrepreneur seizing the opportunity and frustrating not only the leaders but also other policy entrepreneurs.

Who Are the Policy Entrepreneurs?

Not all members of the House are policy entrepreneurs or amateur democrats, even among the recently elected representatives. No single characterization applies to all members, not even that of reelection seekers. A growing number of members simply retire, many complaining that their job is more frustrating than rewarding. Perhaps they are unsuccessful policy entrepreneurs, but many seem uncertain about what they wanted from a congressional career. Another notable group is the members who run for the Senate, even though they may have to give up safe House seats. The situation of Morris Udall (D-Ariz.) is somewhat atypical. Given virtually certain nomination and election to the Senate in 1976, he chose instead to seek reelection to the House, to assume the chairmanship of Interior and Insular Affairs in a Congress when passage, with Presidential support, of strong strip-mining legislation was virtually ensured. Udall, who earlier had sought power within the House, did not enter the contest for Majority Leader. Instead, he seized the opportunity of the new House structure to pursue his policy interests.

Thus, policy entrepreneurs are found not only among the junior members of Congress. Conversely, not every junior member is a policy entrepreneur; some are predominantly concerned with reelection and may have little interest in substantive questions. Others, perhaps unsure of their surroundings or too preoccupied with broader concerns, have not selected a policy specialization. A particularly disturbing situation for a new member, with such an area in mind, involves the discovery that someone else has already monopolized the policy in question. The new member must decide whether to challenge the other representative or seek out another area. The latter course seems most promising if no accommodation can be reached on dividing the responsibilities between the members. Yet another recent change in House procedure has made such accommodation more likely: If multiple committees have jurisdiction over a bill, it can now be assigned to more than one committee. Such a procedure allows greater flexibility for policy entrepreneurs with similar interests, although it does exacerbate the problem of coordinating policy initiatives and may make the Speaker even more important in aggregating interests.

The member, as a policy entrepreneur, is not necessarily unconcerned with other goals. Shepsle (1978) suggests that concern for reelection often can be consistent with a member's policy objectives. In some cases, such mixing of goals may be possible. But members' interest in policy does not seem predicated on the reelection goal, and I believe that the case of a low-seniority, policy-oriented member from a safe district is not atypical. A close associate reported what many observers of the Congress have heard: "He's so frustrated about his constituency. He spends so much time working on issues and then wants to talk to the voters about this work. But they just aren't interested." Nevertheless, the member goes home to his district virtually every weekend to attend weddings and to listen to constituents' personal problems. The worlds of policy formation and seeking reelection seem generally distinct. Members *do* worry about reelection, and they *are* concerned with making good public policy. Observers who insist on the electoral connection as fundamental are observing the members in only one context; members at work in subcommittee or on the floor of the House are in a different world than the one they face either in the district (see Fenno 1977) or when planning reelection efforts in their Washington offices. Some members can coordinate policy and reelection goals, but it is likely that their use of policy considerations in the electoral arena presages a bid for higher office, where elections are more likely to revolve around issues.

Policy entrepreneurship does seem to be the most common orientation of the contemporary House member. Reelection goals, I have argued, can be met simultaneously without impinging upon members' concerns for specific policies. It is not surprising to find many members pursuing policy interests of concern to their districts, since they are themselves constituents and likely to have lived in the district for many years. In some districts, there might indeed be an "electoral connection" between policy specialization (and House voting behavior) and electoral security. The changes in House procedure are more readily explicable by viewing members' orientations toward policy formation and the equitable distribution of power in the House rather than with constituency demands. There has been a sharp increase in the role of incumbency in recent congressional elections (Erikson 1971; Mayhew 1974b; Ferejohn 1977), and constituency service rather than policy agreement seems to be the key to the phenomenal reelection rates of incumbents (Fiorina 1977a), including 72 of the 74 freshman Democrats from the 1974 Watergate landslide who sought another term in 1976.[5] Members can no longer be viewed as "single-minded seekers of reelection" (Mayhew 1974a, p. 5). Instead, because members have become such experts in the science of constituency service, now they may have considerably more freedom to take whatever policy positions they want in (sub)committee or on the House floor (Uslaner 1977a).

Perhaps the largest groups of nonpolicy entrepreneurs are two species approaching extinction: (1) senior Southern Democrats and (2) Republicans. Many of the former are still hoping for the rebirth of a more complacent House. In supporting a successful motion to open Caucus meetings to the press and the public, Joe Waggoner (D-La.), a leader in the Southern conservative wing of the party, stated: "We don't really like sunshine for the Caucus, but we've got to stop this damn Caucus from legislating" (*Congressional Quarterly Weekly Report* 1975, p. 911). As turnover among Southerners occurs, however, the Democratic Party displays fewer tensions over policy questions and, particularly, over procedure. The Republicans are in a different situation. They do not necessarily want to return to a previous era, although they resent the power of the Democratic Caucus. Undoubtedly, many want to participate in policy making, but they are so outnumbered in the House that they have few opportunities to do so. Some GOP members do offer alternative policy proposals to those of their Democratic counterparts specializing on particular issues, but the continuing minority status of the Republicans has led (Jones 1970, p. 192) to the development of a "minority party mentality," in which policy innovation seems a fruitless task and members become concerned with electoral survival. The House minority leader, John J. Rhodes (R-Ariz.), sees the party as immobilized (1976). With the loss of the Presidency in 1976, the incentives for policy innovation among Republicans become even fewer.

The implications of these orientations of House members for policy making depend upon the development of a strong leadership role for the Speaker. The policy entrepreneur is a largely independent actor on questions of substance. On procedural matters, however, the amateur democrat is willing to sacrifice at least part of his/her own influence to the Caucus, as an agent of intraparty democracy, to ensure that each member will get the opportunity to participate in policy formation. Policy entrepreneurs, while not supportive of centralizing power through a body such as the Caucus, may well realize that a certain degree of coordination is necessary in order to get their favored programs through the obstacle course on the House side of the Capitol. The Speaker provides such a potential coordinating mechanism; indeed, O'Neill has been quite successful in two ventures which faced rather long odds—ethics reform and Carter's energy program. The party leadership remains the only potential clearinghouse for such policy aggregation. Independent committee chairpersons no longer have sufficient resources of their own, while the Rules Committee is an arm of the Speakership.

The critical question with respect to party activism on policy formation is whether O'Neill can weld the multiple desires of the policy entrepreneurs into a more or less cohesive party program. If so, the potential for a revitalized congressional party system (at least on the House side) is quite real. The alternative may be such extreme decentralization of decision making that members may give up on the policy-making goal and either concentrate on the constituency service aspects of the reelection goal or retire from Congress altogether. Currently, we are somewhere in between the two extremes, although O'Neill clearly has his sights set upon achieving a more cohesive party structure.

His proposed vehicle for doing so in the 95th Congress was to have been a new Select Committee on Committees (as recommended by the House Commission on Administrative Review), which would attempt to reduce the number of subcommittees and further centralize power in the party leadership. The Democratic Caucus approved the establishment of such a committee, but also created two other review bodies—a subcommittee of Rules and a similar body responsible directly to the Caucus itself. This posed a difficult question for O'Neill: Could he control all three such committees, or any one of them? In mid-October 1977, the situation became somewhat more complicated when 63 percent of the members present (including every GOP representative) voted against the rule which would have allowed consideration of wide-ranging "reform" efforts, including committee reorganization. Like the 1974 attempt, an odd coalition (committee chairmen, the Black Caucus, and all Republicans) voted to kill committee reorganization despite powerful support from the majority party leadership.[6] The press accounts of the defeat of the rule stressed that members seemed unconvinced that previous reforms had any effects on the ethics of members, although the potential to deprive members of their bases of power in subcommittees was also mentioned. Had the rule been adopted, the reorganization would have had an uphill fight since it was a difficult-to-disguise attempt to affect substance through procedural changes. Will members ultimately realize that they need to cooperate with O'Neill to get their programs adopted? Or, will "reform" ultimately destroy what prospects do exist for policy making in the contemporary House of Representatives?

Notes

1. Price (1971) first employed (to my knowledge) this term in discussing the various roles of congressional *staff members* and senators in committees. The

present use of the term is an extension of Price's framework. Thus the approach differs from recent conceptualizations of the principal goals of members (Mayhew 1974a; Dodd 1977). It is, however, consistent with (and similar to) Ripley's (1976) analysis of the Senate and with Ornstein and Rohde's (1978) descriptive analysis of the House. The differences between the two chambers make party-oriented policy formation somewhat more feasible in the House.

2. One reform measure that failed which might be attributed to the reluctance of members as policy entrepreneurs is the 1974 attempt at committee reorganization by the (Bolling) Select Committee on Committees. The new members were reluctant to restructure a system to which they had just adapted, and the proposed reorganization would have affected the potential for individual members (easily identified) to play a major role in the policy-making process. The strongest opposition came from the more senior members, who had accumulated substantial seniority on the existing committees; however, no seniority group in the party gave anywhere near majority support to the Bolling committee proposal. Davidson and Oleszek (1977, p. 252) note that 41 percent of freshman Democrats supported the plan, compared to 36 percent of members who had served from two to seven terms. I considered this to be a "sample" and conducted a difference of percentages test on these data. The results failed to yield significant differences even at the .30 level. Liberal members did tend to favor the Bolling plan (Davidson and Oleszek 1977, p. 255), but the liberalism among opponents was higher than one might have expected. This is indicative of an underlying bimodality in the opposition to the reorganization and also suggests that concern for entrepreneurship crosses the ideological spectrum.

3. Phillip Burton's defeat in his bid to become majority leader in 1977 is generally attributed to personality clashes with many Democrats and his continuing support of Representative Wayne Hays (D-Ohio), whose ouster as chairman of House Administration was recommended by Steering and Policy in 1975 but rejected by the Caucus. Hays' later involvement in a sex scandal caused his downfall, but Burton continued to support him throughout most of the controversy. Another factor probably also contributed to Burton's loss: his advocacy of the use of the Caucus, which he chaired in the 94th Congress, to set policy for the party (*Congressional Quarterly Weekly Report* 1975, pp. 911-15).

4. The differences in *Congressional Quarterly* party unity scores during and after the Vietnam era generally fall into the 5 to 7 percent range for both parties, although they are larger for Democrats than for Republicans.

5. See the description of the constituency service of incumbent members, particularly freshmen, in *Congressional Quarterly Weekly Report* (1976, pp. 2771*ff*) and the discussion below. In 1976, several freshman Democrats were attacked by their GOP challengers (often with support from national conservative organizations) as being "radical." Yet, their constituents overwhelmingly reacted negatively to such attacks, believing that their representative "just couldn't be that sort of person." On the relations between incumbents and their constituents, see Fenno (1975) for a supporting argument.

6. To be sure, the defeat of committee reorganization was part of a broader defeat of ethics reform. The reasons for opposition included the following: (1) the belief that previous ethics reforms had not worked; (2) the opposition from Republicans to strengthening the power of the Speaker through House reorganization and through the continued use of modified closed rules; and (3) the belief by some blacks that the reform proposals did not go far enough toward affirmative acton. Yet, examination of the votes against the rule from Northern Democrats indicated that many (if not most) came from the younger policy entrepreneurs discussed above.

10 Institutional Innovation and Performance Effectiveness in Public Policy Making

Ronald D. Hedlund and
Keith E. Hamm

As their environments change, political institutions must adjust organizationally to continue to be successful in their goal seeking. The range of adjustment varies from superficial "cosmetic" changes, for example, the image an organization projects, to major structural alterations. *Institutional innovation* refers to organizational adaptation patterns most closely associated with this latter, more pervasive type of adjustment.[1]

The question here is the effect of institutional innovation on policy-making performance. The institution is the Wisconsin State Assembly during 1971–1974. The innovation involves three basic changes in the decision-making process affecting the general approach to problem solving. The indicators of output performance assess the effectiveness with which the Assembly made policy in differing substantive areas and in response to differing types of requests.

Our specific interest is in how three innovations in the legislative decision-making procedures, used after the 1971–1972 Assembly session, affected policy making with respect to demands from various interest sectors and across issue (committee) areas. These procedural innovations were intended to speed up decision making, to reduce the prospects for minority delay and veto, and to strengthen the majority party's position. The rationale for them included greater efficiency and increased institutional capacity to decide by majority rule rather than by minority veto. Three major changes were enacted. First, a little-used housekeeping committee—the Rules Committee—was given the power, upon the request of any member, to make any proposal a special order of business with precedence over any other measure. (A simple majority vote on the floor sustained the committee decision.) The committee could limit floor debate and discussion on any bill, could prevent floor amendments, and could select floor

Financial support for our research has been given by the University of Wisconsin-Milwaukee Graduate School, the College of Letters and Science, the Department of Political Science, the Urban Research Center, and the Milwaukee Urban Observatory. Also important has been the ongoing research assistance from the Political Research Laboratory and the Social Science Research Facility (especially Carla Garnham, Paul Keuler, and Jerome Schuh). A number of students also have assisted greatly in collecting these data; most notable have been Patricia Siewart, Judy Titel, Sharon Noftz, Michael Gaulitz, Linda Abdelmanien, and Thomas Pyatt. Comments on an earlier draft were provided by Richard Bingham, Wilder Crane, and Meredith Watts. A special acknowledgment goes to our wives. We alone, however, assume responsibility for the data, analysis, and conclusions.

managers who would oversee debate. Since the floor leaders serve on the Rules Committee, this change tended to give greater formal power to the leadership to control the flow of legislation to the floor. The second rules change involved a discharge petition that would extricate legislation from a committee. If a committee failed to report a proposal it had held for 21 days, a petition signed by at least 50 of the 99 members could withdraw the measure and place it on the calendar. This change supplemented previous provisions that allowed the removal of legislation from committees by majority vote on the floor. The third major change, probably the most effective, placed automatic limitations on debate if the Assembly was one or more days behind its schedule on the calendar. Under these conditions, debate was automatically limited to 20 minutes on any question, with a 5-minute maximum for any speaker. Exceptions to the debate limit had to be made under the hard-to-achieve suspension of the rules.

Performance Indicators: Operational Measures and Hypotheses

The major factor under study here is the Assembly's effectiveness in performing its lawmaking function, our dependent variable. Our primary concern is how institutional innovation influenced the effectiveness with which the Assembly made decisions and solved legislative problems. We will operationalize "performance effectiveness" to maximize comparisons across the two sessions studied (1971-1972 and 1973-1974), using quantitative indicators that objectively measure this dependent variable.

Based on social psychology and management science notions of organizational performance, we divided performance effectiveness into four components: productivity, expeditiousness, efficiency, and adaptiveness (Katz and Kahn 1966; Kelly 1974; Price 1968). We specified each, using multiple quantitative indicators that could be observed directly for each session (see Figure 10-1).

Productivity is an institution's ability to transform inputs into outputs. It measures the institution's capacity to respond to demands by output action. *Expeditiousness* refers to the speed with which the institution acts; it places a premium on making decisions rapidly. *Efficiency* deals with decision-making costs and indicates the investment necessary to obtain certain output levels. *Adaptiveness* concerns the institution's ability to reorient itself; as innovations are implemented, the institution responds and adapts.

Since our interest is in the differential impact these innovations had on various outputs, we selected from the 23 operational measures in Figure 10-1 a smaller number that were relevant. Five measures—bills passed/bills placed on calendar (Calendar success); bills passed/bills introduced (Overall success); days in session from placement on calendar to second reading (Mean days calendar to second reading); days in session from second to third reading (Mean days second

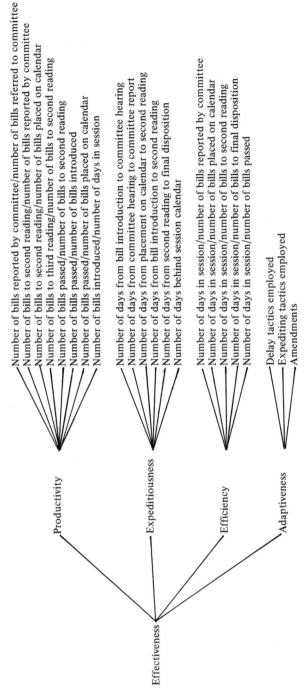

Figure 10-1. Operational Measures and Dimensions of Concept of "Effectiveness in Performing Decision-Making Functions."

to third reading); and days in session from introduction to final disposition (Mean days introduction to final disposition)—representing two components, productivity and expeditiousness, serve as our operational measures of the institution's performance effectiveness. Our analytic strategy is to compare these five measures across the two sessions—one (1971-1972) prior to and one (1973-1974) after the innovation—for different types of legislation. This research qualifies as a time-interrupted, quasi-experimental design (Campbell 1969; Campbell and Stanley 1963). Our analysis involves comparisons using analysis of variance and t tests.

An earlier study of the overall performance effectiveness of the Wisconsin Assembly before and after the innovations, using all 23 measures, showed that the innovations did, in fact, alter the levels of performance effectiveness—the postinnovation session was more productive, expeditious, and efficient—and revealed differing patterns of adaptiveness (Hedlund and Hamm 1977). This research seeks to assess whether differential effects can be detected across types of agents "requesting" legislative action and across different substantive areas of public policy. The presumption that such differences may occur reflects legislators' statements in 1973 that the innovations were intended, and were likely, to benefit certain types of agents and certain kinds of issues. Legislators' opinions at the close of the 1973-1974 session indicated that many members did, in fact, perceive such benefits to have accrued (Hedlund and Hamm 1976).

We examined legislation introduced in each session to determine if each bill had been "Introduced at the request of . . . " If such a statement was included, the bill was coded as a requested bill and the requester was placed in one of nine types—social issue organization, labor organization, the governor, private individuals, legislative committees, state agencies, regulatory/professional/farming interests, city/county governments, or miscellaneous groups.[2] Bills carrying no such designation were coded "no request." In Wisconsin, the designation "Introduced at the request of . . . " generally indicates that a bill is of great interest to some person or group and has been introduced on their behalf; however, this designation should not be taken as a sole indicator of group interest. Much legislation carrying *no* requester designation is of interest to pressure groups and generates much lobbying activity, but without the specific designation we have no reliable method to ascertain which bills or which groups.

In the Wisconsin Assembly, committees have fairly distinct subject-matter areas; bills dealing with a similar topic tend to be sent to the same committee. Thus, committee assignment of a bill is normally a fairly accurate, yet unobtrusive indicator of its subject matter. Where a bill may be referred to more than one committee, its initial committee assignment is usually a reliable indicator of its primary substantive area. In reviewing each of the bills introduced, we recorded the initial committee to which it was assigned and coded this as assignment to one of ten alternatives—Agriculture, no committee, Joint Finance, Transportation/Highways, Health/Education/Social Services, State Affairs/

Municipalities, Commerce/Consumer Affairs, Judiciary/Elections, Environment/ Natural Resources, and Taxation. Committee assignment, then, is our indicator of the subject matter of the legislation.

Four major null hypotheses guide this report:

H_0 No significant across-time change in measures of productivity will be observed by type of requester.

H_0 No statistically significant across-time change in measures of expeditiousness will be observed by type of requester.

H_0 No significant across-time change in measures of productivity will be observed by type of committee to which a bill is assigned.

H_0 No statistically significant across-time change in measures of expeditiousness will be observed by type of committee to which a bill is assigned.

Since we consider events in a natural setting as treatment variables in a longitudinal data collection sequence, we must consider the effects that other potential causal variables might have upon the dependent variable, performance effectiveness. This is critical since we are unable to control these effects. Other studies of organizations have identified a number of factors that affect performance, several of which are compared (Table 10-1) for the two sessions of the Wisconsin Assembly. These data suggest that these other potentially causal variables are fairly stable across the time studied.

In comparing performance effectiveness across the two sessions, using the indicators we have chosen, we assume that the content and complexity of legislative proposals are constant or vary in a random fashion. If more controversial, complex, or sought-after legislation characterized one session, performance effectiveness might be altered; however, our impressions from discussion with many observers indicate that no such systematic difference existed.

Institutional Innovation and Requesters for Legislative Action

During the 1971-1972 session, 34.8 percent of all the bills introduced carried the designation "Introduced at the request of . . ." compared with 32.2 percent in 1973-1974.[3] This substantial number of bills is sufficient to permit anlaysis of the comparative success of different requesters.

Table 10-2 indicates the existence of great variation in the number of bills requested by various groups and persons for each session. Some variation is evident across the two sessions: legislative committees and social issue organizations increased their requests while labor and local governments reduced theirs.

Table 10-1

Control Variables for Each Legislative Session in the Wisconsin Assembly

Control Variables	Session	
	1971–1972	*1973–1974*
System Resources		
Percent in SMSA[a]	58.9	58.9
Percent Employed in Manufacturing[a]	24.8	26.2
Demand Input from Agencies or Interest Groups		
Governor	Governor Lucey	Governor Lucey
	Democrat	Democrat
Senate	20 Republicans	18 Republicans
	13 Democrats	15 Democrats
Interest Groups[b]	394	395
Lobbyists[b]	531	485
Internal Decisional System		
First-Term Members	29%	29%
Number of Previous Terms	2.23 average	2.23 average
(For 1945–1967 Average = 2.25)[c]		
Partisan Balance	66 Democrats	62 Democrats
	34 Republicans	37 Republicans
Leadership		
Speaker[d]	Rep. Huber	Rep. Anderson
Majority Floor Leader[d]	Rep. Anderson	Rep. Earl
Minority Floor Leader	Rep. Froehlich	Rep. Shabaz
Assistant Minority Floor Leader	Rep. Shabaz	Rep. Thompson
Educational Level[c]		
Not beyond High School	20%	18%
College Degree	49	52
Higher Degree	30	31
Occupational Status[e]		
Attorney	20%	19%
Farmer	15	12
Retired	3	4
Other	62	64
Age Average	44 Years	42.5 Years
Informal Norms	Assumed Constant over Period	
Staff Services	Slight Increase over Period	

[a]Figures provided by the Bureau of Research Statistics, Wisconsin Department of Industry and Human Relations.

[b]Figures supplied by the Division of Elections and Records, Office of the Secretary of State.

[c]David Ray, "Membership Stability in Three State Legislatures: 1883–1969," *American Political Science Review*, 68 (March 1974): 110.

[d]On December 18, 1971, Representative Huber resigned from office to accept an executive appointment. He was succeeded as Speaker by Representative Anderson. The majority floor leader became Representative Earl.

[e]Figures provided by the Wisconsin Legislative Reference Bureau.

Table 10-2
Productivity Measures for 1971–1972 and 1973–1974 Sessions, by Type of Requester (*percentages*)

Requester[a]	Calendar Success[b]				Overall Success[c]			
	1971-1972 % Success (N)[d]	1973-1974 % Success (N)	Percent Change[e]	Rank	1971-1972 % Success (N)	1973-1974 % Success (N)	Percent Change	Rank
Social Issue Organizations	14.3 (7)	63.4 (11)	343.4	1	7.1 (14)	35.0 (20)	393.0	1
Labor Organizations	38.5 (26)	61.1 (18)	58.7	3	25.0 (40)	50.0 (22)	100.0	2
Governor	48.9 (47)	62.7 (51)	28.2	8	33.3 (69)	49.2 (65)	47.7	3
Private Individuals	26.7 (30)	50.0 (16)	87.3	2	9.0 (89)	11.0 (73)	22.2	4
Legislative Committees	58.3 (84)	77.2 (92)	32.4	7	51.0 (96)	60.7 (117)	19.0	5.5
State Agencies	42.5 (134)	59.7 (92)	40.5	4	35.8 (159)	42.6 (129)	19.0	5.5
No Requester	39.3 (660)	53.2 (477)	36.4	5	20.1 (1291)	20.6 (1236)	2.5	7
Regulatory/Professional/Farming	56.5 (23)	75.0 (12)	32.7	6	46.4 (28)	42.9 (21)	-7.5	8
City/County Governments	54.7 (95)	58.0 (50)	6.0	9	34.4 (151)	27.9 (104)	-18.9	9
Miscellaneous Groups	53.3 (30)	50.0 (16)	-6.2	10	38.1 (42)	22.2 (36)	-41.7	10
Total	43.0 (1136)	58.0 (835)	34.9		24.7 (1979)	26.5 (1823)	7.3	

[a] "Requester" = Those bills officially designated as "Introduced at the request of . . ." Thus the legislation designated "Governor Requester" were the bills labeled "Introduced at the request of Governor Lucey."

[b] "Calendar Success" = The number of bills for a requester passed by the Assembly as a percentage of the number of bills reported to the Assembly calendar for that type of requester.

[c] "Overall Success" = The number of bills for a requester passed by the Assembly as a percentage of the number of bills introduced to the Assembly for that type of requester.

[d] "(N)" = The total number of bills on which the percentage is based.

[e] "Percent Change" = The percentage change from 1971-1972 to 1973-1974 using the 1971-1972 percent as the base.

The Wisconsin Legislature, like most others, places much responsibility in its committees to discuss, alter, and assess legislative proposals. This action may entail a complete revision or substitution of provisions in a bill. Using a measure of calendar success controls for the effects of committee action.

The greater calendar success for all legislation in the more recent session, 58.0 percent as opposed to 43.0 percent, suggests that the new procedures may have had one of their anticipated outcomes. A greater percentage of the legislation placed on the calendar was passed in 1973-1974 than in 1971-1972. It is difficult, however, to attribute all this increase to the institutional innovations since only one of the changes had any impact upon committee action—the discharge petition—and this procedure was used very sparingly. One contributing factor may have been that committees in 1973-1974 reported a smaller percentage of bills than in 1971-1972, 45.8 percent compared with 57.4 percent. Committees gave all bills greater scrutiny and were more selective regarding what they reported. These committee changes may have had some effect on calendar success, but these influences are very difficult to trace.

In 1971-1972 the calendar success rate for various requesters (or percentage of bills passed out of those placed on the calendar by a committee) varied between 14.3 and 58.3 percent, a range of 44 points, while in 1973-1974 the scores varied between 50.0 and 77.2 percent, a range of 27.2. The narrower range in 1973-1974 suggests that some of the disparity among various requesters' success rates was reduced by the institutional innovations. The 1973-1974 session revealed greater equality in success rates across all types of requesters. Concurrent with these changes is a substantial increase in the lowest calendar success rate from 14.3 percent in 1971-1972 to 50.0 percent in 1973-1974. Such a dramatic increase may result because committees were more selective in 1973-1974, sending fewer "nonpassable" bills to the floor.

Requesters' overall success in 1971-1972 varied between 7.1 and 51.0 percent, a range of 43.9 points, while in 1973-1974 the variation was between 11.0 and 60.7 percent, a range of 49.7. Contrary to the trend noted for calendar success, overall success dispersion actually increased. Further, certain requesters—especially social issue organizations, labor groups, and the governor—enjoyed a much greater success rate in 1973-1974.

Regarding measures of expeditiousness (Table 10-3), we deal with the speed with which the legislature acts. Given the nature of the innovations, we expect these indicators to be valid and sensitive measures of changes in performance effectiveness directly traceable to the procedural changes. The three indicators of expeditiousness focus on important sequences in a bill's history. Obviously the time from introduction to final disposition is an important sequence. So are the time from the termination of committee control (placement on the calendar) to the deliberation and perfection stage for the entire legislative body (second reading) and the delay between meaningful floor action and the final vote (second reading to third reading). By comparing the time used in each sequence

Table 10-3

Expeditiousness Measures for 1971–1972 and 1973–1974 Sessions, by Type of Requester[a] (mean number of "session days")[b]

Requester[a]	Mean Days Calendar to Second Reading			Mean Days Second Reading to Third Reading			Mean Days Introduction to Final Disposition		
	1971–1972	1973–1974	t Test	1971–1972	1973–1974	t Test	1971–1972	1973–1974	t Test
Social Issue Organizations	c	c	c	c	c	c	c	c	c
Labor Organizations	15.6	13.7	.77	2.5	2.4	.40	49.2	32.7	1.53
Governor	19.6	14.1	3.15**	3.7	5.3	-.62	32.1	36.1	-.77
Private Individuals	14.8	9.9	1.60	7.3	0.0	1.00	57.2	25.0	3.04**
Legislative Committees	14.0	10.0	1.53	0.9	3.2	-2.09*	22.9	21.7	.32
State Agencies	19.6	12.7	5.50***	2.8	3.6	-.38	36.1	28.8	1.87
No Requester	16.4	12.7	4.54***	2.7	3.2	-.47	35.5	33.9	.88
Regulatory/Professional/Farming	16.0	13.6	.94	5.6	0.1	1.06	48.7	24.1	2.18*
City/County Governments	16.0	14.2	.93	2.2	0.3	1.12	41.4	33.9	1.27
Miscellaneous Groups	17.7	10.6	1.53	1.9	0.0	.68	43.1	24.3	1.61
Total[d]	16.6 (589)	12.6 (579)		3.1 (566)	3.3 (487)		36.1 (495)	31.1 (483)	
F Ratio	0.71	0.99		0.77	0.83		3.3	1.1	
Significance	.68	.56		.63	.58		.00	.30	

t test significance * = $.01 < p < .05$; ** = $.001 < p < .01$; and *** = $p < .001$.

[a]"Requester" = Those bills officially designated as "Introduced at the request of. ..." Thus, the legislation designated "Governor Requested" were the bills labeled "Introduced at the request of Governor Lucey."

[b]Table entries are the mean or average number of "session days" required for bills to move from one point in the legislation process to another. Session days are defined as those days on which the Assembly met and transacted legislative business.

[c]The number of bills was too small to calculate meaningful averages and a t test.

[d]Bills placed directly on calendar were not included.

across the two sessions and among the various requesters, we assess the effects of the institutional innovations on expeditiousness.

For the time from placement on the calendar to second reading, Table 10-3 indicates nonsignificant F ratios among type of requester for each session, indicating that we have insufficient evidence to conclude that differing requesters experienced differing expeditiousness rates between calendar assignment and second reading. (The range is 5.6 days in 1971-1972 and 4.3 days in 1973-1974.)

Although all requesters received improved treatment, a few experienced very significant changes. Most dramatic are state agency-sponsored legislation and bills introduced without request (t test differences significant at .001 level) and governor-requested bills (.01). These trends indicate that while each type of requester had a more expeditious treatment of its legislation after the innovations, state agencies, "no requesters," and the governor experienced the most significant improvement. In sharp contrast are the findings regarding delays between second and third reading. Five requesters experienced an average decrease in the time period while four experienced an increase. Only one requester, legislative committees, shows a significant change.

The most interesting and important measure of expeditiousness is the average total time from introduction to final disposition. (Final disposition can mean a variety of specific actions including passage, being moved for indefinite postponement, etc.). In 1971-1972 the range was 34.3 days, but in 1973-1974 it was considerably smaller—14.4. While a significant F ratio among requesters exists for the earlier session, the 58 percent decrease in range is associated with a nonsignificant F ratio for the later one. A leveling out of differences among requesters seems to have occurred with the innovations. Such a trend appears primarily because of a reduction in the mean days for the longest delays between 1971-1972 and 1973-1974 for bills requested by labor, private individuals, state agencies, regulatory/professional/farming, local governments, and miscellaneous groups. Only one requester experienced an increase from 1971-1972 to 1973-1974 in the mean days required for treating legislation—governor. While some requesters did benefit from the innovations, in both productivity and expeditiousness, these advantages must be viewed against the background of some equalization of treatment among all requesters. This equalization is most apparent in the expeditiousness with which the Assembly acted upon legislation. On the other hand, inequality seems to have been heightened for productivity, with the primary beneficiaries being social issue organizations, labor, and the governor.

Institutional Innovation and Committee Assignments

In the Assembly, a bill is routinely assigned to one of more than 20 standing committees. Each committee has a fairly well-defined, substantive jurisdiction, and assignment is rather automatic following introduction and first reading. Less than 10 percent of all legislation introduced is not referred to committee.[4]

With regard to calendar success, the 1973-1974 session demonstrated a greater range across committee areas—48.7 points versus 37.9 in 1971-1972 (Table 10-4). Such an increase appears to result because some committees had much improved rates in 1973-1974 while others had more modest changes. All but one committee area—Commerce/Consumer Affairs—did increase, but the increases varied from a low of 8.7 percent to a high of 81.5 percent.

For overall success, as for calendar success, the range across committee areas increased after the introduction of the institutional innovations—42.3 points in 1971-1972 to 74.2 in 1973-1974. This increase is much larger than that for calendar success. Each one-way analysis of variance by committee area shows statistically significant F ratios, indicating that during each session expeditiousness differed considerably among committee areas. Comparing the range across sessions for each measure indicates that some narrowing of the gaps among areas took place: calendar to second reading, 11.6 in 1971-1972 to 7.7 in 1973-1974; second to third reading, 7.5 in 1971-1972 to 6.7 in 1973-1974; and introduction to final disposition, 47.8 in 1971-1972 to 34.1 in 1973-1974. Thus, for each expeditiousness measure, comparatively less dispersion characterized the session after the institutional innovations.

The most striking aspect of Table 10-5 is the parallel trend across sessions for the amount of time between calendar and second reading, and introduction and final disposition. Every committee area except Judiciary/Election experienced less delay in 1973-1974 than in 1971-1972. Further, five of the six committee areas experiencing a statistically significant decrease in the number of days from calendar to second reading also experienced a statistically significant improvement in the time from introduction to final disposition. Finally, if we turn our attention to differences among committee areas, we find a decrease in the range from 1971-1972 to 1973-1974. In spite of this decrease, the remaining differences have statistically significant F ratios. Thus, while the innovations in the 1973-1974 session appear to have reduced the disparity, there remain significantly different expeditiousness rates.

Conclusions and Implications

This research on the relationship between institutional innovation and subsequent performance effectiveness shows that in the period following change, the Wisconsin Assembly appears to have been more productive and expeditious in its treatment of bills. Further, differential effects are noted for groups or individuals who had requested legislation and for committee areas. With regard to various organizational and individual requesters, differential changes are noted for productivity, with social issue organizations, labor groups, and the governor

Table 10-4
Productivity Measures for 1971-1972 and 1973-1974 Sessions, by Assembly Committee Assignment[a] (percentages)

Committee Assignment[a]	Calendar Success[b]				Overall Success[c]			
	1971-1972 % Success (N)[d]	1973-1974 % Success (N)	Percent Change[e]	Rank	1971-1972 % Success (N)	1973-1974 % Success (N)	Percent Change	Rank
Agriculture	43.3 (30)	62.0 (29)	43.2	4	31.0 (42)	47.4 (38)	52.9	1
No Committee[f]	57.5 (146)	84.7 (72)	47.3	2	57.5 (146)	84.7 (72)	47.3	2
Joint Finance	62.9 (27)	68.4 (19)	8.7	9	17.3 (98)	22.4 (58)	29.5	3
Transportation/Highways	38.9 (95)	46.0 (87)	18.3	7	21.9 (169)	27.6 (145)	26.0	4
Health/Education/Social Service	31.3 (239)	56.8 (176)	81.5	1	20.5 (366)	23.6 (424)	15.1	5
State Affairs/Municipalities	53.1 (113)	59.6 (99)	12.2	8	25.3 (237)	28.5 (207)	12.6	6
Commerce/Consumer Affairs	58.3 (58)	56.4 (62)	-3.3	10	24.1 (116)	25.7 (136)	6.6	7
Judiciary/Elections	47.6 (210)	58.9 (173)	23.7	6	23.8 (421)	25.3 (403)	6.3	8
Environment/Natural Resources	41.5 (106)	57.9 (63)	39.5	5	23.0 (191)	22.4 (147)	-2.6	9
Taxation	25.0 (108)	36.0 (50)	44.0	3	15.2 (178)	10.5 (171)	-30.9	10
Total[g]	42.9 (1132)	57.9 (830)	35.0		24.7 (1964)	26.6 (1801)	7.7	

[a]"Committee Assignment" = The Assembly committee to which a bill was sent.

[b]"Calendar Success" = The number of bills for an area passed by the Assembly as a percentage of the number of bills reported to the Assembly Calendar for that type of committee area.

[c]"Overall Success" = The number of bills for an area passed by the Assembly as a percentage of the number of bills introduced to the Assembly for that type of committee area.

[d]"(N)" = The total number of bills on which the percentage is based.

[e]"Percent Change" = The percentage change from 1971-1972 to 1973-1974 using the 1971-1972 percent as the base.

[f]Some legislation that was introduced was *not* sent to an Assembly Committee. The vast majority of this legislation was bills passed by the Senate and sent to the Assembly where "Companion" Assembly bills made committee assignment redundant; the bills were placed on the calendar.

[g]Excluded from analysis were bills sent to minor housekeeping committees like printing, etc.

Table 10-5
Expeditiousness Measures for 1971-1972 and 1973-1974 Sessions, by Assembly Committee Assignment[a]
(average number of "session days")[b]

Committee Assignment[a]	Mean Days Calendar to Second Reading			Mean Days Second Reading to Third Reading			Mean Days Introduction to Final Disposition		
	1971-1972	1973-1974	t Test	1971-1972	1973-1974	t Test	1971-1972	1973-1974	t Test
Agriculture	16.4	12.2	2.3*	0.5	1.2	-.52	35.5	26.4	2.2*
No Committee	8.8	5.7	1.7	0.3	0.1	1.38	9.5	6.1	1.3
Joint Finance	16.0	8.0	1.2	1.2	0.4	.82	27.5	17.4	1.5
Transportation/Highways	20.4	12.2	4.4***	4.9	2.6	.89	48.4	33.9	3.0***
Health/Education/Social Service	16.3	13.5	1.16	3.1	5.1	-.68	41.4	35.5	-1.6
State Affairs/Municipalities	15.5	11.8	2.5*	3.9	2.7	.74	42.5	31.5	2.6**
Commerce/Consumer Affairs	17.0	12.1	3.7***	7.8	4.9	.74	57.3	30.4	4.2***
Judiciary/Elections	14.6	13.4	1.9	0.8	1.1	-1.42	35.6	40.2	1.7
Environment/Natural Resources	18.2	12.3	3.3**	3.7	6.8	-.97	43.8	38.4	1.1
Taxation	19.1	13.4	2.2*	3.9	4.4	.16	48.8	30.3	3.3***
Total	15.6 (678)	11.9 (633)		3.1 (563)	3.3 (489)		36.1 (492)	31.1 (490)	
F Ratio	4.1	4.6		2.1	2.3		11.4	11.2	
Significance	.0001	.0001		.028	.016		.0001	.0001	

t test significance * = .01 $< p <$ .05; ** = .001 $< p <$ .01; and *** = $p <$ .001.

a"Committee Assignment" = The Assembly committee to which a bill was sent.

bTable entries are the mean or average number of "session days" required for bills to move from one point in the legislative process to another. Session days are defined as those days on which the Assembly met and transacted legislative business.

having much greater success for their requested legislation after the innovations. In reflecting on the effects of the changes, at least three-quarters of the legislators report that labor and the governor did, in fact, benefit from the new conditions.

This research also demonstrates that after the innovations, more expeditious legislative action occurred. Legislative working time, as measured in session days, was generally shorter from a bill's placement on the calendar to its second reading. The interval between bill introduction and final disposition was also generally reduced.

In addition to the fortunes of specific requesters under the innovations, certain general trends also are apparent. One of the more interesting is the range of differences among requesters. Under the innovations there were reduced differences among requesters' calendar success rates. A similar trend is seen for expeditiousness, with reduced differences among requesters under the innovations for the time delay between calendar assignment and second readings, and between introduction and final disposition. However, when attention is turned to overall success, this trend is reversed; the disparity among requesters was actually greater after the innovation. In our judgment, any reduction in differences for the other measures, while interesting, is overshadowed by this increasing difference in overall success. Overall success is of greatest importance to requesters, legislators, and the public because passage of legislation is a prerequisite for changes in public policy. Expeditiousness and calendar success are less relevant if the bills do not pass.

Focusing on legislation in specific committee areas underscores several important trends. Substantial change in productivity across the sessions is apparent among different committee areas. The across-time changes in overall success produced greater differences among areas after the innovation than had been the case previously. Innovation did not reduce differences here.

In summary, big gains in productivity, as measured by overall success, under the innovations were experienced by social issue organizations, labor, the governor, and in the Agriculture, Joint Finance, and Transportation/Highway areas. Losses were evident for regulatory/professional/farming organizations, city/county governments and miscellaneous groups, and in Environmental/Natural Resources and Taxation areas. Very significant differences exist among areas for expeditiousness in 1971-1972. Although after the innovations some of these differences were reduced, others remained and continued to be statistically significant. Sizable improvements were noted for private individuals and regulatory/professional/farming groups. And although Commerce/Consumer Affairs, Taxation, Transportation/Highways, State Affairs/Municipalities, and Agriculture experienced significant improvements with the innovations in the time required for the Assembly to act on their legislation, these improvements were not sufficient to overcome the time advantages enjoyed by other areas, most notably nonassigned bills and Joint Finance legislation. This evidence fails to confirm our four null hypotheses.

We have noted certain other institutional and environmental trends and relevant hypotheses, not associated with the innovations, that may have had some impact on the performance effectiveness measures. Fewer bills were introduced into the 1973--1974 session, reversing a 10-year trend. Also the committees seem to have performed in a somewhat different manner during 1973-1974 than in 1971-1972. In the later session, they reported a smaller percentage of the bills sent to them, thus decreasing the quantity of legislation for the entire chamber to consider. While these factors may have had some effect on performance effectiveness, other evidence indicates that the innovations did, in fact, play a major role in producing the changes in productivity and expeditiousness. Also, since partisan control of each chamber and the governor's office were the same for each session and since the leadership in the Assembly and the executive remained basically unchanged, we find insufficient evidence to attribute the changes in performance to partisan or personnel factors. Rather, partisan concerns and leader perceptions seem to have been largely responsible for implementing these innovations.

Regarding the effects of these innovations on representative government, one could argue that the changes in the rules provide the majority with decision-making procedures and approaches to problem solving that facilitate a more effective performance in policy making. Such organizational control by a majority might foster greater organizational responsibility and responsiveness to citizens, or it might lead to greater insulation and unresponsive legislative action. Regardless of such long-term consequences, any minority in the 1973-1974 Assembly, no matter how vocal, rarely prevailed when the majority (with the consent of the leadership) was committed. If the majority party failed to produce substantive policy, minority obstruction in the Assembly could no longer be blamed. This general statement would not have been *as applicable* in past sessions of the Assembly. On the other hand, these innovations also may reduce the discretion of the individual representative to implement his/her constituents' demands. One might argue that these innovations limited too severely the representative's opportunity to voice and work for the specific interests of his/her constituents, especially when these interests were contrary to majority sentiment in the Assembly. For example, the innovations were used to counteract effectively the intentions of some members to extract compromises from the leadership, using dilatory tactics, during deliberations on the 1975 state budget.

As our evidence shows, the institutional innovations did affect positively the productivity and expeditiousness of Assembly action and did have a differential impact on both requesters and committee areas. Some benefited more than others. As a consequence of these innovations, representative government in the Wisconsin Assembly and the substance of public policy also probably changed. The direction of this change seems to be toward majority rule, which currently favors Democratically oriented policy; toward party accountability and responsibility; and away from individual and minority bargaining and veto in policy decisions.

Notes

1. Some argue that innovation implies that the change itself is novel and has never been attempted (invention). While we find some merit in such a definition, the problem of determining whether some change or series of changes has *ever been used before* seems time-consuming and not very important. Our current approach is to evaluate the degree to which change departs from past practices and to determine whether it is innovative in terms of the *amount of change*. Our sense of innovation seems consistent with its usage elsewhere (Gray 1973; Walker 1969).

2. In addition, the Governor's public statements were reviewed to determine other legislation in his legislative program.

3. For each session we were able to determine that some bills without the designation "Introduced at the request of Governor Lucey" were largely the result of the Governor's initiative. These additional bills were included as Governor requested.

4. Primary among these "non-referred bills" is Senate companion legislation already sent to the floor. Excluded from our analysis are those bills of a routine, housekeeping nature referred to one of the three legislative affairs committees (Printing; Revisions, Repeals and Uniform Law; or Rules). Because many committees handled a comparatively small number of bills, we collapsed categories and formulated nine committee areas:

Agriculture = Agriculture

Joint Finance = Joint Finance

Transportation/Highways = Transportation, and Highways

Health/Education/Social Services = Education, Health, and Social Services; Labor; Veterans and Military Affairs; and Retirement Systems

State Affairs/Municipalities = State Affairs, Municipalities, and Tourism

Commerce/Consumer Affairs = Commerce and Consumer Affairs, and Insurance and Banking

Judiciary/Elections = Judiciary, and Elections

Environment/Natural Resources = Environmental Quality and Natural Resources

Taxation = Taxation, Excise Fees, and Tax Exemptions

11 The Impact of Reform: The House Commerce Subcommittee on Oversight and Investigations

David E. Price

Congressional oversight of the executive and independent agencies, Representative John Culver declared during the hearings of the Select Committee on Committees in 1973, "really doesn't exist on any serious, sustained, systematic basis." "It [is] no contest," a former OMB official told members of Congress. "You are outgunned, outmanned, and outmemoed almost consistently." It was a refrain the Select Committee on Committees heard often and with remarkable consistency. Its response was to recommend that each standing committee be required to establish an oversight subcommittee.[1] This proposal was rejected in its mandatory form by the Democratic Caucus and by the full House, but by 1977 the number of House committees designating separate "oversight" and/or "investigations" subcommittees had increased from 6 to 9.[2] This chapter will ask whether, and under what conditions, such an organizational device is likely to prompt more extensive congressional oversight. I will focus on one of the longest-lived of the House units, the Oversight and Investigations Subcommittee of the House Interstate and Foreign Commerce Committee.

The Commerce subcommittee, which dates from the 85th Congress (1957–1958), has been a focal point of controversy and criticism from the beginning. Early charges against it ranged from an accusation by its own chief counsel (later fired) that the members were attempting to "smother" an investigation of bribery and favoritism on the Federal Communications Commission (FCC) and other regulatory commissions, to a charge by the Republican National Chairman that Presidential Assistant Sherman Adams, under investigation for his relationship with industrialist Bernard Goldfine, was being subjected to "a campaign of political persecution" (Schwartz 1959, p. 100; *Congressional Quarterly Almanac* 1958, p. 691). The subcommittee's public visibility was maintained through the 86th Congress by investigations of television quiz show rigging and "payola" in the music industry. But with the coming of a Democratic administration came a decisive waning of investigative vigor (Scher 1963, pp. 533, 537-39, 549-50). Criticisms of the subcommittee through the 1960s thus came to focus on its

An expanded version of this chapter is available as Working Paper 4782, Institute of Policy Sciences and Public Affairs, Duke University. I am indebted to Steve Haeberle for research assistance, and to staff members of the Oversight and Investigations Subcommittee, particularly former Chief Counsel Michael Lemov and Office Manager Betty Eastman, for their generous furnishing of documents and information.

decreasing level of activity, the narrowness of its inquiries, and the degree of control exercised over the oversight process by successive full-committee chairmen Oren Harris (D-Ark.) and Harley Staggers (D-W.Va.).

Harris took over the subcommittee in 1958 after its stormy first year. Staggers, who succeeded him in 1966, continued the practice of chairing both full committee and Investigations subcommittee. Criticisms of House Commerce's oversight performance have been intertwined with more general complaints about Staggers's leadership. These, in turn, have been linked to the rising dissatisfaction in the House as a whole with the ability of committee chairpersons to control the flow of House business and to restrict the roles of subcommittee chairpersons and junior members. Accordingly, when Democrats on House Commerce in 1975 moved to "reform" and repair the oversight function, they replaced Staggers with John Moss (D-Cal.) as subcommittee chairman. At the same time, in both House and committee caucus, they voted for rules changes that increased vastly the authority and resources available to Moss and other subcommittee chairpersons. It is my purpose to examine the impact of these changes. How has the subcommittee's conduct of oversight changed? In what ways has it remained the same? How does congressional "reform" compare with other factors in explaining performance? Exploring these questions should shed some light on the roots of congressional behavior and on the problems and possibilities of altering it.

The Subcommittee before Reform

Few Commerce Committee members expected Harley Staggers to be a dynamic or innovative chairman, but many welcomed his accession as promising less conservative and controlling leadership. At first it looked as though he might breathe new life into the Investigations subcommittee, whose level of activity had fallen off drastically after the 86th Congress. Staggers added three new slots to the subcommittee and appointed several assertive, relatively senior representatives to membership. He doubled the size of the professional staff, from 6 in 1965 to 12 by 1967, and, most importantly, brought Robert Lishman, who had headed the staff during the subcommittee's earlier heyday, back to the chief counsel's post. Such hopeful signs largely came to naught. Lishman developed an extensive plan for the continual scrutiny of the commissions, but was able to implement it fully only with respect to the Interstate Commerce Commission (ICC). Two staff men spent the bulk of their time during the 91st Congress at the Commission, examining files pertinent to cases on the dockets and attempting to ascertain the basis of Commission decisions. They initially developed a critique of the ICC's willingness to allow the decline and discontinuance of passenger train service. Staff work then came to focus on what Lishman termed "undue fraternization" between regulators and regulatees, culminating in a drawn-out series of hearings on the attempt of the secretary of the ICC to cover up several transactions.[3]

Lishman also assigned staff members to the FCC, and a series of hearings and reports on trafficking in broadcast licenses and construction permits, the regulation of political broadcasting, and the staging of network news documentaries resulted. This latter area, which initially involved investigations of a Chicago station's staging of a "pot party" and of television coverage of the disturbances surrounding the 1968 Democratic National Convention, caught Staggers's interest and eventually claimed a major share of subcommittee time and resources. But policy areas and agencies elsewhere in Commerce's jurisdiction were covered sporadically or not at all.

Lishman's health, meanwhile, began to decline, and he died of cancer in late 1970. Daniel Manelli, an investigator who specialized in communications matters, was elevated to Lishman's slot only after an embarassingly long period as acting chief counsel. His retention was widely seen as an indication that Staggers anticipated few changes in what had come to be regarded as a relatively moribund oversight operation. The subcommittee's activities during the 91st and 92d Congresses gradually deviated futher and further from the Lishman model. "I'd say the main change was that we got [away from the emphasis on continuing agency scrutiny and] into more 'major' cases," one aide recollects. "The use of drugs in sports would be one example, and of course news rigging, which was Manelli's first love."

Subcommittee members became increasingly critical of Staggers's failure to develop a more extensive program of oversight. As Moss recalls,

We were continually frustrated by Staggers' failure to get anything significant going. The subcommittee's role had been narrowed by Harris from the broad oversight responsibility envisioned by [Speaker] Rayburn in setting it up, and it wasn't broadened again until I took over last Congress. Lishman was a good investigator, but he was never given enough resources. And as Lishman got sick, the subcommittee's focus became even narrower. . . . We got to the point that we were simply looking at railroads and a few broadcasting matters. . . . We just had no coverage of most of the areas under the Committee's jurisdiction. . . . I tried continually to change things, but the Chairman had complete control. My access to Lishman was fine, but I had no voice in how the staff was used or what we investigated.[4]

Few suggested that Staggers held back the oversight operation out of a simple desire to protect "the interests"; in fact, he could be quite resistant to pressure, as when the staff's investigation of a Boston FCC case began to come uncomfortably close to some associates of House Speaker McCormack. Staggers's hesitancy seemed to stem more from a reluctance to stir up controversy and from an apprehension that "opening up" the subcommittee would result in a loss of control. Members and staff commonly recall suggesting various lines of inquiry and never receiving any response. One staff member recounts the process by which the subcommittee finally aired charges that employees of CBS News, in the process of filming a documentary, had assisted a group of expatriates planning an invasion of Haiti: "We had *seven* executive hearings before Staggers finally agreed to open it up to a public hearing. Members began telling him that if he delayed any longer, he'd be accused of covering up for CBS."

Member discontent reached a peak during the 91st Congress. Staggers had consented to appoint an Investigations Subcommittee of 16, including the chairpersons of all four legislative subcommittees. Conflict was not the only problem: the subcommittee's size was unwieldy, and quorums were difficult to assemble. "We've got too much of this business of people being on several subcommittees, not being able to handle the work on any adequately," Staggers said. Accordingly, in 1971 he extended the committee rule that prohibited service on more than one legislative subcommittee to the Special Subcommittee on Investigations as well, and reduced the membership of the latter unit to 5. There was surprisingly little resistance—partly because, as Moss notes, there was "really no forum for effective resistance," but also because of an accommodation Staggers worked out on another front: the chairpersons of the legislative subcommittees were given one professional staff slot each. Moss, who as chairman of the Commerce and Finance Subcommittee was one of the scheme's beneficiaries, denies that he was thereby deterred in his determination to do something about the oversight problem. But most members seemed willing to see the battle for committee decentralization and democratization shifted to this new front.

According to most indicators (see Table 11-1), the Investigations Subcommittee's level of productivity reached a low point after this reorganization,

Table 11-1

Selected Indicators of Activity, Subcommittee on Oversight and Investigations, 91st through 94th Congresses

	91st	*92d*	*93d*	*94th*
Days of Hearings	17	16	23	71
Reports Issued	5	3	8	10
Published Staff Studies	2	2	0	5
Number of Members	16	5	5	14
Professional Staff Members	11	9	10	17
Salaries and Operating Expenditures ($1000s)	462	653	721	1182

Source: Data are taken from the relevant calendars and other materials furnished by the Interstate and Foreign Commerce Committee. If anything, the table probably underestimates the quantitative changes, for the eight reports recorded for the 93d Congress include five interrelated studies of Amtrak operations, while a 749-page report on regulatory practices in nine agencies during the 94th Congress is counted as a single item. Otherwise, the figures seem roughly comparable across Congresses as measures of output. For data on earlier Congresses, see Price (1975, p. 310).

which took place early in the 92d Congress. There was some increase in both the volume and the range of activity in the 93d Congress—perhaps in response to criticisms, perhaps as a result of Manelli and other aides settling into their roles. The subcommittee held a series of widely praised hearings on air safety, investigating several recent disasters. The handling of the controversial ITT case by the Securities and Exchange Commission (SEC) was probed, and a "comprehensive study" of that agency's enforcement programs was launched. Prompted by storage tank and tank-car explosions, the subcommittee examined the adequacy of federal safety regulations for the storage and transporting of natural gas.[5] And, partly as a result of a rebuke Staggers received from the full House, the preoccupation with deceptive news programming faded.[6] But this increased activity was not sufficient to head off the changes that were to come in 1975. At that point, discontents that had been simmering within the committee converged with electoral trends and reform efforts that were affecting the House as a whole. The Commerce Committee, and particularly its Investigations Subcommittee, was destined to undergo major changes.

The Subcommittee in Transition

"If the Subcommittee could be entrusted to an honest and independent Congressman like John Moss," wrote deposed Chief Counsel Bernard Schwartz in 1959 (p. 258) of the then-junior subcommittee member who had been one of his few defenders, "then the country might at last get a full probe of the regulatory commissions." Sixteen years later, Moss, as third-ranking Democrat on the Commerce Committee, attained the investigations post, articulating goals not unlike those Schwartz had expressed. Several factors led to his victory. First, Commerce was forced to reorganize its subcommittees by the shifts in its jurisdiction effected by the Committee Reform Amendments of 1974. Rejecting most of the jurisdictional recommendations of the Select Committee on Committees, the House nonetheless shifted aviation and surface transportation (except railroads) from Commerce to a reconstituted Public Works and Transportation Committee, while giving Commerce some additional health and energy jurisdiction. These shifts, as a staff member noted, "created a tremendous imbalance in the four legislative subcommittees. That forced the hand" (Ornstein and Rohde 1977, p. 215). Subcommittee lines were redrawn, one additional legislative unit was created, and senior members began negotiating about who would take which slot. Moss was inclined at first to bump Paul Rogers for the Health and Environment chairmanship. But Moss also had a long-standing interest and considerable experience in oversight—not only on Commerce, but also as a Government Operations subcommittee chairman—and Rogers was anxious to retain his position. Therefore it was in the interest of Rogers and others in line for subcommittee slots to work out an agreement whereby Moss would challenge Staggers for Investigations.

Second, Moss's victory also depended on the procedures for selecting subcommittee chairpersons adopted by the Democratic Caucus in 1973. Committee Democrats had the right to bid, in order of seniority, for subcommittee chairs; their bids would be accepted or rejected by vote of the majority caucus of the committee. Staggers had declined to follow this procedure at the beginning of the 93d Congress, continuing to appoint subcommittee members and chairpersons himself. But in 1975 the committee caucus demanded that the bidding procedure be followed. And while most members assumed that the bids of the most senior members should normally be accepted, they could suspend that presumption when a strong argument existed for doing so. Hence their willingness to deny Staggers's Investigations bid.

Third, Moss's selection would not have occurred without the addition of 12 new Democrats to the Committee. Commerce Committee membership has remained stable at 43 since 1971. But the shift in party ratios after the 1974 elections added 4 new Democratic slots, and defeats, retirements, and transfers opened up 8 more. These new members were more reform-minded than either those they replaced or their senior colleagues. Their presence clearly created the margin of victory for Moss, who defeated Staggers by a 15–13 vote after seven ballots. Staggers, of course, had the usual inducements to offer, and Moss had incurred the enmity of several committee members (Ornstein and Rohde 1977, pp. 200, 215–18). In fact, he had been decisively defeated two years earlier as he attempted to rewrite committee rules to conform to the House Caucus reforms. But in 1975 new members, new rules, accumulated discontent with Staggers's leadership, and a pervasive sentiment for reform combined to give Moss the victory.

In rewriting their rules, Commerce Democrats built on actions taken by the House majority caucus. In 1971 the Caucus voted to allow each member to chair only one subcommittee (this forced Moss to give up his Government Operations subcommittee) and to permit each subcommittee chairperson to hire a professional staff member of his or her own choosing. This latter provision was mirrored in the accommodation Staggers reached with his senior members in 1971. The more extensive set of reforms adopted by the House Caucus in 1973, including the "Subcommittee Bill of Rights," was not immediately implemented by the Commerce Committee. Moss's futile effort to change the rules focused on Staggers's failure to follow the requirement that each subcommittee have a ratio of Democrats to Republicans at least as favorable as that obtaining on the full committee.[7] Bidding procedures for subcommittee chairmanships and memberships were explicitly contradicted by a committee rule that "all appointments to subcommittees shall be made by the chairman of the committee and may be changed by him from time to time as he determines."[8] Democratic Caucus requirements that legislation be automatically referred to subcommittees, that subcommittees "be authorized to meet, hold hearings, receive evidence, and report to the committee," and that each subcommittee should "have an adequate budget" were imperfectly mirrored in committee rules and occasionally violated in practice by virtue of Staggers's continuing control over the referral of bills, the scheduling of subcommittee meetings and hearings, and the allocation and expenditure of funds.

The Commerce Committee rules written at the beginning of the 94th Congress resolved these anomalies and in several respects went beyond the Caucus requirements.[9] Subcommittee chairpersons were given final authority to set hearing and meeting dates; favorable majority-party ratios on all subcommittees were mandated; automatic and "immediate" subreferral of "legislation and other matters" referred to the committee was provided for (unless a majority of the full committee voted otherwise within five days); and bidding procedures were established for subcommittee chairmanships and memberships. The Democratic Caucus rule that subcommittee chairpersons "insofar as practicable" manage legislation reported by their subcommittees on the floor was adopted in nonconditional form. The chairperson was directed simply to "combine" the budget proposals of the subcommittee chairpersons for majority caucus and full committee approval. Subcommittee chairpersons were given the right to appoint, in addition to the single aide authorized in 1971, such staff members as were provided for in their budgets and to supervise full-committee aides assigned to their domains. And the rule limiting members to service on one subcommittee was rescinded.

These rule changes sealed trends toward the decentralization of authority and dispersal of resources that had been in evidence on House Commerce for some time (see Price 1975, pp. 41–50). The chairman has by no means been left totally powerless: he still schedules and presides at full-committee markups, and conceivably could exert considerable influence as subcommittee budget, personnel, and other requests come to the full committee for approval. But the reforms of 1975 effectively secured the subcommittees' control over their own operations against the discretion of the full-committee chairperson. Staggers, according to a senior colleague, accepted the changes relatively gracefully:

He has relaxed a lot. He's finally done what I advised him to do some time ago: I told him he had a good committee, lots of talent, and that he should preside over it all and enjoy it. There's just no way he can really run the committee. I think he's accepted that. At first he was determined to get the Investigations Subcommittee back [in the 95th Congress]. But he didn't even try.

"Staggers," Moss confirms, "has not interfered at all." Accordingly, as Moss set about his new task in 1975, he was free of the constraints that had plagued him in the Commerce and Finance chair. The new rules surely could not force subcommittee leaders to be effective legislators or vigilant overseers. But they did guarantee subcommittees the autonomy and resources to carve out their own distinctive roles; whatever effectiveness and industry they could muster would be primarily up to them.

Dimensions of Change

The impact of Moss's accession and of the rules change seems obvious enough in Table 11-1. The subcommittee's membership tripled between the 93d and 94th Congresses, and the professional staff was increased to its 1959-1960 level. The subcommittee budget grew by 64 percent, and Moss held as many days of hearings in two years as Staggers had held in the previous nine. But such quantitative measures at best only suggest the impact of "reform" on the character and effectiveness of House Commerce oversight, and they can be quite misleading. Therefore, one must look more closely at several dimensions of subcommittee operation and performance.

Membership and Participation

The Oversight and Investigations Subcommittee now ranks with Energy and Power, and Health and Environment, as the most sought-after of Commerce's subcommittees. Under the new bidding procedures, size is a good indicator of subcommittee desirability; these three had 14 members each in the 94th Congress, while in the 95th Oversight had 17, ranking behind Energy (20) but ahead of Health (14). Both the rules changes and Moss's accession undoubtedly have contributed to subcommittee growth. Many members, especially new members, have been attracted by Moss's promise of a vigorous oversight operation, and they have no longer been forced to choose between Investigations and a legislative subcommittee assignment. This contrasts markedly with the situation under Staggers: the small size (5) of the subcommittee and the junior stature of its members during the 92d and 93d Congresses were the results of both his desire for a manageable group and the reluctance of members to accept such an assignment.[10]

The change, however, is not as stark as it appears at first. First, Investigations still tends to attract relatively junior members. This is partly because the 1975 committee rules permitted legislative subcommittee chairpersons to serve on no other subcommittees. But neither did any other senior Democrat choose to bid for the Moss subcommittee in 1975, with the sole exception of fourth-termer Bill Stuckey (Ga.).[11] On the minority side, Investigations initially attracted somewhat more senior members, but proved less able to hold those it did attract. Full committee ranking Republican Samuel Devine (Ohio) appointed (the Republicans did not follow a bidding procedure) James Collins, a fourth-termer from Texas who ranked sixth in seniority among Commerce Republicans, to the ranking minority slot on Investigations. Norman Lent (N.Y.), who had come to the subcommittee in 1973, agreed to stay. But the other Republican slots have been filled by freshmen and second-termers and have been subject to frequent turnover.[12]

Second, Oversight has not been the first priority of most of those who have elected to join it. Caucus procedures now permit Democrats to choose as many as three subcommittees, and most of Oversight's present members chose it on their second round of bidding. A number of members value their slot for the opportunity it provides for involvement and visibility across the Commerce Committee's expansive policy spectrum. "It's appealing," Richard Ottinger (D-N.Y.) says, "because of the hunting license it gives you to range over a very wide jurisdiction." Albert Gore, Jr. (D-Tenn.), one of the few members for whom oversight was first choice, notes that the subcommittee's work "fits in with this new political mood, being sceptical of government's ability to solve every problem, seeing what works and what doesn't." But most seem to feel that the political payoffs are generally quite modest: "My investigations work hasn't gotten much play back in the district." Many members describe subcommittee inquiries as often tedious and complex, difficult for them and the public to muster much interest in. Legislative work is seen as more tangible, more understandable, and hence likely to crowd out oversight commitments. "I've gotten more and more involved with the Energy Subcommittee," says one member:

That's a terribly demanding assignment, with hearings every day lately, and, unlike Investigations, you can look toward a tangible product. . . . *[Oversight] was a lesser assignment for me in the first place, and it's even more so now.*

For minority members, subcommittee activity has an even more dubious political aspect. Oversight "is not generally considered a very attractive subcommittee assignment," Collins says. "You have no staff and no voice in what the subcommittee does . . . and you've got issues that it's very hard [for the minority] to look good on. It's very bad politics to defend business these days, especially the oil companies."

Third, the level of participation in subcommittee functions is still relatively low. Under Staggers, a normal hearing might find three of the five members in their chairs, but hearings with one or two representatives present were not uncommon. Under Moss, the expansion of the subcommittee to 14 has put more bodies in the chairs, and increased activity has placed heightened demands on the subcommittee's members. But the percentage of members participating in meetings and hearings has dropped. Attendance at the subcommittee's ten "open" business meetings during 1975–1976 averaged a fairly respectable nine, but four members missed over half of the sessions. Highly publicized hearings on matters such as uranium price fixing and the Arab boycott can stimulate high participation, just as air safety and the ITT case did under Staggers. But for each of the subcommittee's two longest series of hearings during the 94th Congress, 13 days on natural gas supplies and 22 days (exclusive of field hearings) on regulatory reform, only five members dropped in on an average day. This is partly attributable to the removal of the one-subcommittee limitation; members simply have more conflicting responsibilities now. Some have been alienated by Moss's mode of operation. But the main conclusion to be drawn is simply that the incentives to extensive oversight activity remain rather weak for most members.

Staffing

The oversight staff now numbers 19 professionals. Twice as large as it was under Staggers, it also is more specialized. As Chief Counsel, Moss chose Michael Lemov, who had been his top Commerce and Finance Subcommittee aide since 1971. Working with him, and more directly with Moss after Lemov left the subcommittee in late 1977, were three "task force" heads responsible for the major areas of activity that the subcommittee mapped out in 1975—health, energy, and regulatory reform. Each of these directed the activities of some four staff members. In addition, several "floating" aides were available for assignment wherever the needs of the moment dictated.

A comparison with Staggers's staff roster[13] reveals striking differences in patterns of recruitment, although under neither regime has Investigations been a repository for political appointees. Four of the ten professional aides working for the Investigations Subcommittee in 1974 had FBI backgrounds, and three had occupied legal positions in one or more of the regulatory commissions. By 1977, only one FBI man remained, and few aides could claim experience in the agencies or commissions. "Oversight" and the kind of background relevant to it were conceived somewhat differently. Moss's staff came from three main sources: congressional offices, "public interest" organizations, and the universities. The result was a staff more conspicuously reformist in inclination than their predecessors, more broadly focused on policy questions, more sensitive to the political requisites of having a policy impact, and more inclined to carry on their investigations in a public forum.

Aides now play a more active role in developing inquiries than they did under Staggers. Lishman expected his people to keep their eyes and ears open for possible new areas of investigation, but they were very much "on assignment" and their focus on agency operations and procedures limited the sorts of problems they were likely to bring up. With the shift, under Manelli, to more topical, case-oriented inquiries, came a further narrowing of the staff's role to digging out the "facts" on a matter already established as suspicious or problematic. Of course, much investigative work is intrinsically of this quality; thus one would not, in any case, expect to find "policy entrepreneurship" of the sort that has become the norm on some legislative staffs (see Price 1975, pp. 22–41). But an examination of the sources of the subcommittee's inquiries during the 94th Congress reveals an instigative staff role of major importance. Regulatory reform, for example, was suggested by Lemov, sniffing the winds of Presidential debate, as the subcommittee mapped out its areas of concentration in 1975. Unnecessary surgery, the health issue that attracted the most notice to the subcommittee during the 94th Congress, was proposed, also during the 1975 agenda-setting period, by top health aide Elliot Segal on the basis of his experiences while employed at the Yale–New Haven Medical Center.

The staff's ties to individual members are closer than they were under Staggers but fall short of what is sometimes found on more decentralized staffs. Moss has often been responsive to members who wished to take the lead in a specific line of inquiry; this has led members and their staffs to work directly with subcommittee aides and the latter, in turn, to suggest additional areas of potential interest. Subcommittee aides also exercise considerable discretion as to which members they should "line up" and prime with background information for a given inquiry. But their instigative role has been limited by the extent to which subcommittee communications have been filtered through Moss and Lemov and priorities set at the top.

Two further kinds of staff activity are more conspicuous under Moss than they were under Staggers, and both are worthy of note. The first is cultivation of the press. Under Moss, the public hearing has become the major vehicle for developing cases and for stimulating policy change, and top aides frequently prepare background packets on subcommittee hearings and brief reporters "to make sure they got the main point" of an inquiry. Lemov is quick to deny charges of "sensationalism":

We do get lots of coverage, but we don't have to go after it that way. They know we have good hearings, and we package them well, so they'll make a good story. We often use the human interest element to lead off, for example actually bringing in a woman who was given an unnecessary hysterectomy. But if we do something sensational like that, you can be sure there's a serious general problem behind it. . . . Now of course I'll call [reporters from the *Post, Times,* etc.] if a hearing is coming up that we know they're interested in. [Special Assistant] Kirk Smith spends maybe half his time making sure the press is informed. After all, this is a fast league up here; there's a lot going on. You have to make sure people know what you're doing. . . .

A second staff role, one that sometimes conflicts with the desire for "well-packaged" hearings but which Moss has nonetheless perpetuated and expanded, is that of hearing examiner. Staff often lead off in the questioning and "develop the record" for as long as an hour, and aides who have researched a case are sometimes brought to the witness stand themselves. The subcommittee pays a price in terms of member restlessness and media interest for such a procedure. But one looking over the transcripts produced by the subcommittee during the 94th Congress cannot help but be impressed with the qualitative difference, in the development of a systematic line of questioning and the possession of a factual background, between staff and member examinations. For an investigations unit, and especially one suspected of grinding ideological axes, such a staff role would seem to be, whatever its other political drawbacks, an important source of credibility.

Leadership and Partisanship

Under both Staggers and Moss, members have portrayed the subcommittee as sharply mirroring the priorities and style of its chairman: "It's pretty much a one-man show." With Staggers this indicated a certain indecisiveness and eclecticism in planning subcommittee activity, as well as considerable anxiety about sharing power. Occasionally members were able to put pet items on the agenda—for example, J.J. Pickle's investigations of freight car shortages—but Staggers resisted the efforts of members to push him and in 1971 reorganized the subcommittee in a way that minimized the need for him to deal with such initiatives. Moss's members, by contrast, portray him as a stronger and more decisive chairman, but also as one—here the Republicans would dissent—more willing to see others contribute to the agenda and share the spotlight.

Moss's colleagues describe him as a "fierce partisan," a champion of congressional prerogative ("Sometimes he seems to think Congress can do anything it wants, that it can actually *run* the government"), a stickler for procedure ("He presses points that most of us would let pass by"), scrupulously fair as a presiding officer, and determined to uphold his own and the subcommittee's authority. They agree he is a hard man to cross, either from within the subcommittee or from the witness stand. One observer recalls the treatment James Scheuer got when he suggested decentralizing subcommittee operations:

Scheuer suggested that we might go much farther in this direction of having separate task forces at work, letting members *convene hearings in their areas of interest more or less independently. Nobody much took the idea up, and Moss could have let it drop. But as usual he carried it out to its logical extreme, accusing Scheuer of wanting to set up "mini-subcommittees" and hitting him pretty hard on it.*

Most majority members, however, seem relatively well satisfied with the role they are able to play on the subcommittee. Remarkably few, even in private, echoed Scheuer's discontent. "The subcommittee is heavily Moss's show," said one of his colleagues, "but I and other members have had no problem putting forward matters for investigation." Five members were able during the 94th Congress not only to put the staff onto matters of interest but also to conduct hearings on problems such as power rates and natural gas shortages in their home districts. Moss is content to share the limelight at hearings, and on several occasions he has helped members he regards as especially promising to gain public exposure. "They had asked Moss to appear on 'Good Morning America,' " Gore reports, "but he urged them to get me instead. He really pushed it. So I was on for a fifteen-minute debate with a doctor on unnecessary surgery."

Minority members of the subcommittee present a contrary picture of Moss's generosity, a far more negative interpretation of his "strength" as a chairman, and a confirmation of the impression—readily gained from reading subcommittee hearings and reports—that "reform" has resulted in a heightening of partisan conflict. Of the 16 reports approved by the subcommittee in the 91st through 93d Congresses, only three (19 percent) carried minority views. By contrast, eight of the ten reports issued by the subcommittee during the 94th Congress were approved on a divided vote. Staggers's hearings could occasionally hit the minority close to home; Devine and Lent, for example, accused him of prejudging the role of the White House and the SEC in the ITT affair.[14] But, in general, the issues Moss tackled were more likely than Staggers's agenda to keep partisans of a Republican administration on the defensive.

Shifts in subject matter only partially account for the increased conflict. In fact, the most persistent minority complaints have focused not on substance but on process, the way the subcommittee is run. The note was struck in the re-constituted subcommittee's first hearings, a hastily called inquiry into Federal Energy Administration conduct in a Jacksonville, Florida, fuel case. Subcommittee Republicans considered boycotting the hearing, and then attended only to press a series of bitter complaints about the lack of due notice, the one-sided nature of the case developed by the staff, the lack of time for members to examine background materials thoroughly, and the chairman's failure to consult them on the subcommittee agenda. Lent, as a subcommittee member, "for two years last past," made the contrast with the previous regime explicit: under Staggers, he said, "we were taken into the confidence of the committee chairman and given a general idea of the areas of investigation and we had broad contact with the staff of the subcommittee."[15]

Much of the minority opposition on substantive issues, in fact, is less solid than it appears at first. There were a few occasions during the 94th Congress when subcommittee Republicans banded together as an opposition bloc—against subpoenas to the Departments of Commerce and HEW, for example. But most of the divided votes and minority reports found Collins acting alone or, on some energy matters, with fellow Texan Robert Krueger. Most of the Republicans were hesitant to vote against subpoenas, and they often voted aye or simply absented themselves when controversial reports were approved. "Sometimes I just think it's better not to stand in the way," said one. Many of the subcommittee's issues, Collins explains, place the opposition in a difficult political position: "I don't make a big effort to get the minority members to sign my views. I know how unpopular it is to defend business. Rinaldo has told me that whenever I need him, to call on him. But I don't lean on him." Adds minority counsel Bernard Wunder: "You can't expect a member to display high enthusiasm for signing a report that might make him appear to be *for* unnecessary surgery. Collins has no hesitancy, but some of the others do. A lot of these are tough political issues. Fuel adjustment clauses is another one; Rinaldo didn't sign the minority report. After all, nobody likes fuel adjustment clauses."

Minority members, however, are considerably more united in their grievances about how the subcommittee is run. Most of their complaints have been aimed at Moss and Lemov, and they have touched on both style and procedure:

Moss can be very dictatorial in the way he runs the subcommittee. He's smarter than Harley, of course, but also quite enamored of himself. He's been here a long time and has this attitude that these young whippersnappers have no business asserting themselves. He's very condescending toward junior members, and brooks no opposition. I've been gaveled down by him several times myself. . . . [Freshman Republican Marc Marks was recently "very gently" questioning a witness called by the majority in executive session.] Moss gaveled him down and accused him of "badgering" the witness. "Mr. Chairman," I said, "since when don't we badger witnesses on this subcommittee?" Moss is of course a master at it, and so is Lemov. . . . It does seem like a pretty hopeless situation sometimes. I don't think its surprising at all that Madigan and Moore chose to transfer off.

Much disputed, for example, has been Moss's strict construction of the House rule ensuring to all members access to "all committee hearings, records, data, charts, and files." In limiting the access of the subcommittee's minority counsel and prohibiting photocopying, Moss and Lemov restricted the minority's capacity to inform themselves and build the opposition case in hearings. But they saw such restrictions as necessary to prevent the "tipping off" of prospective witnesses, claiming that information had been leaked from executive sessions to oil companies and downtown agencies and thus that their concerns were not illusory. A second sticking point has been Moss's unusual practice of appending a rebuttal to the subcommittee's printed "minority views." Wunder complained:

I know of no other subcommittee where such a practice is followed. I see no way they can do it under the rules, for we're all under the same three-day limit [for submitting views supplemental to a subcommittee report] and we invariably get ours in at the very end of the 72-hour period.[16]

But Moss stoutly defended the practice: "In our system the majority rules, and I'm obliged, as chairman, to correct any obvious distortions of the record on behalf of the majority."

The Work of the Subcommittee

The "reform" of the Investigations Subcommittee, as already noted, resulted in both heightened *levels* of activity and an increase in the *proportion* of activity conducted in or for a *public* forum—hearings, reports, and so forth. Tables 11-2 and 11-3 point up, in addition, significant shifts in the *policy areas* covered. The figures for the 91st Congress reveal a heavy emphasis on transportation and communications, while those for the 93d reflect the belated broadening of focus that characterized Staggers's final term. The 94th Congress saw a quantum jump in the time spent on energy matters—an area to which Staggers, had he been re-elected, might have felt constrained to pay increased attention—but nothing like that prompted by the priorities of Moss and many of the subcommittee's new members. In addition, for the first time the subcommittee began to give sustained attention to questions of health policy. Transportation figures, of course, reflected the loss of jurisdiction inflicted upon the committee in 1974. Other changes were less dramatic, with activity in the SEC, consumer/FTC, and communications areas remaining at modest levels.

These figures reflect the subcommittee's decision to concentrate activity and staff resources in the health and energy areas. Meanwhile, the task force on regulatory reform has become the main vehicle by which the subcommittee maintains its reach over other areas of Commerce Committee jurisdiction. Staggers had begun to pay more attention to such matters as CAB and FPC rate decisions and the regulatory lag at the FTC, but the task force device has institutionalized such scrutiny and rendered it less sporadic. In fact, one result of Moss's accession and other changes on the subcommittee has been a partial return to the notion of oversight put forward by Lishman. One can distinguish,

Table 11-2
Subject Matter of Hearings, Subcommittee on Oversight and Investigations, 91st through 94th Congresses

	Days of Hearings, by Congress			
	91st	*92d*	*93d*	*94th*
Communications, FCC	8	8	0	2
SEC	0	1	6	4
Energy, FPC	0	0	5	33
Surface transportation, ICC, Amtrak	9	7	1	2[a]
Aviation, FAA/CAB	0	0	8	—[a]
Health, environment, FDA	0	0	0	17
Consumer, FTC	0	0	3	6
General regulation and other	0	0	0	7
Total	17	16	23	71

[a]Commerce Committee jurisdiction in these areas reduced or eliminated before 94th Congress.

Table 11-3

Subject Matter of Reports and Published Staff Studies, Subcommittee on Oversight and Investigations, 91st through 94th Congresses

	Number of Reports and Studies, by Congress			
	91st	92d	93d	94th
Communications, FCC	7	2	1	0
SEC	0	1	0	1
Energy, FPC	0	0	1	8
Surface transportation, ICC, Amtrak	0	2	5	1[a]
Aviation, FAA/CAB	0	0	1	–[a]
Health, environment, FDA	0	0	0	3
Consumer, FTC	0	0	0	0
General regulation and other	0	0	0	2[b]
Total	7	5	8	15

[a]Commerce Committee jurisdiction in these areas reduced or eliminated before 94th Congress.

[b]Includes "regulatory reform" report with approximately 50 pages each on the FCC, SEC, ICC, FTC, and five other agencies.

if only provisionally, among three types of inquiry: (1) examining agency *processes* and practices, often in relation to a line of decisions regarded as problematic (for example, "undue fraternization" on the ICC or the accuracy of the FPC's natural gas reserve estimates), (2) probing an extraordinary *case* or crisis which may raise broader questions of agency malfeasance (deceptive programming, air crashes, uranium price fixing), and (3) attacking an unresolved *policy problem* (inadequate protection for investors in failing railroads, unnecessary surgery, natural gas deregulation). Table 11-4 shows the incidence of subcommittee hearings falling under each of these headings. In the four years (92d through 93d Congresses) between Lishman's death and Moss's election, Staggers and Manelli led the subcommittee toward a primary focus on highly publicized disasters, scandals, and abuses. Under Moss, the attentiveness to the regulatory *processes* has returned, albeit in a more public forum than Lishman would have chosen. The subcommittee, to be sure, is still quick to seize the main chance on "cases" such as the Arab boycott and natural gas withholding, and ostensibly routine agency probes are often "packaged" in a fashion that highlights newsworthy instances of alleged malfeasance—the FPC's failure to prevent fuel shortages, for example, and FDA's hesitancy to ban a class of suspected carcinogens. But the subcommittee has become less dependent on such events and situations to stimulate its investigations and set its agenda. At the same time, there has been a modest increase in the third mode of inquiry, as the subcommittee has opened up several major policy questions, especially in the health area. Some of Moss's critics regard these latter moves as too few and too limited; he has been too slow, they argue, to look beyond the integrity of existing

Table 11-4

Types of Inquiries Undertaken by Subcommittee on Oversight and
Investigations, 91st through 94th Congresses

	Days of Hearings, by Congress			
	91st	*92d*	*93d*	*94th*
Monitoring Agency Processes and Practices	8	3	6	50
Investigating Major Case or Crisis	8	7	16	10
Examining Long-term Policy Problem	1	6	1	11
Total	17	16	23	71

processes to the resolution of persisting policy dilemmas, and he has tended to assume that the cleaning up of processes and procedures *constitutes* an answer to broader problems.

This raises the more general question of the *scope* of the subcommittee's work. The reforms of 1975 were accompanied by a change in the subcommittee's name from Investigations to Oversight and Investigations which, if it denoted no change in formal responsibilities, still suggested a desire to get beyond the case approach. Some members, looking at the focus of Moss's inquiries rather than their quantity or their distribution across policy areas, still complain of the "narrowness" of the subcommittee's work. As one Republican puts it,

Under neither *Staggers nor Moss has the subcommittee really done* oversight. *We haven't gotten down to the nitty-gritty of looking at how regulation works and doesn't work, and how we might cut down on some of this needless bureaucracy. What we ought to be doing is bringing in the regulatees, the people who bear the brunt of all this. They have justified gripes, and we ought to hear from them. Instead, we've squandered the resources of the subcommittee on these headline-grabbing ventures, like this flammable nightgown issue, or worrying if some commissioner owns a few shares of forbidden stock.*

The critique of a liberal Democrat, while less harsh and of a different ideological hue, is not totally dissimilar:

I have some criticisms of Moss and how the subcommittee is operated, but not enough to make me think my vote [against Staggers in 1975] was mistaken. . . . It's just this tendency Moss has to nit-pick, to zero in on some very narrow issue and drive it hard. He will rip to shreds some oil executive or push these conflict-of-interest restrictions, but I'm not sure where that gets us [in developing adequate policy]. Sometimes we lose the forest for the trees.

But a task force head, acknowledging the force of the criticism, turns it to positive account. The subcommittee's critics, he says, are using criteria which properly apply to *legislative* units: "Perhaps what we *should* be doing is this grubby business of investigating conflicts of interest, etc.—and leave the broader policy questions to others."

This is not the place to attempt a detailed assessment; suffice it to say that on the "narrowness" question, the evidence seems mixed. The subcommittee's initial plans[17] called for exploration of major energy issues—alternative means of energy conservation in the "middle term" and the longer-range question of building incentives for new energy sources. Regulatory reform was subdivided into four areas of inquiry: agency independence, agency performance and procedural reform, the economic impact of agency regulation, and fundamental questions about the future role and organization of the agencies. Subcommittee aides readily acknowledge that this prospectus did not accurately predict their activities for the 94th Congress. Energy hearings dealt predominantly with natural gas withholdings and the alleged defaults of the FPC, while the regulatory reform inquiries stressed the first two "process" areas at the expense of broader assessments of regulatory impact or the likely consequences of proposed changes.[18]

In some instances, however, the Moss subcommittee examined policy impacts and contributed to basic policy debates—probing the effects of gas shortages and uranium pricing on utility rates, for example, and examining the unregulated intrastate natural gas market—in a way that went beyond the exhortations to agency vigilance and propriety characteristic of the Staggers era. Some of the regulatory reform hearings, on the ICC and Environmental Protection Agency, for example, were notable for the range of major policy issues addressed and agency difficulties aired. There was also some broadening of the range of witnesses Staggers had generally heard from, at least on the "consumer" side. But the typical oversight hearing still consisted of testimony only from agency officials and gave irregular coverage to their policy terrain. The regulatory reform series, for example, included two days on the FCC. No outside witnesses were called. Subcommittee members took up a potpourri of issues with Commission officials—Scheuer on communications services for the elderly, Maguire on a disputed New Jersey case, Rinaldo on the decline of Western Union service, Moss on "equal time" enforcement, Waxman on television violence— while staff questioning focused on such "process" matters as how consumers were represented before the Commission and how equal employment opportunity cases were handled. But critical, longer-range questions, such as the future of cable television, the opening up of the UHF spectrum, cross-media monopolies, and the relationship of the FCC to the White House Office of Telecommunications Policy were barely touched upon.

Critics of the subcommittee also claim that Moss's accession has resulted in an increased *bias* against industry and the health establishment and agencies perceived to be protecting their interests. We have already noted Republican complaints along these lines. Here is a more moderate majority variant:

There's a knee-jerk quality to much of what Moss and Lemov do. We assume that the oil companies or the agencies must be wrongly motivated. There are all sorts of conspiracy theories floating around. . . . The subcommittee may well be right on natural gas withholding. But there was that same knee-jerk quality to the interpretation, ready to assume in advance that the oil companies were deliberately withholding. I really think this sort of reaction reduces the subcommittee's credibility in the House. There's an attitude that much of what Moss produces is predictable.

It was presumably concerns of this kind that led Santini to move (successfully) to soften language concerning Mobil's motivations in the report on the company's failure to deliver natural gas to the interstate market.[19]

If one attempts to code hearings conducted under Staggers and Moss for expressions of hostility toward administration and commission witnesses, it is not clear that there has been a great deal of change in the range of attitudes expressed by members. Shifts in presumptions and priorities are more clearly visible at an earlier stage, in the agenda set by the subcommittee: "natural gas withholding," "unnecessary surgery," "shortchanging children," and so forth. The subcommittee has become more aggressive in *ferreting out* the problems it wishes to examine and in *defining* them in terms of program failure or the victimization of the public, and it has generally proved willing to work with explanatory hypotheses that point to willful agency and/or industry default. Much of this, of course, is a common American (and congressional) way of thinking; every problem must have a villain. In any event, such thought patterns are very prominent on the Moss subcommittee, and while they may in some instances prove fruitful, they seldom lead to totally satisfactory explanations. Such working hypotheses, moreover, do create problems of credibility for the subcommittee, and they may divert attention from other factors more relevant to long-term policy solutions.

Thus we arrive at the difficult question of *effectiveness*. Clearly, the subcommittee has a visibility now that it has not enjoyed since the days when it examined vicuna coats and the $64,000 question. "One thing you can say for Moss," Collins acknowledges, "He gets their attention down there [in the bureaucracy]. They really sit up and take notice." Staggers did not generally seek such exposure, and there are those who defend his less flamboyant mode of operation. "He had materials for a sensational set of hearings on the use of drugs in sports," one observer said of an investigation that in 1972 involved as much as three-fourths of the staff. "But Staggers was concerned that youngsters might try to emulate their sports heroes by using drugs themselves. So he proceeded in a low-key way, bringing in the heads of the various leagues and getting them to pledge themselves to an informal housecleaning." It is difficult to imagine Moss making such a decision. And one of his aides, arguing on grounds of effectiveness, describes it as, in fact, a misguided decision:

Staggers talked about keeping it low key so as not to disillusion the "youth of America." Regardless of why he did it, I think it's pretty clear that nothing has happened since. This "low-key" approach actually just lets everyone off the hook.... Did you ever see anything get done in this town without publicity?[20]

The Staggers subcommittee could point to scattered instances where their work influenced agency decisions and procedures.[21] After the 1974 air safety investigations, for example, the FAA ordered ground-proximity warning devices installed on all commercial aircraft. But many subcommittee reports, partly as a function of the focus on particular cases and crises, had a "Don't let it happen again" quality. Moss's regulatory reform report, by contrast, contained some 125 specific suggestions for altered agency procedures which should provide, among other things, a basis for continued subcommittee scrutiny and assessment. Those working in the health area have been similarly attentive to follow-up: "We didn't get much out of [former HEW Secretary David] Mathews," Segal noted in mid-1977, "but we've served notice on [Secretary] Califano that we expect some movement [on the development of regulations that would curtail unnecessary surgery]. We'll have him up here in a couple of months, and if there are problems, we'll ride him hard." When HEW officials appeared before the subcommittee a few months later, they announced that the federal government would thereafter pay the bill for Medicare patients who wished to obtain a second medical opinion before surgery.

Subcommittee effectiveness, both as an investigative arm of the full committee and in devising follow-up measures, requires cooperative relationships with the legislative subcommittees. Staggers sometimes stepped on the toes of the Communications subcommittee leadership, but occasionally he conducted studies of which this and other legislative subcommittees made use. But investigations work was generally only loosely connected with what went on elsewhere in the committee. This has not changed dramatically under Moss; the legislative subcommittees develop their own oversight agendas and do not systematically call upon the oversight unit for support services.[22] Less conflict has developed than one might have predicted, given the expansion of the Oversight subcommittee's agenda. There has been some sniping, particularly at the staff level, between Oversight and the Energy subcommittee, but the personal and ideological affinity of Moss and Energy Chairman John Dingell, plus a heavy overlap in membership, has made it possible to work out a mutually agreeable division of labor.[23] The strongest hints of conflict have come in the health area, where Rogers guards his turf carefully and often differs from Moss's policy views. Here

the sharing of plans and information has been limited, and at least one proposed Oversight inquiry, on the need for standards for clinical laboratories, has
been derailed by the objections of Rogers's chief subcommittee aide.

Moss, while often arguing that what is needed is simply for agencies to
meet "the responsibilities they *already* have under the law," has nonetheless
introduced more corrective legislation than Staggers did. Bills to facilitate
Medicaid cost control and to broaden the powers of the Comptroller General in
the conduct of energy-related audits were passed in the 94th Congress, with the
cooperation of the Health and Energy subcommittees, respectively. But the
lagging of follow-up on more complicated measures—notably regulatory reform,
which was relevant to every Commerce subcommittee and to several committees besides Commerce—suggested that lacunae still existed between the performance of oversight and the devising of specific corrective measures.

Concluding Observations

The House Commerce Committee evidence suggests, first, that the designation
of a separate oversight subcommittee can significantly increase a committee's
capacity for and propensity to oversight and, second, that the House reforms of
the 1970s have generally been conducive to increased activity by such subcommittees. Morris Ogul (1976, pp. 11–22) has identified several "opportunity
factors" that maximize a committee's proclivity toward oversight—the possession of formal authority; adequate staff resources; a decentralized committee
structure; and members, particularly high-status senior members, highly motivated to undertake the task. These factors are generally enhanced by the appointment of a separate subcommittee: the committee's vague responsibilities
for oversight are assigned to specific members and, for this group, given precedence over competing obligations; a staff whose prime concern is oversight is
instituted; the conduct of oversight is freed from the competing priorities that
might eclipse it at the full-committee level; and several members, including at
least one relatively senior member from each party, are placed in a situation
where their self-interest—the reputation and leverage they wish to gain in committee, in the House, and in the governmental establishment—is more likely to
require them to take their oversight responsibilities seriously. The House reforms, which gave to Oversight and other subcommittees increased resources
and authority, have generally extended these positive effects.

It is important, however, not to overestimate the capacity of such structural devices to prompt vigilant oversight. Ogul (1976, p. 184), surveying the
state of oversight on three committees, concluded that "the best boost for an
active oversight effort is a committee chairman who puts a high premium on
oversight and has the skill and resources to do something about it." Certainly
the Commerce case bears this out. By far the most important factor in altering

the role of the Investigations subcommittee was the selection of John Moss as chairman. The rules changes made it possible for committee Democrats to make a deliberate choice for the position, and they increased the autonomy and resources Moss enjoyed after he won. But the "reforms" themselves would have had little impact on performance had the swing vote on that seventh ballot gone to Staggers.

Moss's goals and methods as a leader have contributed to various changes in the complexion and operation of the subcommittee—the attraction of more members, particularly junior members of a reformist bent, and an increase in contributions to the agenda from down through the ranks; the assembling of a larger staff, more inclined to ferret out areas of inquiry and more attentive to the political requisites of making an impact; and a heightening of partisan awareness and conflict. All this has made for alterations in the subcommittee's product and performance—heightened levels of activity, with more of it conducted in a public forum; increased attention to highly visible and controversial health and energy issues; some movement from a case approach to the broader scrutiny of regulatory processes; a heightened tendency to frame problems and inquiries in terms of agency and industry malfeasance; and more concern to make inquiries newsworthy and to provide effective follow-up.

The changes are indeed substantial, but as we have seen, there is much that has not changed as well. The low incentives which members generally have for oversight as opposed to other forms of activity[24] have been only partially overcome; few members regard the Oversight subcommittee as their first choice, and participation tends to be sporadic. The members' desire for newsworthy hearings of topical interest, and their tendency to seize on readily understandable diagnoses in terms of "villains," are still at odds with the standards of "comprehensiveness," long-range significance, and objective analysis to which lip service is paid. And the difficulty of establishing complementarity between oversight and legislative units remains.

To note that congressional behavior is more intractable in some of its aspects than reformers have assumed is not to minimize the importance of what has happened on House Commerce and other committees. The rules changes of 1973 and 1975 provided an impetus and critical conditions for these changes. But just as they are of only limited utility in "explaining" the shape of oversight as it has emerged on the Moss subcommittee, so does reform, as it is generally conceived, hold little promise for correcting such remaining (or new) flaws as critics might detect.

To be sure, our look at the Commerce Committee suggests certain "structural" needs—increased minority staffing, for example, a limitation (to two) of the subcommittees on which members can now serve, improved mechanisms for translating oversight findings into legislative remedies. But few such problems could wisely or easily be solved by dictates of the full House or its majority caucus. The critical second front of reform for congressional oversight and, I suspect, for other aspects of the legislative process is the committee itself. Devising rules and structures is part of this, but no longer the most important part. The important questions for units like the Commerce Committee and its Oversight subcommittee have to do with what sorts of issues will be raised, what kinds of hypotheses will be developed, what range of interests will be heard, what kind of expertise will be mustered, what kind of solutions will be devised, what sorts of follow-up will be pursued. Members must decide how much time, energy, and resources to devote to oversight, what kind of leaders to choose, what patterns of member participation and accommodation to develop. The quality of congressional oversight will depend on how such questions are answered. They will not, however, be given predictable answers by the adoption of ever more refined rules and procedures. Rather they will be answered anew day after day as members, individually and in their committees, decide what kind of job they wish to do.

Notes

1. "Committee Organization in the House," *Hearings* of the House Select Committee on Committees, 93d Congress, vol. 2, pp. 261 (June 22, 1973), 396 (July 11, 1973); *Report* to accompany H. Res. 988 (March 21, 1974), pp. 62-71. For discussions of the Select Committee's work on oversight, see Price 1974, pp. 605-06; and Davidson and Oleszek 1977, pp. 96-99, 143-44.

2. To Agriculture, Armed Services, Commerce, Post Office, Public Works, and Small Business were added Banking, Interior, and Ways and Means.

3. This case largely overshadowed Lishman's attempt to establish a general *pattern* of "commission personnel accepting transportation, accommodations or other gratuities from parties to a hearing before them." See "Inquiry into Certain Procedures of the Interstate Commerce Commission," *Hearings* of the Special Subcommittee on Investigations, House Committee on Interstate and Foreign Commerce (hereafter SI Subcommittee), 91st Congress, June 16-August 13, 1970, part I, p. 64 and *passim*.

4. Quotations without citations are taken from interviews conducted in mid-1977 with seven members of the Oversight and Investigations Subcommittee, seven present or former staff members, and several others acquainted with the subcommittee's work. A few interviews have also been utilized from an earlier study carried out in 1972-1973 by the author for the Congress Project. The quotations are taken from a transcript, as nearly verbatim as possible, drawn up from notes immediately following each interview.

For an account of the subcommittee based on the Congress Project research and focusing on the 92d Congress, see Price 1975, pp. 309-21, 326-28.

5. See House Committee on Interstate and Foreign Commerce, *Report* on Activities for the 93d Congress, January 2, 1975, pp. 61-70.

6. When Staggers attempted in 1971 to subpoena CBS President Frank Stanton to relinquish the outtakes of "The Selling of the Pentagon," he was defeated 226-181. See Price 1975, pp. 225, 314.

7. For a detailing of Staggers's violations of Caucus rules in the 93d Congress, see Joan Claybrook, "Consumer Protection," in Price 1975, pp. 99-102. On the problems the composition of his Commerce and Finance Subcommittee posed for Moss as he attempted to report consumer legislation, see pp. 96-100, 122-25.

8. *Report* on Activities, 93d Congress, p. 2.

9. *Report* on Activities, 94th Congress, January 3, 1977, pp. 2-8.

10. Staggers, with difficulty, induced J.J. Pickle (D-Tex.) to stay on the subcommittee to give it seniority and stature, but the other majority slot was filled by Ray Blanton (92d) and Charles Carney (93d), both relatively junior and inactive legislators. The minority slots were filled by William Springer (92d) and Samuel Devine (93d), ranking full-committee Republicans who, like Staggers, could serve on Investigations without losing their ex officio voting rights on the legislative subcommittees, and by two committee freshmen, Richard Shoup (92d) and Norman Lent (93d).

11. Two of the new majority members, James Scheuer (N.Y.) and Richard Ottinger (N.Y.), were returning to Congress after previous periods of service, but the remaining six—Robert Krueger (Tex.), Toby Moffett (Conn.), Jim Santini (Nev.), Henry Waxman (Calif.), Philip Sharp (Ind.), and Andrew Maguire (N.J.)— were all freshmen. Most of this class of 1975, excepting only Ottinger, bid for Investigations again in 1977. Charles Carney (Ohio), who had served on the subcommittee under Staggers, replaced Stuckey (who left Congress) as the only senior Democratic member; otherwise, the new members—Thomas Luken (Ohio), Douglas Walgren (Pa.), and Albert Gore, Jr. (Tenn.)—were again all freshmen.

12. Second-termers Matthew Rinaldo (N.J.) and Edward Madigan (Ill.) accepted appointment in 1975. Madigan, however, left the subcommittee in 1976 and was replaced by freshman Henson Moore (La.); Moore, in turn, transferred off the subcommittee in 1977. His place and the subcommittee's new minority slot are currently occupied by Commerce's two freshman Republicans, Dave Stockman (Mich.) and Marc Marks (Pa.).

13. Staff data for 1974 and 1977 are in Price 1975, p. 27; and in table 2 of the Working Paper cited above, p. 133.

14. "Legislative Oversight of SEC: Agency Independence and the ITT Case," *Hearings* of the SI Subcommittee, 93d Congress, June 14, 1973, p. 219; June 27, pp. 230-31.

15. "FEA Enforcement Policies," *Hearings* of the Oversight and Investigations Subcommittee, House Committee on Interstate and Foreign Commerce (hereafter O/I Subcommittee), 94th Congress, April 9, 1975, p. 9 and *passim*.

16. Moss and Lemov acknowledged that the rebuttal could not be written by the same deadline as other supplemental views but asserted that it did not need to be, for it was written in response to the minority statement rather than the report proper. "On that the rules are silent." This was a defensible position, but somewhat incongruous for a member whose first complaint about the Staggers years was that "back then the Committee operated without rules"; it should have been simple enough to write rules that established the majority's right of rebuttal.

17. *Minutes* of the meeting of April 17, 1975, on file in subcommittee office.

18. The eclipse of the "economic impact" idea is attributed by regulatory reform task force head Lowell Dodge both to the "monumental" difficulties of measuring "the impact of regulation on consumer prices, product diversity, etc." ("We know about these studies, but we don't try to do them ourselves") and to an ideological commitment against applying "narrower sorts of cost-benefit analysis" in the area of health and safety. For an example of the extremes to which Moss and Maguire were willing to take this latter argument, see their questioning of National Highway Traffic Safety Administration officials, "Regulatory Reform," *Hearings* of the O/I Subcommittee, 94th Congress, vol 4, February 27, 1976, pp. 447-52, 511.

19. *Minutes*, February 3, 1976.

20. Staggers's defenders insist that his approach produced results. "The leagues and teams tightened rules, imposed severe fines, called for an accounting of all drug purchases. And the National Football League subsequently brought strong disciplinary action against several members of the San Diego Chargers."

21. See Price 1975, pp. 316, 318; *Report* on Activities, 93d Congress, pp. 67, 69.

22. For the oversight plans of the legislative subcommittees for the 95th Congress, see "Oversight Plans of the Committees of the U.S. House of Representatives," *Report* of the House Committee on Government Operations, 95th Congress, March 4, 1977, pp. 70-73.

23. For a critical comparison of the work of the Dingell and Moss staffs on energy matters, see Malbin 1977, pp. 27-31.

24. Researchers have consistently found member incentives to oversight to be relatively low; cf. Scher 1963, pp. 531-40; and Ogul 1976, pp. 19-21, 181-83.

12 New Powers of the Purse: An Assessment of Congressional Budget Reform

James A. Thurber

Introduction

The Budget and Impoundment Control Act of 1974 (P.L. 93-344) established five major congressional reforms: two new budget committees, a new office providing information and analysis (Congressional Budget Office), a new time-table for the budget process, procedures for Congress to determine national budget policies and priorities, and a process to review Presidential impoundments. Before this reform, congressional spending decisions were made in isolation, one at a time, without concern for the impact of the aggregated spending decisions. Each appropriations subcommittee, revenue committee, and authorizing committee made spending and revenue recommendations with only rare reference to what the others were doing. Congress could not describe the total appropriated funds for a particular fiscal year until after the beginning of that year. In fact, Congress could not appropriate funds for many programs before the beginning of a fiscal year, so it frequently passed continuing resolutions to allow programs to survive until the final spending decisions were made.

The new Budget Act raises a number of questions about congressional reform. What were the major causes of budget reform? What are the major characteristics and objectives of the new budget process? And two more difficult questions: What is the impact of the reform on congressional institutions and behavior? What are the consequences of budget reform for public policy?

Some Causes of Budget Reform

The Budget Act represents the first successful congressional recapture of its past control over spending and revenue decisions in a single committee since 1865 when the House Ways and Means Committee's responsibility for spending was transferred to the newly created Appropriation Committees.[1] Conservatives as well as liberals criticized the old budgeting process, described by Shick (1974) as a war between the parts and the whole; and a variety of factors, both internal

I am grateful to Louis Fisher of the Congressional Research Service, John Ellwood of the Congressional Budget Office, and Terence Zinn of the U.S. Senate Budget Committee for helpful suggestions in the development and writing of this chapter.

and external to Congress, led to the enactment of the new congressional budget process. The major conditions that contributed to its passage will be discussed briefly (for a more complete explanation, see Ellwood and Thurber 1977a).

A primary factor behind the reform was Richard Nixon's abuse of Presidential power, which triggered a strong congressional counteraction. One month before the 1972 Presidential election, Nixon challenged Congress to cut $6 billion from the already authorized budget for fiscal 1973, demanding authority to make whatever spending cuts he found necessary. This, coupled with his impoundment of $8.7 billion in January 1973, gave Congress the courage to refuse the President blanket authority to cut the budget and to set up a joint study committee on budget control as the first step in the development and passage of the new Budget Act. Nixon's public castigation of Congress as "big spenders" and "fiscally irresponsible" established an unprecedented political challenge to Congress, as Nixon's Vietnam, Watergate, and impoundment troubles were growing.

Many in Congress also feared the rise in spending and deficits. Federal spending had doubled from 1956 to 1976 (even in constant dollars), and the government had run a deficit 15 out of 19 years from 1956 to the passage of the Budget Act.

Congress also realized that special interests could not continue to have increasingly larger amounts of the federal budget. Congress had discovered the need to set spending priorities, but lacked a mechanism. Liberals wanted to reduce defense spending, conservatives to reduce spending for social programs; both factions pushed for a process to help pursue their policy objectives more effectively. They turned to a new congressional budget process.

Many members realized that Congress had no way to challenge the dominance of the executive branch (and the Federal Reserve Board) over fiscal policy and felt that Congress should be directly involved in setting the "proper level" of economic stimulation or restraint through a congressional budget. Members wanted better control over macroecnomic policy to deal with inflation, unemployment, recession, and other national economic concerns (see Fisher 1977b).

Congress also felt a need for an independent source of budgetary information and analysis. It was always difficult, and at times impossible, to get information about the President's budget from other than the Office of Management and Budget, which is, of course, part of the executive office of the President. Increasingly distrustful of the "imperial Presidency," Congress felt a need for an independent budget and for an objective source of information, analysis, and expertise to establish that budget. Thus, there was a strong desire to establish an independent analytical institution like the Office of Management and Budget (OMB), but responsible only to Congress. Senator Edmund S. Muskie emphasized this desire in 1974: "Congress has seen its control over the federal purse strings ebb away over the past 50 years because of its inability to get a grip on the over-all budget, while the Office of Management and Budget in the Executive

Branch has increased its power and influence" (*National Journal*, May 29, 1976, pp. 742-43).

Members of the appropriations and revenue committees also wanted a new budgetary decision-making system that would limit "backdoor spending" and "uncontrollables." Authorizing committees were increasingly using "backdoor spending" devices such as contract and borrowing authority and entitlements to circumvent the restraints placed on spending by the appropriations committees. The year before passage of the Budget Act, only 44 percent of the budget could be directly controlled by the appropriations committees. Only about 30 percent of all federal spending was allocated by current decisions (that is, during the cycle just before the start of a new fiscal year).[2] Because of the uncontrollability of the budget, appropriations bills were most often passed after the beginning of each fiscal year. For example, in 1971 the regular Transportation appropriations bill was never enacted, and the same was true of the Labor-HEW bill in 1973. Members of the appropriations committees, wanting more control over spending decisions, were major advocates of new deadlines and more discipline in the appropriation and authorization process.

Finally, behind all these factors lurked the rising discontent of constituents with Congress, the ultimate threat to the peace of mind of senators and representatives. A majority of voters believed Congress to be irresponsible in its budgetary and fiscal policy decision making. Congress was held uniformly in low esteem in all major opinion surveys, and members of Congress felt reform of any kind would help the prestige of the institution. The widespread turnover of representatives and senators introduced new norms and values and, in turn, new demands for a more responsible process for making spending decisions. This influx of new members (more than half of the members of the 95th House had been elected since 1970) brought to Washington members of Congress more concerned with making public policy (Bullock 1976) and, thus, with improving the process by which spending decisions were made.

Characteristics and Objectives of the Reform

The Budget Act of 1974 overlays the old congressional "particle" budgeting. It adds new institutions and a new process and replaces none of the old. Spending, authorizing, and revenue jurisdictions were not significantly altered by the reform, but the act created new House and Senate budget committees, the Congressional Budget Office (CBO), and a set of budgetary procedures and deadlines (see Table 12-1). It also requires use of standardized budget terminology and information in the President's budget and establishes new impoundment controls.

The central "driving mechanisms" of the new budget process are the concurrent resolutions and the decision-making deadlines associated with them. On

Table 12-1
Congressional Budget Timetable

Deadline	Action to Be Completed
November 10	Current services budget received
January 18[a]	President's budget received
March 15	Advice and data from all congressional committees to budget committees
April 1	CBO reports to budget committees
April 15	Budget committees report out first budget resolution
May 15	Congressional committees report new authorizing legislation
May 15	Congress completes action on first budget resolution
Labor Day + 7[b]	Congress completes action on all spending bills
September 15	Congress completes action on second budget resolution
September 25	Congress completes action on reconciliation bill
October 1	Fiscal year begins

Source: U.S. Senate, Committee on the Budget, *Congressional Budget Reform*, 93d Congress, 2d Session, 4 March 1975, p. 70.
[a]Or 15 days after Congress convenes.
[b]Seven days after Labor Day.

or before May 15, the first concurrent resolution establishes targets, aggregate levels of taxing and spending for 17 budget categories.[3] A second concurrent resolution is passed by September 15, establishing the final taxing and spending ceilings (see Table 12-1). If a reassessment of spending, revenue, and debt requirements in the second budget resolution is necessary, then Congress has until September 25 to enact a "reconciliation bill." The Budget Act sets October 1 as the beginning of the fiscal year and requires the President to submit a current services budget by November 10 and his budget for the next fiscal year on the 15th day after the convening of each session of Congress. The President still proposes the federal budget, but the final version is Congress'. Authorizing committees must report all new legislation early in the process, by May 15, and the appropriations committees must complete all spending decisions between May 15 and seven days after Labor Day, giving Congress time to enact the second concurrent resolution by September 15. The budget must be internally consistent: Revenues and expenditures must balance, or be accounted for through a deficit or surplus figure; this forces members, for the first time in the history of Congress, to vote at least once a year on a "congressional" budget. If any bill exceeds the expenditure ceilings or revenue floor established in the second (or reconciliation) resolution, it is subject to a point of order if considered on the floor.

Three institutions were created by the new budget act: the House (HBC) and Senate (SBC) Budget Committees and the Congressional Budget Office (CBO).

The HBC consists of 25 members (five each from Appropriations and Ways and Means and one each from the majority and minority leadership). Members must rotate on the committee, with no one serving more than four years during a 10-year period. The sixteen SBC members are selected by the Democratic Steering Committee and the Republican Committee on Committees. Senate Budget Committee members are exempt from the current committee assignment limitations until the start of the 96th Congress, thus delaying senators' decisions about whether to stay on Budget or drop another committee assignment (a good test of the committee's prestige and popularity). (See Ellwood and Thurber 1977a, for differences between the House and Senate Budget Committees.)

The Congressional Budget Office is the primary analytical and informational component of the budget reform. It fulfills four general responsibilities:

1. Monitoring the economy and estimating its impact on government actions.
2. Writing policy analyses of existing and recommended programs.
3. Improving the flow and quality of budgetary information to members and committees.
4. Analyzing the costs and effects of alternative budgetary choices.

CBO meets these responsibilities first by providing information and analysis to the two budget committees (80 percent of the time); second, it provides support to Appropriations, Ways and Means, and Finance (10 percent of CBO's time), in limited degree to other committees (5 percent of its time), and to individual members (5 percent).

The major objectives of the new budget process differ, reflecting the ideological differences in Congress, but most members agree upon the following:

1. To set spending and revenue targets and ceilings under the new deadlines
2. To determine national spending priorities
3. To force early estimates and enactment of authorizing legislation
4. To make timely (well before September 15) appropriations decisions (that is, to eliminate continuing resolutions for department budgets)
5. To allow Congress to establish its own macroeconomic and fiscal policy
6. To have an independent source of budget information and to make objective evaluations of Presidential budgets, programs, and policies
7. To limit the growth of "uncontrollables" in the budget
8. To close all "backdoor spending" by authorizing committees
9. To relate revenue, spending, and deficit decisions to each other
10. To limit Presidential impoundment power and regularize review of impoundments (See Ellwood and Thurber 1977b for a more complete discussion of the objectives.)

Institutional and Policy Implications of Budget Reform

Now that Congress has an overall framework and process to establish fiscal and tax policy and to set spending priorities, how well has it functioned and with what impact for congressional institutions and, ultimately, for public policy? The definitive answer to this question must await more than 2½ years of implementation, but several preliminary observations are possible.

The new process has worked better than most expected, and the elaborate timetable has been met consistently during the first years of its implementation. Total projected spending has been reduced slightly as a result of the new process (FY 1977 spending rose 11 percent compared to an average of 17 percent a year increase for the three previous fiscal years). Congress has also illustrated that it can implement its own spending priorities (deciding expenditures that should be decreased or increased) and fiscal policy (determining the magnitude of federal spending, revenues, and deficit that is best for the economy). The controversy over Presidential impoundments has been confined to a specific set of well-defined procedures that have worked. For the first time, the President no longer unilaterally determines the budget. There has been a cap on new "backdoor spending," and the gap between the level of authorization and appropriation for programs has been closed. The budget process has proved to be independent of a majority President, although the budget committees still get many cues from the executive.

CBO provides sound, objective, independent (some have argued that it is too independent) information, budget estimates, and policy analysis for Congress. The Senate Budget Committee has gained power and realized success through a strategy of bipartisan coalition building and the strong leadership of Senator Muskie, its first and only chairman. The House Budget Committee, weakened by partisanship, rotation of its members, and a liberal-conservative split, has produced budget resolutions that passed with narrow margins only because of the skillful maneuvering of Rep. Brock Adams and Rep. Robert Giaimo (the first two Budget Committee chairmen) and the persuasive hand of the House Democratic leadership. Thus, many of the original objectives of the Congressional Budget and Impoundment Control Act have been met (see Ellwood and Thurber 1976a for measures of success and failure of the new process). The final question remains: What are the institutional and policy consequences of the new congressional budget reform? The institutional and behavioral impact of this process during the first 2½ years, on congressional committees, congressional leadership, congressional power vis-à-vis the President, interest groups, and members' constituency relationships has been remarkable.

Impact on Committees

Implementation of the new budget process has led to significant consequences for congressional committees. In addition to the obvious increased workload for all committees, stemming from both an altered budgetary timetable and the required reports on projected spending and revenues, the gap between authorizations and appropriations has been dramatically reduced. An additional impact seems to be an enhanced ability and incentive of committee staff to conduct systematic oversight of programs resulting from new knowledge of the budget. The reform has also caused some jockeying for jurisdictional turf between the budget committees and the other standing committees, especially appropriations and taxing committees. Finally, the authorizing committees have lost significant power because of the appropriations committees' right to cap new "backdoor spending."

The Budget Act requires each standing committee to submit estimates of spending authority for programs within its jurisdiction by March 15; by May 15 each must submit a final list of spending authorizations to the budget committees. The committees' reports, the most significant reason for their increased workload, provide the major ingredient for the targets that the first budget resolution sets. The committee estimates of authorizations have tended to limit their freedom to pass unanticipated new programs and higher authorizations after May 15. The budget targets set outer spending limits for commitees and force them to state priorities and to make difficult choices among programs very early in the process, rather than to authorize high levels of funding and new programs as a result of strong, well-organized, twelfth-hour lobbying shortly before the beginning of the fiscal year. Before the reform, program authorization levels were commonly (and symbolically) double and even triple the final appropriations. The substantive committees would authorize at very high levels to placate strong pressures from outside Congress, knowing full well that the appropriations committees would push the actual funding down to "reasonable" levels. The authorization committees can no longer play this game as a result of the requirement to estimate total program funding within each committee's jurisdiction. Thus the gap between authorizations and appropriations is now frequently less than 5 percent.[4]

Although Senator Sam J. Ervin, Jr., floor manager of the Senate's version of the Budget and Impoundment Control Act, argued that the budget committees "would not infringe on the jurisdiction of the now existing committees" (Fisher 1977a, p. 1), jurisdictional conflicts have occurred in at least four ways as a result of the reform. First, to arrive at targets and ceilings for the functional categories of the budget, the budget committees must look at specific programs. Thus, there has been an "inescapable invasion" of authorization and appropriation committee jurisdictions by the budget committees when they build their aggregate targets and ceiling figures (see Fisher 1977a, U.S. Senate 1976b). The Senate Budget Committee has avoided setting line-item limits in the budget resolution or its accompanying report (this is not the case in the House); however, the SBC has frequently opposed bills from other committees after passage of the first budget resolution. Second, the Ways and Means and Finance Committees have lost power as a result of the budget reform. Rudder (1977) has shown that the tax committees have lost some control over information, expertise, and issue definition in revenue matters. They have been forced to react to budget committee proposals, therefore losing the power of initiative. [Rudder (1977) shows that this is more observable in the Senate than in the House.] Third, budget committee "scorekeeping" (comparing the cost of legislation reported by committees to the functional targets in the first budget resolution) and keeping committees within the targets are a direct infringement upon the prereform authority of the standing committees. Fourth, the successful power-building strategy of Senator Muskie and the SBC has caused several direct confrontations on the floor of the Senate (see Ellwood and Thurber 1977a, pp. 177–82). Not only did Senator Muskie oppose legislation on the floor of the Senate (which is not the style of the HBC) that would break the targets of the first budget resolution, but the SBC also won several critical battles with the Appropriations Committee, including the right to joint jurisdiction over recession and deferral impoundment resolutions.

The final major consequence of the new budget reform is to close two types of backdoor spending (contract authority and borrowing authority) by the substantive committees (see Fisher 1977a; Pfiffner 1977). Although either house may waive this restriction, the elimination of new "back doors" has increased the appropriation committees' control over spending and thus the freedom for the authorization committees to circumvent the traditional appropriations process.

Impact on Party Leadership

As a result of the sweeping reforms of the 1970s, power in the House of Representatives shifted from committee to subcommittee chairpersons; concurrently, changes in rules and procedures increased the influence of the Democratic Caucus and Democratic Party leadership. Thus, the 1970s brought both decentralization and centralization of power to the House. This was not the case in the Senate. There was a resurgence of the Speakership, and the new budget process stands out as one of his primary tools to coordinate and centralize decision making in the House. House Democratic leaders are forced through the budget process to mobilize members behind budget resolutions that do not always please committee and subcommittee chairpersons, interest groups, agencies of the executive branch, or the President. They must build coalitions and centralize decision making in a House that is highly decentralized. Although Senate Majority Leader Robert Byrd plays a more active role than his predecessor, power in the Senate is still firmly in the hands of the committee chairpersons; therefore, House and Senate party leaders have played widely different roles in the new budget process. The Senate Democratic leadership has taken a "hands-off" approach to the SBC and its budget resolutions; this reflects the bipartisan coalition building of SBC Chairman Muskie and ranking minority member

Bellmon. However, both Majority Leaders Mansfield and Byrd have been strong supporters of the process.

The House leadership has been actively involved in setting budget figures and offering refining amendments to marshal support for the resolutions on the floor. The primary impact of the budget reform on the House majority leadership (under Speakers Carl Albert and "Tip" O'Neill) is that it has forced centralization, coordination, and the construction of a Democratic coalition to support a congressional budget. Majority Leader Jim Wright, the leadership's member of the HBC, has been a primary force in molding workable Democratic budget resolutions. When Speaker O'Neill was majority leader under Carl Albert, he played a key role building the narrow margins needed to keep the budget process alive.[5]

The House leadership has also helped make the budget process independent of the President (an important test of the integrity of the reform under Carter), but not always of the power and expertise of committee and subcommittee chairpersons who put pressure on the HBC to spend more for their pet programs. Defense spending and the confrontation over water project funding typify the House leadership's responsive role in the process. Under strong pressure from House Democratic leaders, the HBC reversed itself and restored funds for water resource projects that President Carter wanted abolished. On March 28, 1977, the HBC voted 13-11 to support the Carter cutback, but three days later majority leaders, under pressure from members, turned the committee around, 14-11, to defeat Carter and to refund the water programs.

The budget process might have broken down in the House several times except for the efforts of the leadership. During 1975, leaders appealed for "support of the process," but in 1977 they based their persuasion on the policy content of the resolution. The latest crisis in the process occurred in spring 1977 when conservatives, claiming too little money was allocated for defense, succeeded in increasing the budget target, thus incurring the ire of House liberals. These same conservatives later objected to the overall deficit and coalesced with liberals who were upset by the high defense spending to defeat the overall budget resolution, the first recommital of a budget bill. A revised bill with strong leadership support later passed the House.

Impact on Congressional-Presidential Relations

A major element influencing the flow of power back to Congress from the Presidency during the 1970s has been the Budget Act. Members can no longer hide behind an archaic budgetary process to explain deficits and expand expenditures, and the traditional monopoly over the budget is no longer held by the President. President Carter must face the reality of a new budgetary process:

If President Carter wants an immediate tax cut, he must first convince the budget committees of Congress to approve it. If President Carter wants to stimulate the economy through increased federal spending, he must first persuade the budget committees to accept this. If President Carter wants to balance the federal budget by 1980, he will have to work continuously with the budget committees to reach that goal (Smith 1977, p. 89).

When Carter lobbies for his budget, he is not working with the Georgia Legislature, as Representative Giaimo reminded him recently, nor is he dealing with the decentralized, uncoordinated Congress that existed before the new Budget Act.

How has the new congressional process worked with a President of the same party as the majority in Congress? Both budget committee chairmen, Senator Muskie and Representative Giaimo, argue that the process has met the challenge of independence by resisting co-option by President Carter. Senator Muskie recently asserted that "It has been a helluva job to maintain the independence of the congressional budget this year, but we've done it" (Russell and Broder 1977, p. A3). Chairman Giaimo also feels the process has been free of the dominance of a Democratic President: "The question was whether we were going to be a rubber stamp or work out our own priorities. I think we've answered that question" (Russell and Broder 1977, p. A3). The chairmen have stressed the independence of the process, but the preliminary evidence suggests a more tempered judgment. Although President Carter and his advisers have lost several major policy battles to Congress, the budget committees seem to be taking their major cues from the President.

Table 12-2 reveals wide disparities between the 1976 congressional budget and President Ford's budget (Congress had 14 percent more outlays), while outlays in the second congressional resolution of 1978 are almost identical to Carter's budget (less than 1 percent difference). Outlays by function show several other significant differences. The 1976 congressional budget exceeds the President's budget in all categories except national defense and international affairs, while the 1978 budget targets vary little in any category from President Carter's budget, except for three distributive policies (community development, agriculture, and veterans' benefits) that are "bread and butter" programs in almost every House district. Congressional budget levels have been consistently higher than President Ford's and consistently lower than President Carter's. Of the possible explanations for the disparity—budget formulation in an election year (1976), Presidential inheritance of a budget that could not be altered in a short time, and a unified congressional-Presidential party—the most important is that the congressional majority party is the same as the President's for the 1978 budget.

However, there is ample evidence that the process has been independent of President Carter. The dynamic conflicts between the President and Congress over spending programs for national defense, water projects, welfare, and energy

Table 12-2
Comparison of Presidential and Congressional Budgets for Fiscal 1976 and 1978 (in billions of dollars)

	1976 Ford Budget	1976 Congressional Budget	1976 Congressional Difference	1978 Carter Budget	1978 Congressional Budget	1978 Congressional Difference
Overall Levels						
Total Outlays	349.4	374.9	25.5	462.6	458.25	-4.35
Total Revenues	297.5	300.8	3.3	404.7	397.00	-7.70
Deficit	51.9	74.1	22.2	57.9	61.25	3.35
Outlays by Function						
National Defense	94.0	91.9	-2.1	112.8	110.1	-2.7
International Affairs	6.3	4.8	-1.5	7.2	6.6	-0.6
General Science	4.8	4.8	0.0	4.7	4.7	0.0
Natural Resources, Environment, & Energy	10.0	11.4	1.4	20.9	20.0	-0.9
Agriculture	1.8	2.8	1.0	4.4	6.3	1.9
Commerce & Transportation	13.7	18.3	4.6	19.9	19.6	-0.3
Community Development	5.9	7.0	1.1	9.9	10.6	0.7
Education, Manpower	14.8	20.9	6.1	27.0	26.4	-0.6
Health	28.05	32.9	4.85	44.6	44.2	-0.2
Income Security	118.7	128.2	9.5	148.7	146.1	-2.6
Veterans' Benefits	15.8	19.1	3.3	18.8	20.2	1.4
Law Enforcement	3.3	3.4	0.1	3.8	4.0	0.2
General Government	3.2	3.3	0.1	4.0	3.85	-0.15
Revenue Sharing	7.2	7.3	0.1	9.7	9.7	0.0
Interest	34.4	35.4	1.0	40.9	41.7	0.8
Allowances	8.05	0.8	-7.25	1.2	1.0	-0.2
Offsetting Receipts	-20.2	-17.1	-3.1	-16.0	-16.8	0.8

reveal budding congressional budgetary power. For example, after the House recommitted the first budget resolution for fiscal year 1978 and President Carter lost both funds for military spending and face with congressional leaders, he apologized for "his own and colleagues' unknowing and unwitting collisions with the congressional process" (Russell and Broder 1977, p. A3). After losing military funds and the water projects battle, Carter's director of the Office of Budget and Management, Bert Lance, added, "I've learned first-hand these last few weeks that this is still a young and tender process and needs to be brought along" (Russell and Broder 1977, p. A3).

One major goal of the reform was to give Congress an objective, independent source of budgetary expertise and knowledge; indeed, the Congressional Budget Office and the budget committees have attained this goal. Now Congress has more specialized knowledge and expertise when it elects to compete with the President. For example, CBO pointed out that President Ford's budget was not adequate for the needs of the economy, and recently that Carter's energy plan was "overly optimistic" (CBO found that oil import savings would be closer to 3.5 million barrels per day in 1985 rather than 4.5 million that the Carter administration projected. Karen Williams, Chief Counsel of the Senate Budget Committee, comments on the importance of the CBO to the competition with the President: "Before CBO, we just did not have the figures to work with. Now CBO studies on defense issues have allowed us to take a really good look at costs. The same goes for proposed food-stamp and social security reform" (*Time*, July 18, 1977, p. 71).

Impact on Interest Groups and
Member-Constituency Relations

There is some evidence that budget reform has had an impact on behavior and attitudes "outside" Congress, on interest groups and on member-constituency relationships. Through open debate and more visible and coordinated votes on deficits, total spending, taxation, and macroeconomic policy, constituents, electoral opponents, and interest groups have new (and probably better) data to evaluate the performance of senators and representatives. No one has been defeated as a result of information from the budget process, but the 1976 election campaign revealed wide use of policy stands on the budget by both incumbents and nonincumbents. The primary influence on constituents, beyond a mini-course in macroeconomics, will probably be unknown for several years, but it is likely the influence will be dynamic, reflecting the salient issues related to reelection goals of members.

Constituents appear to support the new budget process—wondering why it was not instituted before 1974—while many interest groups see it as a threat and have opposed it from the beginning: since the reform forces Congress to set priorities, it guarantees everyone will not always get more. There is a realization that the budgetary pie is not growing rapidly enough to take care of expanding old programs and new expensive programs. Under the new process, tradeoffs between popular programs have to be made, which is not true under the old system of making spending decisions. Large interest groups such as the AFL-CIO have been major opponents of the new process, and most small specialized interest groups have found it difficult to influence the spending levels in their functional areas of the budget. The aggregated, centralized, coordinated approach to budgeting has tended to reduce the power of the "iron triangles" or "clientelism" (the relationship of congressional subcommittees, executive agencies, and interest groups in the same policy subsystem), used to push successfully for expanded programs, more spending, and less oversight.

New broad-based coalitons have also formed to lobby the major budget participants. Their central objective—how can we get more for our functional category in the budget? For example, several health, education, welfare, and union associations have joined forces, hired a staff, and pressured the budget committees to increase spending for social programs and to reduce money for defense. Their language, analysis, and action are at the aggregate level, at the stage of the budget resolution markups, rather than at the program level, the traditional focus of congressional lobbying. Seldom does an internal congressional reform have such a significant effect upon the "external" environment of Congress.

Future Implications for Policy[6]

The major impact of budget reform on public policy is yet to be determined, although fears that the reform would primarily help conservatives oppose spending for social programs and give military spending the upper hand appear not to be realized. Nor is there evidence of a major change in priorities, toward more social spending in the budget, as a result of the new process. However, some observers believe the reform has forced the setting of priorities for major new program initiatives—that is, consideration of tradeoffs between programs of marginal value and new program initiatives. Others argue it has made Congress too cost-conscious, thus killing new programs such as national health insurance.

The reform has given committees and members better tools to evaluate new programmatic demands and economic trends. The new process highlights macroeconomic and macrobudgetary tradeoffs. The issues are more visible, so they can be more readily contested by individuals and groups. A new budgetary consciousness has been brought to the Hill as a result of the Budget Act. However, it is unlikely that the process itself will initiate programmatic changes; it is more likely that initiatives will continue to come from members of Congress, committees, party leaders, executive branch agencies, the President, interest groups, and the public.

Notes

1. An attempt to establish a centralized congressional budget process, authorized in the Legislative Reorganization Act of 1946, failed after one year.

2. This condition still exists, although many members are advocating systemic advanced budgeting to give Congress more control over spending.

3. The Budget Act requires Congress to estimate outlays, budget authority, and tax expenditures for each of the functional categories of the budget. The budget is divided into the following functions (consisting of federal program accounts): (1) national defense; (2) international affairs; (3) general science, space, and technology; (4) natural resources, environment, and energy; (5) agriculture; (6) commerce and transportation; (7) community and regional development (8) education, training, employment, and social services; (9) health; (10) income security; (11) veterans' benefits and services; (12) law enforcement and justice; (13) general government; (14) revenue sharing and general-purpose fiscal assistance; (15) allowances; (16) undistributed offsetting receipts; and (17) interest.

4. Section 402 of the Budget Act provides that any bill or resolution which "directly or indirectly" authorizes enactment of new budget authority for a fiscal year will not be in order if it is reported after May 15 preceding the fiscal year. Waiver resolutions must be approved by the budget committees, thus giving them significant control over late legislation. Section 311 gives the budget committees the authority to reject authorizations or appropriations that would exceed the second or final budget resolution, thus granting the two budget committees extraordinary power to ensure that all regular bills are passed before the start of the fiscal year (see Ellwood and Thurber 1976b).

5. The first concurrent resolution of 1975 passed by four votes, the second concurrent resolution of that year by ten, and the conference report for the second resolution by a slim margin of two votes (see Ellwood and Thurber 1977b). All the budget resolutions through mid-1977 passed easily in the Senate, with bipartisan support.

6. A fuller discussion of the implications of the budget reform for Senate policy making is found in Ellwood and Thurber (1976b). I am grateful to my coauthor for permission to use several sentences from that study in this section.

13 Presidential Impoundment and Congressional Reform

William G. Munselle

Introduction

In recent years, Presidential powers have been broadly exercised and expanded. Presidents have claimed executive privilege, conducted unpopular wars, refused to spend congressional appropriations, and made secret foreign commitments using executive agreements. In the 1970s, Congress has reacted to these developments with a number of measures designed to maintain or restore the power of the legislative branch. In response to the use of secret executive agreements, Congress enacted legislation in 1972 requiring that all international agreements, other than treaties, be transmitted to both houses of Congress within 60 days of their execution. In reaction to the broad exercise of Presidential war powers in Southeast Asia, Congress passed the War Powers Act of 1973, which curtails the President's ability to commit United States armed forces in foreign conflicts without congressional approval. The President's extensive use of the Office of Management and Budget (OMB) as an instrument to increase the President's control of the executive branch resulted in legislation requiring Senate confirmation of the OMB director and deputy director.

One of the most important and controversial areas of congressional-Presidential conflict has concerned the President's use of impoundment to control federal expenditures and Congress's efforts to enact legislations limiting Presidential impoundment powers (Fisher 1970, 1975). Impoundment is an executive branch action or inaction that precludes the obligation or expenditure of funds under budget authority provided by Congress.[1] During recent administrations, the executive refusal to spend appropriations or to use other budget authority was condemned by members of Congress and potential program beneficiaries. These critics claimed that impoundments violated the doctrine of separation of powers, usurping congressional powers and ignoring the constitutional obligation of the President to execute the laws faithfully. They argued that this practice undermined congressional control over appropriations, provided the President with an unconstitutional item veto, and contributed to the excessive growth of Presidential power. Potential recipients of federal funds and

I want to thank Leroy N. Rieselbach of Indiana University and Michael A. Maggiotto, Jon L. Mills, and R. Lee Andersen of the University of Florida for their insights and helpful comments.

173

their congressional supporters complained of programs being reduced, terminated, or placed in uncertain status by impoundments.

Presidents and their supporters responded to criticisms of impoundment in statutory, constitutional, and policy terms. Franklin Roosevelt argued that congressional appropriation acts permit, but do not always require, full expenditures; the Johnson and Nixon administrations made similar arguments. General statutes also specifically authorize or even require some impoundments. For example, the Anti-Deficiency Act (31 U.S.C. 655) permits withholding of funds to provide for contingencies or to effect savings. It has also been argued that under the Constitution spending is an executive, not a legislative, function and that the power to impound stems in part from the President's constitutional powers as Commander in Chief and spokesman for the nation in international relations.

Impoundment also has been defended on political and economic policy grounds. President Nixon characterized Congress as so decentralized that it could not obtain an overview of government expenditures and revenues; he asserted that it was fiscally irresponsible, captured by special-interest demands for increased expenditures. He suggested that the President, on behalf of the country as a whole, must provide an economic overview and bring expenditures in line with federal revenues. The Nixon administration also argued that impoundment made possible savings from programs that were wasteful, inefficient, or unnecessary, and that it provided the necessary flexibility to promote and regulate a healthy economy. Promoting the general economy was cited to justify impoundment in the Truman and Johnson administrations as well. Finally, impoundment has been presented as a proper tool to fight higher taxes and inflation brought about by excessive congressional spending.

Many Presidents—Jefferson, Grant, Franklin Roosevelt, Truman, Kennedy, Johnson, Nixon, and Ford among them—have impounded funds. In some cases, such as Roosevelt's impoundment of public works projects and Kennedy's impoundment of funds for the B-70 bomber, controversy ensued. But for several reasons, impoundment became an intense political controversy during the Nixon administration. Nixon impounded funds provided by a Congress under the control of an opposition party, a Congress with policy goals different from his own. His predecessors had often faced a Congress of their own party and thus aroused less political opposition over cuts. The salience of impoundment increased because both Nixon and many congressional Democrats wanted to make it an issue. Furthermore, Nixon withheld funds from a large number and a wide range of programs, including funds for highways, low-rent public housing, rent supplements, farm disaster loans, rural electricification, water and sewer grants, mortgage subsidies, water pollution control, and education. Many of these programs had more broadly based support than programs affected by earlier Presidents' impoundments. Also, Nixon was viewed as using impoundment more often than predecessors to end programs rather than merely to delay expenditures. Finally, the salience of impoundment increased during the Nixon administration because of the general atmosphere of conflict between Congress and the Presidency.

The Congressional Budget and Impoundment Control Act of 1974

Congressional opposition to executive impoundment and the deep concern of many members over their inability to develop a sufficiently rational and comprehensive national budget led to the passage of the Congressional Budget and Impoundment Control Act of 1974. The first nine titles of this act deal with changes in congressional budget-making processes. Title X deals with impoundment; it requires the executive branch to report impoundments and provides mechanisms for Congress to respond to impoundments.

Title X places all impoundments into one of two categories: rescissions and deferrals. A rescission is a *permanent* withdrawal or cancellation of budget authority by Congress; it is a permanent impoundment. If a President wants Congress to rescind budget authority that it has previously created, the President must send a special message to both houses of Congress, indicating the amount of budget authority to be rescinded, the projects and governmental functions involved, the reasons for rescission, and the fiscal, economic, and budgetary effect of the proposed rescission. The message is to indicate all facts, circumstances, and considerations relating to the proposed rescission and the estimated effect of the proposed rescission on the objects, purposes, and programs for which budget authority had been provided. Congress may agree with the President's special message and rescind the budget authority as requested. A rescission must be passed by both chambers in the same manner as any other statute. If Congress does not pass the requested rescission within 45 days of continuous congressional session after the receipt of the special message, the executive branch must make the budget authority proposed for rescission available for obligation.

A deferral is a *temporary* impoundment; it is a delay in the use of budget authority. A deferral may not extend beyond the end of the fiscal year during which it is proposed. Whenever the President decides to defer budget authority, a special Presidential message is sent to both chambers of Congress providing essentially the same information required in the special message for a rescission. In addition, the special message for a deferral must indicate the period of time during which the budget authority is to be deferred and any legal authority the President invokes to justify the deferral.[2] Any budget authority the executive branch defers must be made available for obligation if either house of Congress passes a resolution disapproving the deferral.[3] In the absence of congressional action, the deferral remains in effect.[4]

Title X provides that copies of special messages for rescissions and deferrals be sent to the Comptroller General of the General Accounting Office who is to review them and report to Congress on the legality of deferrals and the facts surrounding proposed rescissions and deferrals. If the Comptroller General finds that the executive branch has failed to report a withholding of budget authority, he or she may report this impoundment to Congress, which will treat the message as though it were a special message from the President.[5] If a withholding of budget authority is improperly classified, the Comptroller General can reclassify that impoundment. The act also empowers the Comptroller General to sue the executive branch in federal court to require that budget authority be made available for obligation.[6]

After the passage of the 1974 Budget Act, there was disagreement about whether it provides the President with new statutory authority to impound or simply recognizes the limited power the President had under already existing statutes. Senator Edmund Muskie, chairman of the Senate Budget Committee, argued that the act does not provide a new legal basis for impoundments. But the practice of both the Ford and Carter administrations, supported by the opinion of the Comptroller General, has been to treat the Budget Act as a separate legal basis for impoundment. Senator Muskie also argued that the President does not have the legal power to defer budget authority for policy reasons, such as opposition to a particular program. Muskie contended that the President can defer only to effect savings, provide for contingencies, or obey specific statutory requirements to impound. But under both the Ford and Carter administrations, budget authority has been deferred for policy reasons, as well as for effecting savings or providing for contingencies.

The passage of the Budget Act did not end the practice of impoundment.[7] President Ford impounded funds for a large number of projects, including funds for mortgage subsidies, water and sewer facilities, maternal and child health care, Head Start, agricultural conservation of soil and water resources, nutrition programs for the elderly, education for the handicapped, and defense. In fiscal 1975, Ford proposed approximately $4.3 billion in rescissions. Congress approved a little under $1.4 billion of these rescissions, or less than 32 percent of their dollar value. Ford deferred $24.9 billion. Congress disapproved $9.3 billion for a 37 percent disapproval rate. In fiscal 1976, Ford proposed $3.6 billion in rescissions. Congress approved $138 million, less than 4 percent of the dollar amount requested for rescission. In 1976, $8.2 billion was deferred. Congress disapproved $393 million, or less than 5 percent of the dollar amount of the deferrals. Thus congressional refusal to pass rescissions requested by the President during fiscal years 1975 and 1976 prevented the permanent impoundment of over $6.4 billion, but unwillingness to override deferrals allowed the temporary impoundment of approximately $23 billion. During this 2-year period, the largest amount of impounded funds ($14.8 billion) was for housing, environmental, and community development programs. The second largest amount ($11 billion) was for highway and road development. Defense, with $7.1 billion, was the third largest category[8] (Comptroller General's Report 1977, pp. 72-84).

Fiscal year 1977 (which began October 1, 1976) spanned both the Ford and the Carter Presidencies. The last cumulative report for that year reported approximately $1.9 billion in proposed rescissions and $7.5 billion in deferrals. As of September 1, 1977, Congress had accepted $712 million of these rescissions and rejected $187 million, while $665 million was pending. Executive adjustments and withdrawals accounted for the other $363 million. Congress overrode $26 million in deferrals, while routine executive releases and adjustments accounted for another $3.1 billion. Approximately $4.4 billion in deferrals was pending before Congress as of September 1 (*Federal Register* 1977, p. 46247). Most of the 1977 impoundments were initiated by President Ford, who submitted 13 rescission proposals and 52 deferrals (*Federal Register* 1977, p. 4337).

During fiscal year 1977, President Carter proposed seven rescissions, totaling $791 million (*Federal Register* 1977, pp. 46248-49). The largest of these was the proposed rescission of $462 million for the B-1 bomber.[9] Carter initiated 12 new deferrals, totaling approximately $383 million (*Federal Register* 1977, pp. 46249-58).[10] Routine managerial or technical reasons accounted for most of these deferrals, but Carter did initiate policy deferrals of $12.6 million for federal water resources projects and $31.8 million for the Clinch River Breeder Reactor Plant project (*Federal Register* 1977, pp. 17092, 17094, 26396). In the first few weeks of fiscal year 1978, Carter made greater use of impoundment. By November 10, 1977, he had proposed only one rescission for $2.7 million. But he had initiated 46 deferrals totaling $2.4 billion. Most of these deferrals were for routine managerial or technical reasons. Although Carter has made limited use of impoundment in his first eleven months in office, it is too early to determine with certainty what the long-range impoundment policies of the Carter administration will be. If Carter is presented with what he views as excessive congressional spending that undermines his efforts to streamline the federal bureaucracy and balance the federal budget, or if he strongly disagrees with Congress on such policy matters as energy and defense spending, he may make increased use of his impoundment powers.

Consequences for Congressional-Executive Relations

During the Nixon administration, impoundment was used to thwart the will of Congress and to substitute the executive's policy goals. Programs were terminated or greatly reduced in scope by unilateral impoundment. Congress lacked the proper formal mechanisms to override impoundments. The release of impounded funds had to be obtained primarily by informal political pressures on the executive branch and by litigation.[11] The ability of Congress to act as an equal in developing national priorities was threatened.

The passage of the Budget Act was an attempt to regain for Congress a greater voice in national policy making. It was part of a more general reassertion of congressional power. Like the legislation constraining Presidential power to enter into secret foreign agreements and to commit armed forces to foreign conflicts, the 1974 Budget Act was designed to reestablish congressional powers diminished by an aggressive Presidency. Distrust of the Presidency and concern over possible Presidential abuses of power can be seen in several major provisions of the impoundment control legislation. The provision allowing the Comptroller General to report unreported executive impoundments was based upon the assumption that the executive branch might attempt to conceal impoundments from Congress. The provision giving the Comptroller General the power to sue for the release of funds was based upon the assumption that a President might not voluntarily make funds available as required by law. The requirement that even routine, managerial deferrals be submitted to Congress was based in part on the belief that the executive branch might disguise some policy impoundments as routine, managerial deferrals and thus avoid congressional scrutiny.

The 1974 act restored much of the balance of power, damaged by the unchecked use of impoundment. Now Congress is routinely informed of the status of impounded funds, and it has the ability to stop unwanted impoundments by refusing to pass requested rescissions and by overriding deferrals. The impoundment process is now in the open; and, to a large extent, Congress has the formal mechanisms necessary to prevent the executive branch from using impoundment to impose its will.

However, even though Congress's ability to control public policy has been increased by the 1974 reforms, present impoundment procedures still allow the executive branch to delay and hamper the execution of congressional programs and policies. Present rescission practices allow the executive branch to withhold budget authority proposed for rescission until the end of the 45-day period following submission of a special message, even if Congress voted against the rescission before the end of that period. Because the period during which Congress can pass a rescission must consist of 45 days *of continuous congressional session*, the actual number of calendar days during which budget authority is withheld can greatly exceed 45 days. In fiscal years 1975 and 1976, the 45-day provision allowed withholdings pending rescission to average 80 calendar days (Comptroller General's Report 1977, p. 12). Congress could increase its control over policy by forbidding the withholding of funds while a rescission awaits congressional action or by requiring that any such withholding be treated as a deferral. Or Congress could allow the present withholding practice but change the act to require that rescission proposals pend for 30 calendar days rather than 45 days of continuous congressional session.

The delays resulting from proposed rescissions and deferrals can disrupt programs that Congress intends to have operating smoothly. State officials who depend on federal funding report that these delays create uncertainty that results in impaired planning ability, loss of trained personnel in affected programs, diminished staff morale, and decreased efficiency. Also, it is sometimes difficult for Congress to understand fully the impact of deferrals and rescissions on programs and their beneficiaries. The information in special messages is not always adequate, and state and local officials, lacking information and organization, are not always able to indicate the adverse effects with sufficient force to obtain congressional action against impoundments.

A potential barrier to congressional policy control is the fact that late in a fiscal year, a deferral or a proposed rescission may tie up budget authority until it is too late to obligate it that fiscal year. If the authority for these funds expires at the end of that fiscal year, the funds are lost permanently unless Congress reenacts the necessary legislation. However, the executive branch has not yet used this practice frequently.

Congress's ability to see that programs are actually carried out may also be hampered by functional equivalents of impoundment—actions which technically may not be impoundments but which do result in the withholding of budget authority. Agencies may delay funding a program by refusing to promulgate rules which govern application procedures for funds. Or standards for qualifying for funds may be made excessively high to lower the number of recipients qualifying. Another technique used to delay the obligation of funds is called "dotting the i's and crossing the t's," which entails searching for minor errors in funding applications and insisting that applications be revised or resubmitted with these errors corrected. Minor errors are thus used as an excuse to prolong the application procedures and thus to delay the obligation of budget authority. The use of functional equivalents involves gray areas of discretionary authority, and it may be difficult to prove that such actions are implemented for the purpose of delaying the obligation of budget authority.

Conclusion

Presidential impoundment practices contributed to the passage of the Congressional Budget and Impoundment Control Act of 1974. This reform legislation has greatly increased Congress's ability to respond to impoundments and thus to maintain congressional spending priorities. But present impoundment procedures do not maximize Congress's ability to make and control public policy. It is still possible for the President to affect the level of federal expenditures after authorizations and appropriations are enacted into law.

In varying degrees, Presidents will continue to use impoundment in their dealings with Congress. President Carter has made limited use of impoundments

during his first few months in office. But Carter's position may be modified
before his administration is over if he disagrees with Congress on major policy
issues or if Congress enacts spending totals far in excess of Presidential budget
requests.[12] Regardless of Carter's use of impoundment, future Presidents, more
fiscally conservative, may be much more willing to use impoundment procedures
to modify spending policies established by Congress, especially if Congress is
controlled by the opposition party. But impoundment as practiced during the
Nixon Presidency is no longer possible. Congressional reform has greatly modified the use of Presidential impoundment and its impact on congressional-
executive relations.

Notes

1. *Obligation* means a commitment to spend at some time. Appropriations
and contract authority are examples of budget authority. The definition of
impoundment provided here is more accurate than defining impoundment as
"the refusal to spend congressional appropriations" because impoundment may
occur at a budget stage prior to appropriation and because a type of budget
authority other than an appropriation may be involved. For example, the executive branch may impound by refusing to use contract authority, a type of budget
authority that allows an executive agency to contract to have a service performed with appropriations to pay for the service to come later. This type of
impoundment precedes the appropriations stage.

2. In actual practice, special messages usually do not specify a precise
period during which a deferral will be in effect. Most indicate only whether the
deferral will last for part of or all the fiscal year.

3. In both the House and the Senate, the Appropriations Committee
reports out measures to override deferrals or to rescind budget authority.

4. Funds which have not been obligated during one fiscal year because of
deferrals may be used in the following year unless the budget authority for those
funds has lapsed at the end of the year during which the deferral occurred.

5. From July 1974 through June 1977, the General Accounting Office
identified ten impoundments unreported by the executive branch (Comptroller
General's Report 1977, p. 4).

6. From July 1974 through June 1977, the General Accounting Office
sent to Congress three letters indicating the intention to file suit to terminate
impoundments. Two of these suits became unnecessary because of executive or
judicial actions. One suit was actually initiated, but it was dismissed after the
executive branch released the impounded funds (Comptroller General's Report
1977, p. 9).

7. There is a common misunderstanding that the Supreme Court declared
impoundment unconstitutional. Actually, the one Supreme Court case dealing

with impoundment, *Train v. New York* (420 U.S. 35, 1975), was a very narrow decision based on statutory construction, not constitutional interpretation. The Court did not rule all impoundments to be invalid, only that the particular impoundment was invalid because the statute did not allow impoundment at the stage at which it had been exercised.

8. During the Nixon administration, the Office of Management and Budget (OMB) reported $12.9 billion of withheld budget authority, as of February 1971. The OMB reported $12.3 billion of withheld budget authority, as of January 1972 (*Congressional Quarterly Weekly Report* 1972, p. 443). Caution should be exercised, however, in relying on figures for comparative purposes. Differences in assumptions and definitions can greatly affect impoundment totals.

9. Carter's proposed rescission for the B-1 bomber program was rejected by the House Appropriations Committee on September 28, 1977. After the negative vote in the House Appropriations Committee, a rescission of $462 million for the B-1 bomber program was introduced in the Senate as a provision of a fiscal 1978 supplemental appropriations bill. As of the writing of this chapter Congress had not taken final action on this rescission.

10. These figures do not reflect subsequent revisions in deferral and rescission amounts which are transmitted to Congress by special messages. These totals are not significantly altered by these modifications and adjustments.

11. For a discussion of methods used to obtain the release of impounded funds before the passage of the 1974 act, see Mills and Munselle (1975).

12. Democratic control of Congress and the Presidency during the Carter administration will not necessarily stop the use of impoundment. Presidents Franklin Roosevelt, Kennedy, and Johnson all impounded funds while their party controlled Congress.

14 Congressional Change and Reform: Staffing the Congress

Susan Webb Hammond

During the past decade, Congress has undergone rapid change. A major component of that change has been in congressional staffing. New staff agencies have been established, the number of staff in existing offices and agencies has increased dramatically, and the distribution of staff resources has changed considerably.

Staff resources are power resources. Staff gather and analyze information needed for legislative decision making; staff handle casework and federal projects; they are actively engaged in oversight. Staff thus support and assist senators and representatives in carrying out their various responsibilities. The quantity of staff resources and the way those resources are distributed are important to congressional power. In recent years these patterns have changed.

A number of changes in staffing have been closely tied to other recent congressional change. Staff has been both affected by, and contributor to, such change and reform. It is unlikely, for example, that some of the changes would have taken place without the general climate for change evident in Congress in recent years. On the other hand, many staffing changes are incremental and tend to occur without being tied to major reforms; yet the effect of a series of incremental changes, can, of course, also be significant.

This chapter focuses on the staff component of congressional change and examines several aspects of staffing changes in recent years.[1] Specifically, changes in staffing are identified, and the causes and consequences of those changes are examined. The focus is primarily on committee and personal staff, with some reference to support agency staff.

Changes in Staffing Patterns

Virtually every staff group in Congress has increased in size in recent years. Personal staffs in both House and Senate have grown: in the House, for example, 4055 personal staff aides were employed in 1967, in contrast to 6939 in 1977, a 71 percent increase. In the Senate, 1749 were employed on the personal staffs of senators in 1967; in 1977, 3903 (including 393 personal committee aides) were employed, a 123 percent increase. Average office size has increased: in 1967, House members employed an average of nine aides in their personal offices; in 1977, the average number of aides per office had increased to 15.8. Figures for the Senate are similar: 17.5 aides per office on average in 1967 and 35.4 aides per office, on average, in 1977.[2] These figures, of course, do not indicate the variations among the different offices: some members appoint the full complement of aides permitted in the House (18 in 1977); others employ as few as nine. The size of a senator's staff varies from as few as 15 to as many as 75.[3]

Committee staffs have also increased, from 1210 for both Senate and House in 1967 to 3052 in 1977 (an increase of 152 percent). Much of the increase has occurred in the investigative staff, funded pursuant to annual resolutions reported by the Committee on House Administration (House) or the Rules and Administration Committee (Senate) and approved by the respective house, and in the staffs of special and select committees. Data on increases in personal and committee staff of both houses are presented in Table 14-1.

Several other developments should be noted. Within each house, ad hoc informal groups (such as the Democratic Study Group) have continued to form and to appoint staffs. In the House, many of the groups have their own staffs and offices.[4] In the Senate, there are fewer groups, and those that exist are generally staffed by aides based in the personal offices of senators. The aides handle the work of the group as a portion of their job.

The existing support agencies of Congress—the Congressional Research Service and the General Accounting Office (GAO)—have also increased staff in recent years. There has also been diversification of staff, especially in GAO, which has moved to recruit economists, fiscal analysts, and social scientists as well as accountants. In addition, two new support agencies have been established: the Office of Technology Assessment, in 1972, and the Congressional Budget Office in 1975 (see Table 14-2).

In June 1975, the Senate established a new group of legislative aides, passing S. Res. 60 to permit senators who do not appoint committee or subcommittee staff to appoint personal committee aides to assist them with their committee work.

Documenting the increase of staff is a useful starting point for an examination of staffing change. Analysis of the components of that increase sheds further light on the matter. To assist Congress in its traditional functions of legislation, representation, and oversight, what types of staff increase have occurred?

Much of the increase has been for personnel to support the policy-making function of Congress. For example, the number of legislative aides on personal staffs of both senators and representatives has increased. In 1967, few representatives hired aides designated as legislative assistants, although aides in each office did handle work relating to legislation. By 1977, most representatives designated at least one aide as a legislative assistant, and many hired two or three. In addition, legislative correspondents, legislative secretaries, and researchers worked with the legislative assistants on issues, legislative briefing, and other legislatively related matters. In the Senate, there are similar developments.

Table 14-1
Staffs of Congress, Selected Years

	1960	1967	Percentage Increase, 1960 to 1967	1970	Percentage Increase, 1967 to 1970	1977	Percentage Increase, 1970 to 1977
Personal Staff							
Senate	1418	1749	23.3%	2299	31.4%	3903[a]	69.8%
House	2630	4055	54.2	4545	12.1	6939	52.7
Committee Staff							
Senate	497	621	24.9	695	11.9	1184	70.3
House	438	589	34.5	705	19.7	1868	165

Sources: See text note 1. Also, "The Senate Committee System." First Staff Report to the Temporary Select Committee to Study the Senate Committee System, U.S. Senate Committee Print, July 1976; Committee Reform Amendments of 1974, Report of the Select Committee on Committees (Bolling Committee) to accompany H. Res. 988, March 1974, H. Rept. 93-916, Part II, p. 357; Reports (1977) of the Secretary of the Senate and the Clerk of the House.

[a]Includes 363 S. Res. 60 (Personal Committee) Aides.

Table 14-2
Analytic Support Agencies of Congress

	1970	1976
Congressional Budget Office	–	193
Congressional Research Service	323	721
General Accounting Office[a]	4471	5126
Office of Technology Assessment	–	103

Source: Data are drawn primarily from H.W. Fox and S.W. Hammond, *Congressional Staffs: The Invisible Force in American Lawmaking* (New York: Free Press, 1977). Other sources include the following: S.W. Hammond, "The Operation of Senators' Offices," in U.S. Senate, Commission on the Operation of the Senate, *Senators: Offices, Ethics and Pressures* (Washington: GPO, 1976); U.S. House of Representatives, Commission on Administrative Review, *Background Information on Administrative Units, Members' Offices, and Committee and Leadership Offices* (Washington: GPO, 1977); U.S. House, Commission on Administrative Review, *Administrative Reorganization and Legislative Management*, vol. 2 of 2, "Workload Management" (Washington: GPO, 1977); and reports of the Secretary of the Senate and the Clerk of the House, 1977.

[a]Approximately one-third of the GAO workload is assistance to Congress.

Legislative aides on personal staffs increased from 73 to 531 (including S. Res. 60 aides) between 1960 and 1975. Some legislative staffs have grown so that senators have established "legislative departments" to handle all aspects of legislative matters. The personal committee aides (S. Res. 60) also handle legislative work.

The primary focus of committee staff is legislative. Here, too, the growth is phenomenal. One feature of the past few years on the Hill has been large staffs to run committee investigations—the Ervin committee's Watergate investigations, the House impeachment inquiry, the intelligence inquiries in both houses, and the 1976-1977 Korean influence investigations. Some of these investigations have legislative impact as well, of course. But allowing for these large investigative staffs, the total staff of committees—primarily devoted to legislation or to investigations and oversight that eventually result in legislation—has increased. And many of the support agency staff increases have been in personnel available to assist Congress in its legislative function.

Staff increases support other functions of Congress as well. Increases in caseworkers and in federal projects aides directly assist members of Congress to carry out the representative function. Offices that ten years ago managed with one caseworker and perhaps an assistant now have several caseworkers. In the Senate, there are casework "departments" with five or six caseworkers. And in both Senate and House, junior staff have been appointed as Federal Projects Assistants to work with senior aides on matters relating to state and district needs. Press aides, too, have increased in number (Hammond 1976, p. 6).

In the Senate, one other group has increased: office managers. Ten to fifteen years ago, when staffs and allowances were smaller and the volume of work less, office management was generally handled by a senior clerical aide or the personal secretary to the senator. Today in many Senate offices this is no longer the case. With much larger staffs requiring regular coordination and supervision, personnel trained in office management and recordkeeping are employed in an increasing number of Senate offices. This is not, at present, the case in the House, with its somewhat smaller staffs, although House offices, too, are beginning to use assistance in office management techniques (see U.S. House of Representatives 1977d).

In summary, then, staffs handling all aspects of the workload have increased, although staff with legislative responsibilities have particularly increased.

What of the individual attributes of the personnel hired? Although data over time are not available for comparative purposes, the data we have suggest that Hill employees are more expert and more highly trained than previously. First, the increases have occurred primarily in positions that require specific skill training—legislative assistant jobs, committee aides, analytical and research staff of support agencies. Second, data gathered shortly after passage of the 1946 Legislative Reorganization Act indicated that most committees in both House and Senate employed aides who did not have specific education, training, or job experience relating to the professional positions they filled. Committees such as the two appropriations committees were the exception (Kammerer 1951). Today, most committees employ trained professionals; 75 percent hold advanced degrees (Fox and Hammond 1977, p. 175).[5]

Further changes, fully as important as the increase in staff size, are changes in the distribution of staff resources and in the access to staff. There is a wider distribution of staff resources; many more members now have assistance in managing all aspects of their responsibilities and in handling their increasing workload. They have more flexibility in managing their staff, and are more able to participate, *with staff support*, in the work of the Congress.

This change in the distribution and use of resources has occurred in several ways. It has accompanied a weakening of the apprenticeship system (Rohde, Ornstein, and Peabody 1974); rapid changeover in membership, particularly in the House; and pressures to modify the effect of rigid seniority norms.

First, several changes have directly affected the wider distribution of staff resources. In the Senate, S. Res. 60 gave additional legislative assistance for committee work to senators, primarily junior and minority members, who did not control committee staff. The personal committee aides are assured all the rights of access to committee records and of participation in committee deliberations of committee staff.[6]

In the House, several committees (Appropriations, Budget, Rules) now permit individual members to designate associate committee staff members to assist them on committee work. Thus, junior members who do not otherwise control committee staff (by virtue of committee or subcommittee chairmanship or ranking minority member status) have legislative assistance directly responsive to them.

These changes have been significant. In spite of recent changes in appointment procedures that require the majority or minority caucus of the committee to approve staff appointments, in fact, 68 percent of committee staff report that their primary responsibility is to the committee or subcommittee chairman or ranking minority member. Personal committee aides appointed under S. Res. 60, or as associate committee staff designated pursuant to committee rules, change the situation considerably.

Similarly, House and Senate requirements that the minority be allotted minority staff have resulted in wider staff resource distribution. In the House, the provision applies to standing committee permanent (statutory) staff; the minority slots for other committee staff groups vary. In the Senate, S. Res. 4, approved in February 1977, extends provisions for minority staff appointments to investigative staff as well.

Second, increases in staffing allowances for personal staff have given more resources to junior and minority members, thus equalizing assistance available. More junior members of the House, for example, use all their staff allotment, thus enabling them to offset the greater control of committee staff by senior members (U.S. House 1977d).

Third, congressional reforms have resulted in more equal distribution of staff resources. In the House, the diffusion of subcommittee chairmanships, in conjunction with House and caucus rules changes allotting staff to subcommittees, has had a direct effect on who obtains committee staff resources. The House rules change, which requires all committees of more than 20 members (except Budget) to establish subcommittees and the limit on the number of subcommittee chairmanships one member can hold, resulted in more members holding subcommittee chairmanships. In turn, requirements that subcommittee chairpersons and most ranking minority members be permitted to appoint at least one subcommittee staff aide gave these new chairpersons and ranking minority members staff assistance. In the Senate, virtually all Democrats in recent Congresses have chaired subcommittees and most Republicans have served as ranking minority members.

In summary, (1) all staff groups, and staff assisting on all congressional functions, have increased; (2) staffs have changed in character (for example, becoming more professional); and (3) the distribution of staff resources has changed. The overall impact of these changes has been to bring about vastly larger staffs with augmented policy capability. Moreover, such changes have contributed to the increasing autonomy (discussed below) of subcommittees in both chambers.[7]

Why Staffing Change?

The reasons for the changes in staffing are closely related to the various causes of other congressional reforms. First, Congress has responded to concern about its role in the political system, and more specifically, to the perceived imbalance of the power of Congress and the President. The Vietnam war, impoundments, and Watergate brought about specific legislation, internal reform efforts, and so forth from Congress. *If* Congress is to play a more equal role in relation to the President and the executive branch, then it needs (it was argued) increased staff support to give it independent analytical and research capability and thus to decrease its dependence on the executive.

Second, the focus on reform of congressional procedures and structures is also a response to internal pressures. Studies of committee jurisdictions, or concern with administrative rationalization and coordination, lead naturally to concern about staffing arrangements.

Third, changing congressional career patterns and a large group of junior members are also responsible for a focus on reallocation of internal congressional resources. Changes in the seniority system and in the selection of committee and subcommittee chairpersons, for example, are directly linked to staff support, as Obey Commission studies make clear.

Finally, the workload of the Congress has increased tremendously in recent years. Both houses spend more time in committee and on the floor; there are more bills introduced and more committee meetings. Legislative decision making has become far more complicated, as Congress has sought to deal with increasingly complex technological and social developments. A more sophisticated electorate is writing, telephoning, and visiting members of Congress more often, to discuss issues and to request assistance on a variety of problems. Congress has needed assistance to handle the workload resulting from these increasing demands, and increasing staff has been a logical result.

Consequences of Change

A number of consequences result from the changing distribution of staff resources and from the increases in the number of staff appointed.

First, senators and representatives are using added staff resources. Most senators appoint personal committee aides (S. Res. 60 aides); this includes chairpersons and ranking minority members of committees, who appoint personal committee aides to assist them on the work of other committees of which they are members.[8] In the House, many junior members of the Appropriations, Budget, and Rules Committees designate associate committee aides. Other committees have considered this kind of arrangement, and other proposals have been made that would have a similar effect (see U.S. House 1977d). Not all members use all their staff slots or their entire clerk-hire allowance, of course, but many are taking advantage of the added resources and using the additional resources of the support agencies as well.

Second, the wider distribution of staff resources, especially in conjunction with increased resources, has had important consequences. The changes have undoubtedly contributed to the growing autonomy of subcommittees. In the House, most subcommittees have some staff assistance. The growth of subcommittee staff, appointed by and working for the subcommittee rather than the full committee, has been typical of Senate staffing patterns in recent years. Although procedures are changing somewhat, in a number of instances subcommittees have operated with their own budgets submitted as a separate item in the full committee's request for annual inquiries and investigations funding.

Junior members have been able to participate more in committee decision making. Freshman members (Joseph Fisher and Robert Kreuger in the House are two examples) in the 94th Congress often played important roles in the legislative arena. In the Senate, where freshman Senators generally can expect to control some committee staff and also have larger personal staff resources, freshman senators have been very active in the work of the Senate. S. Res. 60 itself was a product of the freshman senators' group, which now numbers over 60 percent of the Senate and includes senators in their second term; renamed the Caucus for an Effective Senate, it continues to be an important force in Senate reform.

The increase in the size and salary allotments for personal staff has meant that members of Congress have more flexibility to meet their perceived staffing needs. Senators are able to appoint a foreign policy, a nuclear weapons, or an energy expert if they wish—and many do so. In the House, several legislative assistants are now found on many House personal staffs. In short, members of Congress can be better prepared to participate in legislative decision making. The fact that assistance is often given by staff responsible to individual senators and representatives has, of course, contributed to congressional decentralization and to the lessening of the apprenticeship norm.

Third, data indicate that larger staffs are more active staffs (Fox and Hammond 1977, chap. 9). For example, the three largest Senate committee staffs communicate more with nearly all groups (bureaucracy, interest groups, other congressional groups, Presidential staff) than the staffs of the three smallest Senate committees. Committees with larger staffs hold more hearings and meetings and report more legislation.

Fourth, organizational consequences flow from these changes. Some elements of bureaucracy are increasingly present on Capitol Hill: for example, more specialization is possible, and staffs are being "departmentalized." Hierarchy is somewhat more evident in staff organization. A second organizational consequence is the evident need for management practices. Traditionally, Congress has been a nonhierarchical organization, with decentralization a central element in its organizational structure. Within the subunits, a similar organization has prevailed, with direct access to the principal actors by professional aides. As staffs increase, this becomes less possible, but Congress has been slow to realize this. A number of aides often report directly to the member; often, that number far exceeds the span of control accepted as optimal. Recent recommendations from the two congressional commissions (the Commission on the Operation of the Senate and the House Commission on Administrative Review) have recognized the need for management assistance.

Conclusion

Two major themes run through recent congressional reform efforts: responsiveness and representation, and centralization-decentralization of decision-making processes. Changes in staffing relate to both.

With regard to responsiveness and representation, more staff handle more casework; more staff communicate more and can meet more frequently with constituents and citizen groups. Changes in personal office allowances permitting reimbursement of aides for travel are also evidence of a concern with meeting constituents, citizen groups, and experts outside Washington on government problems and policy issues. Present staffing resources enable senators and representatives to respond to constituent concerns rapidly and to handle problems effectively. More links to the citizenry are possible. The effect of the information obtained through these links continues to be tempered, of course, by other factors such as the congressman's view of the job and the role of educator, leader, and overseer of government programs.

Whether changes result in centralization or decentralization depends to a large extent on where that staff operates. How staff resources are distributed and who has access to them are significant vairables. Staffing subcommittees, and increased staffing on committees, have had decentralizing consequences, as has the more equitable distribution of staff resources to individual members. Centralization can be enhanced by increasing central party and leadership office staffs. Certainly, this has led to increased coordination. The growth of ad hoc informal groups has had similar consequences, at least for groups of members, although the existence of additional and often important subunits has at the same time contributed to decentralization.

On balance, then, the effects have been somewhat contradictory. Staffing changes do not fit a neat model of congressional reform. At the same time, the effect of the changes has been significant, and future changes can be expected to be considered more carefully for long-term effect as well as for immediate, problem-solving capability.

Overall, the Congress in 1977 may be very different from the Congress of ten or fifteen years ago. No small part of that change reflects staff changes. Each change, in itself, has not appeared a major change. As is typical in the history of staffing, change has generally occurred gradually. But the cumulative effect has been significant—for congressional operations, for legislative decision making, and for the role of Congress in the political system.

Notes

1. The data on which this chapter is based are drawn primarily from Fox and Hammond 1977. Other sources are Hammond 1976; U.S. House of Representatives 1977c and 1977d; and Reports of the Secretary of the Senate and the Clerk of the House, 1977.

2. Figures from Legislative Branch Appropriations Hearings, FY 1968 and FY 1978; U.S. House 1977d; and Report of the Secretary of the Senate, 1977.

3. In the House, members received a "clerk-hire" allowance, in September 1977, of $255,144 per session, one-twelfth of which is available each month, with which to appoint up to 18 personal staff aides. In the Senate, allowances per session for staff vary according to the population of the state: from $449,063 for states with less than 2 million to $902,301 for states with more than 21 million in September 1977; there is no ceiling on the number of aides who may be appointed. In September 1977, about three-fourths of the Senate received allowances of $534,000 or less. Effective October 1, 1977, the start of the 1978 fiscal year, the allowance for S. Res. 60 aides (personal committee aides) was merged with the allowance for administrative and clerical staff, so that allowances will vary according to population and committee assignment (with those not appointing committee staff receiving funds for personal committee aides).

4. In the House, the staffs of the informal groups are carried on the personal office payrolls of group members even though they may have their own offices. In September 1977, the Commission on Administrative Review (the Obey Commission) proposed to change the system for staffing informal groups to report the staff of these groups separately, rather than as personal staff of House members.

5. For aggregate data on education of all House personnel, see U.S. House 1977d.

6. Aides are appointed according to a formula based on committee assignment. Beginning with FY 1978 (October 1, 1977), the dollar allotment for S. Res. 60 aides was merged with the senator's allowance for administrative and clerical personal office aides. See note 3.

7. The House Committee on Administrative Review (Obey Commission) made several recommendations relating directly to staffing (legislative assistance

for members for committee work, limitations on the increase in committee investigative staff, increased flexibility in personal staff allotments and allowances, for example) and suggested others relating to information that indirectly affects staffing patterns. The proposals were never considered by the House, since the rule setting the terms of debate on H. Res. 766 (the Obey Commission resolution) was defeated in October 1977.

8. By December 1975, 75 senators employed 187 S. Res. 60 aides; this includes 40 percent of the most-senior senators (see Hammond 1976, p. 15). In September 1977, 90 senators employed such aides.

15 Money in Congressional Elections

Gary W. Copeland and
Samuel C. Patterson

Public policy dealing with political campaign expenditures has grown extensively in recent years, based upon the principles of reporting and disclosure and limitations on contributions and spending. Lawmakers have found themselves in a unique position in the last few years as they have been called upon to revise the rules of the game in which they are active and concerned participants. In 1971, Congress enacted the Federal Election Campaign Act, which replaced the Corrupt Practices Act of 1925. The new law was amended in 1974 and 1976; the 1974 amendments, among other things, established a ceiling on congressional campaign expenditures. In effect, the 1974 amendments limited contests for seats in the U.S. House of Representatives to an expenditure of $168,000 (subject to fluctuations in the consumer price index), including both primary and general elections (Alexander 1976, pp. 140-52). The probable impact of this limitation on House campaigns (and Senate races, which are subject to spending ceilings, too) has been discussed extensively, with some arguing that the limitations protect incumbents by limiting the amount a challenger can spend to overcome the considerable advantages of incumbency. Critics of the spending limits have characterized the 1974 amendments as an "Incumbent Protection Act." If these charges are true, the implications are serious. In this chapter, we present the results of an analysis of House campaign spending in the 1974 congressional election to assess whether spending limits advantage incumbents and disadvantage challengers.

Analysis of Campaign Spending

It is sometimes claimed that little is known about the political impacts of campaign spending. Once true, this is no longer the case. We now have at least some systematic evidence to demonstrate the following:

1. Campaign spending is considerably more productive of electoral support in primary than in general elections (Welch 1976, p. 348).

This chapter is based in part on our analysis in "Reform of Congressional Campaign Spending," *Policy Studies Journal* 5 (Summer 1977):424-31.

2. In general, spending is substantially higher in politically competitive districts where outcomes are marginal than in safe districts (Agranoff 1976, pp. 225–26).

3. Parties and candidates invest heavily in contests for "open seats," where there is no incumbent, and minority parties predictably invest more in such races (McKeough 1970, p. 109; Crain and Tollison 1976).

4. Although economy of scale in campaign spending might be expected as a function of the sizes of electoral districts, this does not appear to be the case (Welch 1976, pp. 347–48).

5. There is a significant correlation between campaign expenditures and turnout, so that in 1972 "each $1000 of total expenditures generates an increase in turnout of between 1 and 1.6 percentage points, other things being equal" (Dawson and Zinser 1976).

6. Campaign expenditures do have effects on electoral outcomes. These effects have an important bearing upon whether the spending limits advocated in the Federal Election Campaign Act amendments of 1974 are regarded as inappropriately protective of incumbents.

Concern about Congressional Campaign Reform

The purposes of this research are twofold: to examine how money affects congressional campaigns and to argue the polemic issue of the impact of spending ceilings on the electoral results. The first problem is divided into two parts: Who is able to raise and spend large amounts of money? and How do these expenditures affect electoral outcomes? The result of that analysis will be used to address the second issue, but first we will review the background of the amendments, the debates surrounding them, and the current standing of spending limits. No attempt will be made to persuade the reader to a particular point of view, but we believe that empirical evidence can be used to investigate the area which has been most highly debated—whether spending limits imposed by the 1974 amendments are high enough to permit successful challenges.

Spending Limits

Prior to the enactment of the 1974 amendments, much debate centered on limits to spending. Even many of those who favored spending limits were concerned about the exact levels of those limits. If the limits are set too high, spending will be encouraged, not discouraged; if the limits are too low, candidates entering congressional races as unknowns may not have a reasonable chance to emerge as victors. The following exchange in the Senate hearings elucidates these concerns:

Mr. Hemenway (of the National Committee for Effective Congress): . . . By all means, don't report out a bill with limitations that will prevent a challenger from making a reasonable race. This would be a terrible subversion of the system. Incumbents have always liked limitations.

Sen. Cannon: . . . I personally do like limitations, but my question is whether or not the limitations in the bill at the present time, the 25 cents formula plus a minimum for the smaller states, whether that, in fact, isn't too high. . . . So my question is whether this figure should be 20 cents per person rather than the 25 which is now in the formula. . . .

Mr. Hemenway: The maximum amounts to which you have just referred are not out of line with some campaigns that have been waged recently. . . .

Sen. Cannon: But that's just my point. Too much money has been spent in these campaigns. I spent more than I think I should have spent in my last campaign. But you have to pace yourself based on what your opponent is doing.

Mr. Hemenway: Senator Cannon, you are a national figure, someone probably known to everyone in the State of Nevada, and you really don't have to spend much. But if you're just entering the political arena and totally unknown, you must make yourself known to the voters. Sometimes it's necessary to spend money.

I don't think we should talk necessarily about too much money, but a fair amount of money. And what is fair for a well-known incumbent is not fair for an unknown challenger (U.S. Senate 1973, pp. 250–51).

That exchange clearly states the problems lawmakers faced in trying to work out an equitable solution, a decision necessarily based more on speculation than on data.

Advantage of Incumbency

After the law was enacted, many critics maintained that the limits are unfairly to the advantage of incumbents. Ralph Winter, Yale law professor and counsel for Eugene McCarthy and James Buckley in their Supreme Court challenge of the 1974 law, charged at a recent American Enterprise Institute Public Policy Forum that "House incumbents continue to engage in the scandal of using perquisites such as the frank and staff for campaign purposes while their opponents are limited by the law in the campaign they can wage" (American Enterprise Institute 1977, p. 4). Another critic, basing his conclusions on extensive data analysis, claimed that the 1974 amendments "may indeed have generated nothing more than an Incumbent Protection Act" (Jacobson 1976, p. 31). The effects of this law have been much debated, and appropriately so, because the rules of the game are being changed by those who may be advantaged by the rule changes. We will discuss the arguments on both sides of the issue and consider the implications of these charges, if true, before examining the data from the 1974 election that help to evaluate the validity of the claims.

Concern about Electoral Reform

Legislators' concerns over election reform can be traced to three underlying causes: public demands for changes, the belief that electoral outcomes are being influenced in an undesirable way, and the dangers from large amounts of campaign money that appeared in connection with the Watergate scandals. High levels of expenditures do not necessarily lead to unethical activities, but the potential increases with the volume of money. Dangers exist at both the income and expenditure ends of campaign financing. On the income side, there is the danger of trading government favors for campaign contributions. Many allegations of this kind were made in connection with Watergate: the Vesco case, the milk fund, the selling of ambassadorships, and corporate contributions. On the spending side, large sums of money increase the possibility that money may be spent for questionable activities, such as for the Watergate break-in, the plumbers, and dirty tricks. The 2000-plus page Senate Watergate report delved into these charges and concluded that the potential for abuse is great; it recommended, among other things, that campaign spending be limited.

Other observers of Congress became concerned about electoral reform because of fears over the way spending did or might affect electoral outcomes. Many reformers believe that as spending levels increase, the advantage of the incumbent increases. On the one hand, for a number of reasons, it is generally easier for incumbents to raise money. As a result, many proponents of reform of campaign finance conclude that the electoral advantage of incumbency has further increased. On the other hand, incumbents fear what might happen to them if they encounter a well-financed opponent. They fear that a challenger could undertake a media blitz and add former members of Congress to the unemployment rolls. The answer to both problems appeared to be to limit the amounts that can be spent in pursuit of office.

Increased public dissatisfaction with American political processes and demands for revising the electoral system have accentuated discussions of campaign spending reform. As confidence in political institutions reached an all-time low, support for electoral reform reached new highs. Gallup polls in 1974 and 1976 indicated that nearly two-thirds of the American people thought that changes were needed in the way political campaigns are run. After Congress had taken such a critical position concerning Watergate abuses, many citizens challenged the Congress to act positively by enacting legislation limiting the possibility of such abuses in the future. Many officials felt compelled to respond to the challenge.

Arguments for Reform

These factors combined to present Congress with compelling arguments in favor of reform. The main alternatives appeared to be (1) full disclosure of contributions, (2) limits on spending, and (3) public financing of campaigns. Legislation requiring disclosure of contributors had been enacted previously and appeared to be too blunt an instrument to prevent the abuses evident in the system. It is difficult to show conclusively that a contribution is linked with a policy decision; further, disclosure does nothing to limit the spending of candidates, a concern of many of those advocating reform. The alternative of financing elections through the public treasury, favored by many of the reform-minded legislators, was included in the Senate-passed version of the 1974 reform, but was dropped from the version reported out of the conference committee. House leaders feared that public financing would lead to an increase in the number of congressional candidates, causing narrow plurality victories. They also feared an influx of "one issue" candidates such as the antiabortion Presidential candidacy of Ellen McCormack. Limiting the amount candidates can spend was a less extreme reform that appeared to address most of the serious criticisms of the current system. Combined with a set of other measures, limiting spending is expected to lessen the impact of "big money" and lower the potential for abuse. That proposal garnered the most support and became the backbone of the new legislation.

Criticisms of Reforms

Even that proposal was not without its detractors. Criticism of that approach centered on two themes: incumbents will be unnecessarily advantaged by spending limits, and such limits are a violation of constitutional rights. The argument that incumbents will be advantaged is based on the supposition that money is just one of many resources available during a campaign. For challengers, money and volunteer workers account for nearly all available resources, but incumbents can go beyond those resources and use the advantages of their office to provide other resources. Not only are incumbents better known than challengers, but they can also take advantage of franking privileges, increased press coverage, office staffs, and other services available to incumbent members of Congress (Stokes and Miller 1966). If the amounts an incumbent and a challenger can spend are the same, these additional resources tip the balance in favor of the incumbent.

The second criticism, and one tested before the Supreme Court, is that the law violates the First Amendment guarantees of freedom of speech and the right of association.[1] By limiting the amount an individual can spend to advance a political cause (or, in this case a particular candidate), one's freedom of speech is being abridged. Further, by limiting the number of committees that can support candidates, it was claimed that the legislation violated the right of free association. At the same time, proponents argued that Congress has the right to regulate elections. Other constitutional questions were raised, such as whether Congress could establish an independent regulatory commission and whether ceilings unconstitutionally discriminate against challengers and minor parties. In early 1976, the Supreme Court heard these and other arguments and decided a whole series of constitutional issues. Briefly, the Court ruled that limitations on contributions are valid; that truly independent spending for political purposes is protected and therefore cannot be limited; and that anyone who accepts government funding can be compelled to limit expenditures. As a result of this decision, the 1976 Presidential candidates were limited in their expenditures (since both Ford and Carter decided to accept federal funds), but congressional candidates were free to go beyond the limits. If Congress decides to limit spending for candidates in all congressional races, it will probably be through a system that provides federal funding, as in Presidential contests.

As the law now stands, congressional candidates may exceed the spending limits included in the 1974 legislation, although congressional action may change this prior to the 1978 elections. If limits are imposed, the argument that incumbents are favored by spending ceilings will arise anew. By now, however, enough data are available that the decision can be based on more than mere speculation. To aid in this analysis, in the rest of this chapter we will examine two aspects of money and politics: who spends and what effect does spending have? The data will also be used to address the question of whether the limits originally advocated in 1974 amendments are high enough for challengers to have a legitimate chance of victory.

Analysis of 1974 Campaign Spending

The conventional wisdom is that money wins elections. Millions of dollars are spent on congressional races, and frequently it is assumed that "money talks." Congressional candidates in the 1974 election spent a total of nearly $74 million, about $29 million in the primaries and $45 million in the general election (see Table 15-1). Within this total, significant variation can be found in the amounts individual candidates spend to achieve victory. In 1974 many candidates spent absolutely nothing, while Robert Krueger (D-Tex.) spent $311,953 in his narrow victory. Some variation can be identified, such as differences between parties (Democrats outspent Republicans by $3 million), but the major reason for this difference is that incumbents (more of whom were Democrats than Republicans) outspent challengers. This difference between incumbents and challengers is one way in which variance in expenditures can be explained.

Table 15-1
Average Campaign Spending in U.S. House Contests

Party and Incumbency Status	1972	1974
Democratic Incumbents	$50,009	$47,458
Republican Incumbents	$51,947	$78,911
Democratic Challengers	$28,865	$70,090
Republican Challengers	$33,587	$35,430

Source: Congressional Quarterly, *Dollar Politics* (Washington: Congressional Quarterly, Inc., 1974), p. 75; *Congressional Quarterly Weekly Report*, 1975, pp. 789–94.

The other way is to examine the relationship between the closeness of races and expenditure levels. Each of these alternatives will be examined to understand who spends large amounts of money to get elected to Congress.

Winners and Losers

Candidates, of course, cannot spend large amounts of money unless that money is somehow made available to them. The most common source of funding is contributions from private sources to individual candidates or to political committees. The motivations behind these contributions are multifaceted and not always clear, but one generalization is easily supportable: money flows to where money matters (Heard 1962, pp. 60–85; Welch 1974). Conceptually, we can separate candidates into three groups: sure winners, sure losers, and marginal candidates. Sure losers have the most problems raising funds, for few contributors want to invest heavily in an obviously doomed campaign. Sure winners have a far easier time raising funds, but they rarely make a concerted effort to raise and spend all the money that might be available to them. Further, investors often prefer to invest in races where their contributions are more likely to affect the outcome. Marginal candidates feel the need to spend heavily, and contributors are generally willing to provide the necessary funds, believing that their contributions are significant to the candidate.

If all this is true, those who get the fewest votes should spend the least. Expenditures should increase as the vote percentage increases and should peak as the percentage rises just above 50 percent. The data from 1974 show that this is the case (see Table 15-2).[2] The highest average expenditure is $95,302 for those who polled 50 to 55 percent of the vote; the lowest average is $9146 for those who received less than 10 percent of the vote. The comparisons in Table 15-2 show that expenditures are greatest in marginal districts and that winners have more money to spend than losers do.

Table 15-2
Votes and Expenditures in 1974 U.S. House Contests

Vote Percentage	Mean Expenditures	Range	Number of Cases
90+	$16,634	$0–81,915	54
70–90	$40,832	$400–301,135	113
65–70	$51,807	$14,306–166,441	43
60–65	$67,153	$0–192,058	51
55–60	$85,090	$9,660–223,163	69
50–55	$95,302	$8,254–311,953	92
45–50	$91,441	$7,606–251,249	93
40–45	$68,185	$3,619–166,203	70
35–40	$46,528	$2,013–136,810	56
30–35	$28,895	$133–143,895	46
10–30	$11,032	$0–85,680	125
–10	$9,146	$0–31,904	9

Incumbents and Challengers

The second contention is that incumbents are capable of raising and spending more than challengers. Several reasons exist for this. The most obvious is that incumbents rarely lose a reelection bid. In ten congressional elections prior to 1974, only 8 percent of all congressmen desiring reelection failed to get it; incumbents tend to be winners (Jewell and Patterson 1977, p. 91). As shown above, winners are capable of raising money relatively easily. Further, incumbents are a known quality. After having served as representatives, their financeers are likely to be better acquainted with their abilities, policy preferences, and the advantages of their seniority. Moreover, incumbents should be more experienced campaigners. They should know how to raise and spend resources effectively and where to seek those resources. The expenditure advantage of incumbents is clear in Figure 15-1. In 1974, a majority of both incumbents and challengers spent less than $60,000, but nearly half of all challengers did not even exceed $30,000 (only a quarter of all incumbents spent that little). A plurality of incumbents spent between $30,000 and $60,000, and incumbents spent more in the moderate range. However, above $90,000 little difference exists between spending by challengers and incumbents, as most of these large expenditures are in competitive districts.

Certain conclusions can be drawn from these data: (1) large amounts of money are being spent to get elected to Congress, but many candidates spend very little; (2) incumbents tend to spend more than challengers; (3) winners tend to spend more than losers; and (4) more money is spent in close races than in races where no serious competition exists. This pattern would be completely changed if federal funding of congressional races is enacted. The spending advantage of incumbents would be erased, but at the same time large amounts of money would be spent in districts considered safe. Since it is doubtful that

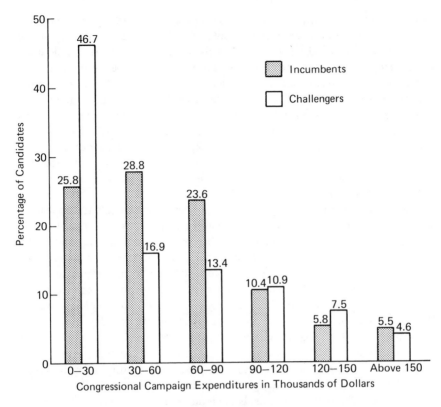

Figure 15-1. Expenditures of House Incumbents and Challengers in 1974.

increasing spending in many of these districts would change the partisan balance, large amounts of money would be spent where the outcome would not be affected.

Expenditures and Election Outcomes

Since money is not everything in congressional elections, to what extent, *ceteris paribus*, do expenditures affect election outcomes? The data presented above indicate that there is a relationship between expenditures and the results of an election, but that there are differences between incumbents and challengers. Therefore, we use regression analysis, separating incumbents from challengers, to see what the vote patterns look like for those who spend varying amounts of money. Analysis of the effects of spending on election results using linear regression shows a negative regression coefficient for incumbents and a positive coefficient for challengers. These relationships are not puzzling; in fact, they make strong theoretical sense. Incumbents who do not face serious challenge have no reason to spend much money on their reelection bids. Such candidates are ensured a large percentage of the vote for a minimum expenditure of money. If, however, incumbents face serious challenge, they may be forced to spend a large amount of resources. Thus, when the percentage of the vote is going to be lower, the incumbent spends much money. A challenger who has no substantial chance of winning has problems raising money (Adamany 1972, pp. 192-94). Then the challenger spends little and gets few votes. If a challenger is able to pose a serious threat to the incumbent, more money can be raised for the contest, more money can be spent, and more votes are likely to be produced, within limits (Ben-Zion and Eytan 1974).

However, linear regression models are not really appropriate to the analysis of the production of votes through campaign expenditures. It is clear that the law of diminishing returns applies to this production function. Obviously, congressional incumbents have an enormous electoral advantage before they spend any money on their campaigns. Most challengers undoubtedly need to spend money to achieve visibility, but for them at some point increased spending becomes decreasingly productive of votes (Welch 1974; Lott and Warner 1974). The question of whether the expenditure limits provided in the 1974 legislation are high enough to permit successful challenges to incumbents needs to be examined in light of these diminishing returns. If campaign expenditures provide decreasing returns at or below the legal expenditure limits, it can be concluded that those limits are high enough that they do not preclude successful challenges. The real question is, Is the legal expenditure limit high enough so that challengers are capable of mounting serious efforts to win elections?

The impact of campaign spending can best be analyzed using a natural logarithmic transformation of the independent variable. In addition, quite a different curve may be expected for incumbents than for challengers. Accordingly, we analyzed the expenditure and voting data for the 1974 congressional election. Our analysis included 326 incumbents and 439 nonincumbents who faced opposition in 1974. Of course, some nonincumbents faced other nonincumbents rather than challenging incumbent members of Congress, but the difficulties facing them are basically the same as those facing an incumbent. For both groups of candidates, the percentage of the two-party vote received serves as the dependent variable; the actual dollar amount spent in 1974 is the independent variable. We do not standardize the independent variable on a per capita basis, since congressional districts are very nearly equal in size. The expenditure variable is logged. These operations produce the scatter plot that provides the curvilinear relationships between spending and votes shown in Figure 15-2. Note that, as expected, incumbent spending increases produce diminishing proportions of the vote, while up to a point challengers gain votes with increasing spending.

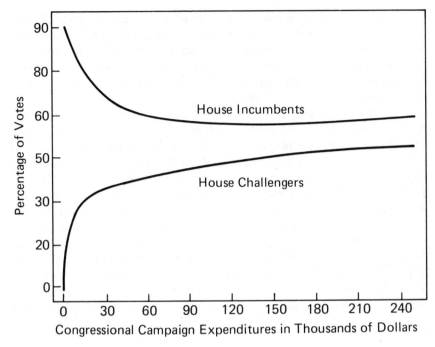

Figure 15-2. Congressional Campaign Spending and Electoral Support, 1974.

The regression equations for incumbents and challengers are as follows:

Incumbents $Y = 93.82 - 2.87X_1 + e$

$$(.59)^a$$

$$t = -4.86$$

$$r^2 = .07$$

Challengers $Y = .74 + 3.82X_1 + e$

$$(.28)$$

$$t = 16.61$$

$$r^2 = .38$$

where Y = the percentage of the two-party vote

X_1 = log transformation of the actual dollars spent by the candidates

e = random disturbance term

---

[a]Standard error.

For incumbents, the regression equation shows a significant negative relationship, but very little variance is explained. For challengers, campaign expenditures clearly are more important; they alone account for 38 percent of the variance in the vote for challengers. Clearly, campaign expenditures are significantly related to the vote for both incumbents and challengers, but they are a much more important determinant for challengers.

The vote productivity of expenditures interests us, but it is not too meaningfully stated in terms of logged expenditures. Since the relationship between expenditures and votes is roughly linear between expenditures ranging from $0 to $125,000, we have calculated the productivity of expenditures within that range, doing so for 293 incumbents and 409 challengers. These 1974 data indicate that an incumbent who spends nothing should, other things being equal, get 73 percent of the vote. Since incumbents spend more as the race gets closer, every $10,000 in additional expenditure by incumbents is associated with a 2 percent drop in votes. Challengers, on the other hand, gain votes with increased expenditures up to $125,000. A challenger who spends nothing should get about 28 percent of the vote on average; and $10,000 in expenditures produce a 2 percent increase in the vote. Challengers must spend to gain visibility and thus votes; the fate of incumbents appears to be more directly tied to their own record and the district strength of their parties.

A Fair Chance for Challengers?

But our main concern is not with how much the average challenger needs to spend to be ensured of winning, or how much is produced by way of votes from the expenditures of incumbents and challengers. Rather, we are mainly concerned here with how much a challenger needs to spend to have any reasonable chance to contest the election. Examination of the scatter plot for challengers indicates that the log curve levels off to within a few percentage points of 50 percent at approximately $125,000, and it stays below 50 percent until expenditures reach about $400,000. No one, of course, spent $400,000; yet, some challengers were successful. To see whether extreme expenditures are necessary to permit victories, we compared the success rates for candidates who spent between $125,000 and $168,000 to the success rates for those who spent more than $168,000. Thirty-one challengers spent in the $125,000 to $168,000 range; 21 were elected. Eleven candidates spent more than $168,000; 8 won.[3] Their respective victory rates were 68 and 73 percent, a rather small difference. Because the expenditure-vote curve is very close to the 50 percent mark beyond expenditures of $125,000, and because the success rates are similar for relatively high and very high levels of expenditures, we conclude that the 1974 limit is sufficiently high to permit a successful challenge.

Other things being equal, challengers who spend up to a threshold amount (about $125,000 in 1974) improve their vote-getting ability by enhancing their name recognition and putting their issue positions before voters. Beyond the threshold, increased expenditures have a decreasing effect for both incumbents and challengers. Of course, other things are not equal; incumbents have quite an electoral advantage apart from campaign expenditures and limits upon them. Most of the advantages of incumbency in congressional elections have little to do with campaign expenditures, but rather have to do with the perquisites of office (Jacobson 1976; Palda 1975). The effects of incumbency are substantial and growing; nevertheless, a considerable proportion of the members of Congress (more than 40 percent of those elected in 1972) get elected in the first instance by defeating an incumbent or the candidate of the incumbent party (Kostroski 1973; Erikson 1976). The pure advantages of incumbency can easily be overstated, and safe elections, which of course frequently return incumbents, depend upon party strength in congressional districts. Our findings provide little support for the claim that the 1974 amendments would constitute, in themselves, special protection for incumbents.

Conclusion

We think that it is reasonably well established that (1) incumbent expenditures are higher than those of challengers; (2) winners spend more than lowers; (3) the highest expenditures tend to be found in close, races; (4) campaign expenditures are a significant determinant of election support; (5) expenditures are more important for challengers, since they must spend some minimum amount to make their names, issue positions, and images known to the public; (6) expenditures are subject to a threshold effect, and after the threshold is reached, expenditures provide decreasing returns in terms of votes; and (7) the spending limit advanced is beyond the threshold which enables challengers to mount successful election bids. The levels advocated in the 1974 amendments would not protect incumbents to the detriment of challengers.

Notes

1. *Buckley v. Valeo*, 424 U.S. 1, 96 S. Ct. 612, 46 L. Ed.2d. 659 (1976).

2. *Congressional Quarterly Weekly Report*, 1975, pp. 789-94, is the source of the expenditure data used in this chapter.

3. The 1974 amendments did not apply to candidates in the 1974 election, but to future elections. Of course, the Supreme Court decision has kept a ceiling from being imposed as of this date; however, Congress is expected to consider a

number of proposals concerning campaign finance prior to the 1978 elections. Nevertheless, in 1974 only 22 candidates, evenly divided between incumbents and challengers, exceeded the $168,000 limit included in the 1974 amendments. Of the 40 challengers who unseated incumbents in 1974 39 did so on less than $168,000.

16

Congress in the Sunshine

Charles S. Bullock III

Unlike most recent congressional reforms, the move to greater openness in Congress is part of a broader effort to give citizens greater access to and more information about their government. Some extensive changes have occurred in the congressional arena, particularly involving activities of decision-making units, campaign financing, and personal ethics. These reforms have the potential to change legislators' relationships with constituents and interest groups, and the kinds of policies they enact. This chapter will deal with three aspects of openness reforms. The first section lays out some rationales behind the changes; the second briefly explains the more important reforms, both those instituted and those not yet beyond the discussion stage; and the final section discusses some potential consequences of these changes.

Openness Arguments

At least four major justifications have been offered for greater congressional openness. One is the belief that Congress operating in the sunshine will help dispel popular distrust of the institution, thereby restoring public confidence. Congress, like other institutions, experienced a sharp decline in public opinion polls after the mid-1960s. By early 1977 there had been an improvement in Congress's public image, but only 22 percent of a national sample rated Congress as pretty good or excellent (U.S. House 1977b). It is argued that if the interested public observes exemplary behavior among the members, this should lead to heightened confidence and levels of support. Dissemination of more information about members of Congress should dispel any notions that the indiscretions of Wilbur Mills (D-Ark.) and Wayne Hays (D.-Oh.) or the malfeasance of Cornelius Gallagher (D-N.J.) or Andrew Hinshaw (R-Cal.) are the norm.[1]

A second argument for opening Congress to closer scrutiny is that it will reduce the number of instances in which members abuse their offices. Making records and actions accessible to inquiring reporters should cause members who might be tempted to violate their trusts to have second thoughts.

A third proposition is that legislators will perform better when they act in public. Knowing that they can be held accountable for their words and deeds

This chapter benefited from a number of discussions with Catherine Rudder and Fran Steckmest about change, openness, and Congress, and what they mean for our political system.

may induce them to be better prepared and to be more conscientious in carrying out their responsibilities.

A fourth reason offered for sunshine reforms is that traditionally powerful interests, for example, big business and big unions, will have less of an advantage when lobbying for legislation. Requiring legislators to act in public may force them to respond to interests other than those with extensive financial resources. Special interests that have flourished in private may find legislators less responsive if the details about decision making, finances, and lobbying are available for critical appraisal. Therefore openness reforms have generally been supported by those, such as Common Cause, who want to see power reallocated.

Openness Reforms

Policy Making

A relatively early congressional reform increased the number of policy decisions on which members had to take public stands. A first step, instituted by the 92d House, provided that at the request of 20 representatives, teller votes in the Committee of the Whole would be recorded. Two years later the potential for recording representatives' preferences was enlarged when electronic voting apparatus was installed. Since this innovation reduced the time required to record the preferences of the House by half (to 15 minutes), the number of questions that could be voted on in the chamber during a given period doubled. Consequently many items that would have been decided by voice or standing votes (for which there are no records of individuals' preferences) could now be recorded votes. During the first five months of 1977, the number of recorded votes was up 17 percent from 1976 and 49 percent above 1975 levels (Southwick 1977). From 1972 to 1976 the number of recorded roll calls rose 100 percent.

In addition to forcing House members to take public stands on a larger number of issues on the floor, both chambers removed the shroud of secrecy from most committee activities. In 1973 the House agreed to open most committee meetings, including markup sessions previously conducted almost exclusively in executive session. Moreover, members' votes on issues coming before a committee must be kept and made public. Even House Democratic Caucus discussions of proposed legislation are open unless members vote to close them. Two years later the Senate followed the House's lead and greatly curtailed the use of closed committee sessions. Once both chambers had adopted sunshine reforms for their committees, it became possible to make conference committee sessions public, and this change was accomplished in 1975. In that year, 93 percent of all congressional committee sessions were open, including 72 percent of the Senate markups and 98 percent of the House markups (*Congressional*

Quarterly Weekly Report 1976, 152-55). Even the House Appropriations Committee, where as recently as 1970 all meetings were closed, opened 94 percent of its sessions in 1975.

While the vast majority of the formal meetings of Congress are now conducted in public, a few exceptions remain. The Republican Conference still convenes behind closed doors. Also both parties carry out the most critical phase of their committee assignment processes in private. The deliberations of both parties' Committees on Committees in the House and the Senate are closed, not only to the public but also to legislators not on the committees.

The resolutions opening up committee proceedings specify conditions under which executive sessions may be held. These exceptions are based on those in one of the first federal sunshine laws, the 1966 Freedom of Information Act, although congressional exemptions are less extensive. House and Senate committees can meet *in camera* to deal with national defense; foreign policy; trade secrets and other confidential commercial and financial information; the investigatory files of law enforcement agencies; individuals' personnel, medical, or other files where publicity would constitute an unwarranted invasion of privacy; and internal personnel files of Congress, its members, committees, or supporting organizations, for example, GAO. Finally, sessions will be closed when required by legislation.

Sessions dealing with these topics are not closed automatically; a committee majority must decide to use executive sessions, meeting in open session so that any member who might habitually wish to exclude the public, thereby violating the intent of the openness reforms, can be held accountable. Senators can vote to close sessions on a single topic for up to 14 days. In the House a separate vote is required for each day on which an executive session is to be held. Provisions for closing conference committees are much broader. Upon the request of a majority of either chamber's conferees, meetings will be closed to the public. In closing conferences, members are not limited to the types of subject matter listed above.

Campaign Financing

Since 1972, congressional candidates have had to make public growing amounts of information about their campaign finances, on both contributions and expenditures. Name, address, occupation, and place of employment are needed for all contributors of $100 or more; less comprehensive records are required on contributions of $50 to $100. For payments of $10 or more, candidates must report the name and address of the payee and the amount paid. Smaller sums need not be reportedly individually, although candidates must reveal their total receipts and expenditures on the primary and general elections as well as any debts remaining after the campaign. The legislation further requires reports on in-kind contributions, loans, and proceeds from fund-raising activities. Reports are also required from political committees, organizations that spend $2000 or more in an election to influence the votes of their members or stockholders, groups that distribute analyses of incumbents' voting records to influence the outcome of an election, and individuals who contribute $100 or more to some entity other than a candidate or political organization.

Reports must be filed quarterly (unless expenditures or income totaled less than $1000) and 10 days before and 30 days after each election. Copies go to the Federal Election Commission, the candidate's secretary of state, and either the Clerk of the House or the Secretary of the Senate.

While campaign finance disclosure legislation has certainly made far more information available concerning sources and amounts spent and has perhaps prevented some influence peddling, it has not reduced campaign expenditures.[2] In the 1976 congressional elections, candidates received $22.6 million from interest groups, some $10 million more than two years earlier (*Frontline*, April–May 1977). The 1976 general election cost congressional candidates $93 million.

Conflict of Interest

While both houses created "Ethics Committees" during the 1960s, these bodies have been reluctant to investigate allegations of misconduct. The House Committee on Standards of Official Conduct was so reticent about looking into charges of Korean influence peddling among members that the chairman, John Flynt (D-Ga.), was stripped of many of his prerogatives and the chief counsel, Leon Jaworski, given almost a free rein.[3] This was not the first time that the Flynt committee had drawn criticism for tardiness in grappling with charges of misconduct. Just the year before, the committee delayed an investigation that culminated in a formal reprimand of Robert Sikes (D-Fla.) until confronted with a complaint drawn up by Common Cause and signed by 45 House members (Freed 1976b). Further evidence of the failure of either Ethics Committee to act aggressively is the fact that although one senior and at least ten representatives have been indicted or convicted of misconduct since the committees were created, neither committee investigated any of these former members.

Since Congress has shown little stomach for rooting out and punishing misbehaving members, another strategy has been employed. In 1977 each chamber passed a resolution designed to dissuade members from activities that might lead to conflict of interest. As shown in Table 16-1, provisions for the two houses are not identical; nonetheless, their objectives are the same. Believing that one way to discourage malfeasance is to require members to file public records, the codes require disclosure of income and gifts of $100 or more that members of Congress and their top staff people receive. Members must also identify their property holdings, securities, and debts and roughly indicate the value of each. The Senate has directed the Comptroller General to audit each senator's financial reports at least once each six-year term.

Other provisions restrict the ability of members to enjoy additional financial gain from their positions. The maximum earned from outside sources is 15 percent of one's salary, or $8625 annually in 1977. The maximum honorarium for a single speech or article—included in the 15 percent limitation—is $1000 for a senator and $750 for a representative.

One tradeoff increased House members' office accounts by $5000 a year while banning slush funds. The Commission on Administrative Review (U.S. House 1977a) estimated that 40 percent of the members had slush funds (more generally called "unofficial office accounts") in which unexpended campaign funds and other contributions were collected to defray expenses such as newsletters and trips back to the district. Some funds were thought to be as large as $60,000.

Additional Proposed Openness Reforms

In addition to these changes, two proposals, currently under consideration, seek to increase the sunshine in which Congress operates by many candlepower. One would expand television coverage of congressional proceedings; the other would bring more sunshine to lobbyist-legislator interactions.

During the 94th Congress, proposals for live television coverage of Congress failed. Critics warned that during an election year, some members would abuse the situation, using the coverage as a free platform from which to campaign. Others feared that the image of Congress recorded by the cameras would not be flattering. Tip O'Neill (D-Mass.) cautioned, "If you think the public's rating of Congress is low now, just wait till we get TV" (reported in Freed 1976a, p. 323).

A year later O'Neill's fears had sufficiently moderated that he authorized a 90-day trial for live television coverage of House floor proceedings. During this period a closed-circuit system will operate as technicians search for camera angles that will not disclose small attendance and inattention to debate often characteristic of floor activities. A possible reason for the leadership's shift on television coverage is a poll, conducted by the Commission on Administrative Review (U.S. House, 1977b), reporting that 68 percent of a national sample thought that debates on major legislation should be televised.

A more sweeping change would be reform of the 1946 Lobbying Disclosure Act. In 1976 both houses passed legislation requiring more extensive disclosure of lobbying activities. The legislation died, however, when chamber differences could not be resolved before adjournment. During the first third of the 95th Congress, House committee hearings have been held on a bill similar to the one passed last year and on several other proposals. Lobbying legislation is being considered again in the Senate.

Table 16-1
Provisions of 1977 Ethics Resolutions

House	Senate
Disclosure	
Members and principal staffers must report source and amount of all income and gifts of $100 or more. Excluded from reporting provision are personal hospitality, food, lodging, and transportation worth less than $250.	Same as House
Must identify and classify by category the value of property, securities, commodity futures, and investments worth more than $1000. Categories used are as follows: less than $5000; $5000 to $15,000; $15,000 to $50,000; $50,000 to $100,000; more than $100,000. Liabilities of more than $2500 must be identified and classified by category.	Must identify and classify by category the value of property, securities, and commodity futures worth more than $1000. Categories used are the same as for the House to $100,000; thereafter: $100,000 to $250,000; $250,000 to $500,000; $500,000 to $1 million; $1 million to $2 million; $2 million to $5 million; more than $5 million. Categories to be used in reporting other income are the same as in the House except at the lowest level where subcategories of $1000 to $2500 and $2500 to $5000 are substituted. Liabilities of more than $2500 must be identified and classified by category using the categories for property, etc., above. Holdings of blind and other trusts must be reported, and the dissolution of blind trusts was encouraged.
	Comptroller General is to audit at least 5 percent of the reports annually with each senator audited at least once per term. A copy of each senator's tax return is also to be filed with the Comptroller General. Audit results to be forwarded to the Ethics Committee.
Unofficial Office Accounts	
Unofficial office accounts (slush funds) and personal use of campaign funds prohibited.	Same as House
Outside Earned Income	
Cannot exceed 15 percent of member's salary. No limitations on unearned income (returns on investments).	Same as for House, except that book royalties are considered to be unearned income.
Maximum of $750 per appearance, article, or speech.	Maximum of $1000 per appearance, article, or speech.
	Staffers earning more than $35,000 can earn no more than $1500 annually and $300 per speech or article. Committee staffers earning more than $25,000 must get rid of any holdings which may be affected by their committees.

House	Senate
	Former members are banned from lobbying the Senate for a year after their service ends. Former staffers cannot lobby in the office or committee where they worked for a year after leaving their Senate jobs.

Gifts

House	Senate
Gifts from lobbyists with an aggregate annual value of more than $100 in a year are not to be accepted. Also applies to staff.	Same as House for members.

Those who judge the 1946 legislation to be inadequate want more extensive reporting of lobbying activities. Supporters of new legislation generally call for expanding reporting requirements to cover:

Lobbying paid for through one's personal or corporate funds in addition to that financed with funds raised from others.

Lobbying carried out by organizations whose primary function is not lobbying; for example, the National Association of Manufacturers need not register under the current legislation.

Grass-roots lobbying; for example, the National Rifle Association is not presently required to register although it boasts that it can flood Capitol Hill with hundreds of thousands of letters in less than a week.

Lobbying limited to preparation of testimony or other informational services.

Juding from the 1976 lobbying disclosure bills, any reform package enacted will close these loopholes. It is also likely that rather than having individuals register, organizations that employ lobbyists will have to register with the General Accounting Office. Reports, which would probably be filed quarterly, would describe the organization, its public policy interests, and how it arrives at its policy positions. Lobbying organizations would also have to identify their agents and expenditures for meals, gifts, etc., for members of Congress or congressional staff. It might also be necessary to indicate the issues on which the organization was active, the legislators or staff members whom it contacted, and who made the contacts.

A major disagreement between House and Senate has been over which groups will have to register (Hager 1977). In 1976 the Senate required organizations initiating a minimum of 12 written or oral contacts per quarter with legislators or staff to register. The House version required registration of organizations that spent more than $1250 per quarter on lobbying or had an employee who spent more than a fifth of his or her time lobbying. Fearing they would be required to register under the more stringent provisions of the Senate bill, a number of public interest lobbies, which rely heavily on volunteers, opposed it. Some combination of these different approaches is likely if legislation is enacted by the 95th Congress.

Consequences of Congressional Openness

Most of, if not all, these openness reforms have been designed, at least in part, to change the reference groups to whom members of Congress respond. An underlying suspicion that our national legislators have heeded too little the preferences of their rank-and-file constituents has triggered efforts to redistribute influence.

While it is still too early to do much more than speculate, it appears that legislators are becoming more attentive to constituent preferences. Greatly increasing the number of decisions made openly decreases the likelihood that members will intentionally vote against the preferences of a sizable share of their constituents, or against the intensely held preferences of a smaller segment of their constituents. Consequently on items salient to their districts, legislators will have less latitude in their decisions in committee (because most committees now act in public), on the floor (because decisions are increasingly arrived at through recorded votes), and in conference committees.[4]

Increasing the visibility of congressional decision making enhances the likelihood that legislators will come to perceive themselves as delegates rather than trustees. While some research (for example, Hedlund and Friesema 1972; Jones 1973) suggests that representational role perceptions are unrelated to variations in constituency voting, Kuklinski and Elling (1977) raise serious questions about these findings. They find, among California legislators, that on high salience issues delegates do indeed vote with constituent preferences more often than do trustees. For Congress we can postulate that openness will cause more members to behave as delegates, resulting in more voting with constituent preferences on items salient to the constituency. And since it is not always possible to determine a priori what issues are salient to one's constituents (compare Miller and Stokes 1963), the impact of greater acceptance of a delegate role may be larger than would be otherwise expected.

Concern about voting to please one's constituents has implications for congressional policy making. Fear that a wrong vote may antagonize an important segment of the constituency, thereby forging a significant link in what Kingdon (1973) refers to as a fatal string of votes, may make legislators more reluctant to reach compromises. Legislators who might be willing to accept half a loaf, or even a crust, in private may hesitate to settle for anything less than a full loaf in public for fear they will be charged by some future challenger with selling out the district. The old system—where compromises reached behind closed doors were protected on the floor by defeating proposed amendments on unrecorded votes, or if lost on the floor were restored in the privacy of a conference committee—may prove to have been more conducive to policy making.

Openness may delay decision making because in an open system more people are allowed to participate. Indeed, one reason for open meetings is to encourage better preparation and greater participation. It is a well-accepted precept that increasing the number of participants is useful if the objective is to expand the number of alternatives available for consideration. However, the more people who are involved, the more difficult it becomes to reach a decision.

Proposals to televise floor proceedings and to identify whether speeches were actually given on the floor or were simply inserted into the *Congressional Record* may create pressures for more members to participate longer in floor activities. In the House, these pressures could lead to rules providing for longer periods of debate, which might necessitate additional hours or days of floor sessions and leave less time for committee and constituency work.

Openness may have a conservative bias for policy making in two ways. First, to the extent that reforms delay decisions, they permit current policies to persist. Second, by inducing members to heed constituent preferences more closely, openness may lead more members to vote more conservatively. For example, on civil liberties issues, elites tend to be more liberal than the masses (Stouffer 1955). Indeed, heightened accountability may explain some of the conservative actions of the 95th Congress, for instance, reducing the use of federal funds for abortions.

Opening committee sessions, increasing the number of recorded votes, restricting lobbyists bearing gifts, and proposing to require more extensive disclosure of lobbying activities all will probably change the requisites for successful lobbying. Interests of some newer lobbying groups (say, environmental groups) and of constituents may assume greater significance. New tactics may come to the fore among successful lobbyists.

At a minimum, one of the coziest lobbyist-legislator arrangements will be broken up. With most markup sessions conducted in the sunshine, it is unlikely that the lobbyists of powerful concerns will be allowed to participate in markups while representatives of lesser organizations are excluded. Thus openness should help place interest groups on a more equal basis when trying to influence legislators.

More generally, the consequence of open lobbying for legislators will depend on whether the preferences of a particular lobbyist coincide with those of a particular legislator's constituency. When they do coincide, the legislator will feel greater compulsion to vote with the interest group when the decision is made in public, even if there is a conflict with personal preference. If perceived constituency preference is at odds with what a lobbyist seeks, decision making in the sunshine will increase the likelihood that, *ceteris paribus*, the legislator will vote as the district prefers. At the very least, openness will create some cross pressures that were absent in the past.

By restricting the influence of money and gifts, openness may accentuate interest-group use of other techniques. Environmental Action—which identifies the "dirty dozen," a list of members who support unsound environmental policies—has enjoyed remarkable success in defeating opponents. In 1976, three incumbents on its list were defeated. The organization boasts that after its first three lists—it began the practice in 1970—77 percent of the incumbents who had been singled out were no longer in the House (*Congressional Quarterly Weekly Report* 1976, p. 765). More recorded voting gives interest groups better insights into where legislators stand on the issues; restrictions on campaign contributions (where powerful groups could flex their muscles) enhance the potential influence of well-orchestrated campaigns to publicize voting records on topical issues. Another tactic that may assume greater significance is grass-roots lobbying. If the financial resources of affluent groups become less of a factor, then groups that mobilize their members to exert pressure on legislators will loom larger on the policy horizon.

The combination of powerful new interest groups concerned about new issues and the need to take stands on a larger number of issues may force members to increase their electoral efforts. This seems likely, since with more roll calls and more groups monitoring roll calls there are more opportunities for each legislator to antagonize some set of constituents. In time this may create a coalition of minorities that could defeat the incumbent (compare Mueller 1973; Parker 1977). Following Fiorina (1977b), we hypothesize that to offset the influence of additional monitoring of voting records, greater personal and staff resources will be invested in casework.

Heightened electoral concern may also become manifest in members' committee preferences. The trend toward greater interest in committees for policy reasons (Bullock 1976) may be reversed. Members may feel additional pressures to turn their attention to committees that pay handsomer electoral dividends. A harbinger of this change may have been the difficulty encountered in filling Democratic vacancies on the Judiciary Committee in 1977. In past years, Judiciary has been popular, attracting more members from other committees than it lost (Bullock 1973; Jewell and Chi-Hung 1974). The decline in attractiveness reportedly stems from a widespread perception that regardless of what Judiciary did, involvement with its subject matter would likely be harmful electorally. Sensitive matters such as school desegregation and penal reform fall in the domain of the committee, and on these topics any stand a member takes may antagonize some constituents.

Sunshine laws may combine with committee reforms to make the role of the House Rules Committee more sensitive. If representatives act increasingly as delegates, the likelihood will increase that legislation, currently popular but with potentially negative consequences in the long run, will be approved by the House. Moreover, the weakened position of committee chairpersons reduces the probability that they will stand in the way of popular legislation even if they believe it to be unwise. Consequently, the Rules Committee may be the only place that will be dominated by members secure enough to block proposals until popular passions cool (Oppenheimer 1977a).

Thus far the discussion has involved issues salient to an important portion of a legislator's constituency. Openness reforms may also have implications for issues having little salience for voters or their legislators. These issues, lacking either electoral or personal significance, fall within the legislator's zone of indifference. It is under these conditions that a legislator, having no opinion on a matter, would be particularly susceptible to a plea for assistance from a lobbyist. Dexter (1969) even suggests that since legislators work in a world where favors are commonly are exchanged, lobbyists might be more successful if they ask legislators to support their position as a favor, rather than because it is in the public interest. Consequently, members of Congress who received some benefit— a trip or stereo—from an organization with an interest in the outcome might be willing to vote as the lobbyist asked. The receipt of such kindnesses from each lobbyist has been limited to an aggregate annual value of $100.[5] Legislators with no reason to do a favor for a lobbyist may now lack an important cue when passing on items about which they are indifferent. To fill this vacuum, the advice of party leaders, fellow members, and staff may assume greater significance.

Since the 1977 ethics legislation reduces the gifts and services lobbyists can provide to members, such lobbying may come to focus more on staffers. Gifts totaling $100 in value may mean little to a member, but may make a lasting impression on the legislative assistant in a member's office who handles the topic of interest to a lobbyist. In the absence of contrary reasons, the legislator may vote as the staffer recommends.

Although it has often been argued that sunshine reforms will expand opportunities for political participation, some fear that the additional paperwork required may actually make it more difficult for some to participate. For example, while all federal candidates face the same requirements, compliance may be particularly burdensom for challengers, who lack a tax-supported staff and who have had less experience with the reporting requirements. One Senate challenger claimed that 30 percent of his staff's time was consumed filling out the reporting forms (Wagner 1976). Some interest groups have complained about reporting requirements in proposed lobbying legislation. Organizations with limited financial resources fear that they might have to hire additional staff to handle the paperwork. The costs involved might be excessive. The director of litigation for Nader's Public Citizen warns that "the NAM can hire 14 more secretaries to comply with reporting requirements. [Small public interest groups] can't" (*Business Week*, May 17, 1976, p. 39).

Finally, we come to the question of whether openness reforms are likely to help Congress ascend in the public opinion polls. If people become convinced that the congressional landscape is so open that there is no place for a miscreant to hide, then public confidence in the institution may rise. Limiting outside earnings and requiring that members reveal their financial holdings and sources of campaign funds should reduce the frequency with which members participate in decisions where there is potential conflict of interest.

On the other hand, a number of likely consequences of the reforms seem unlikely to heighten public esteem for our national legislature. Increasing participation in decision making and more extended floor deliberations will not expedite the legislative process. Most Americans believe that Congress's primary responsibility is to approve what the President proposes (Davidson, Kovenock, and O'Leary 1966, pp. 56–57). Public approval of Congress has been high when the legislature expeditiously ratified Presidential programs; for example, the second highest rating between 1939 and 1974 came in 1965 when Congress was rubber-stamping President Johnson's Great Society proposals (Parker 1977). Consequently, slowing down the legislative process is likely to cause further criticism of the institution.

While careful monitoring of members' finances, the funding of their campaigns, and their contacts with lobbyists may prevent misconduct, it seems likely that the emphasis on openness will lead to discovery of additional misdeeds of past or present legislators (the Korean probe is a case in point). The short-term impact of such revelations is likely to be lower public confidence. The discovery of White House abuses under President Nixon caused public confidence in the President to plummet to levels from which it has yet to recover. In sum, then, if openness improves public ratings of Congress, it will probably take a while.

Summary

This chapter has presented some of the concerns of proponents of greater openness in Congress. It has described several reforms that have forced members of Congress to operate more in public and noted some pending reforms. These reforms have reduced the secrecy surrounding committee deliberations, floor decisions, member finances, and campaign funding. These changes are likely to redistribute influence, with some groups, powerful in the past, losing influence and some newer groups, legislators' constituents, and perhaps staff members being the beneficiaries. Greater delays in arriving at decisions also appear likely.

Notes

1. Wilbur Mills and Wayne Hays had highly publicized encounters with Fanne Foxe and Elizabeth Ray. Gallagher went to jail after pleading guilty to

perjury, conspiracy, and tax evasion, and Hinshaw was sentenced to 1 to 14 years for bribery.

2. Other provisions of the campaign finance legislation restrict the amounts individuals and organizations can contribute to candidates and committees.

3. There have been charges that the Ethics Committee proceeded so slowly at least in part because the Democratic leadership hoped the issue of Korean influence buying would go away. Speaker O'Neill has denied all such charges. The regional composition of the committee does, however, fuel speculations that the leadership prefers a committee that will not aggressively pursue wrongdoing. Standards of Official Conduct is the least regionally balanced of all House committees with five of the six Democrats, as well as half of the six Republicans, from the South. [In contrast, only 27.8 percent of the members of the House are Southerners. Of seven committees analyzed by Bullock (forthcoming), on none—including Interior and Insular Affairs—was any region as overrepresented as the South is on Ethics.] If the Democratic contingent were composed of liberal Northerners, the likelihood of a more active committee would be greater.

4. While there is certainly no guarantee that opening up the congressional decision process will make constituents more attentive to their legislators' activities, legislators cannot safely assume that they will never be held accountable. Indeed, often they may not know which issues will be significant to their constituents or which votes some future challenger might seize upon. Therefore, while many incumbents may emphasize casework more than policy stands, they must anticipate issues likely to be important in their districts, and on these they may perceive little latitude when voting.

5. Campaign contributions are not considered here. A past contribution or the hope of one in the future would make the issue salient to a legislator.

17

Legislative Quality and Legislative Policy Making: Some Implications for Reform

Raymond Tatalovich

During the late 1960s a good-government organization, the Citizens Conference on State Legislatures (CCSL), undertook a comprehensive and comparative evaluation of all 50 state legislatures (Citizens Conference on State Legislatures 1973). It analyzed all legislatures according to five performance standards: functionality, informedness, independence, representation, and accountability. Each state legislature was ranked on each criterion, and an overall ranking from 1 to 50 was produced on the basis of all five standards.

Functionality measured the use of time, staff, facilities, and legislative procedures in the process of lawmaking. Informedness focused on each legislature's capability to study legislation in committee, to draft laws, and to exercise fiscal oversight. Independence appraised the assembly's autonomy vis-à-vis the executive branch and lobbying groups; and representation was the standard to assess the qualifications, diversity, and effectiveness of individual legislators. Accountability evaluated constituents' ability to understand the internal workings of the legislature and to gain access to its proceedings.

This study reflected the dual assumptions that the state legislatures historically have been "ill equipped" to discharge their responsibilities and that proposed "reforms" can make them "democratic decision-making bod[ies]." One may question whether the Citizens Conference on State Legislatures' proposals, in fact, constitute reform, but nonetheless the CCSL perceives them to embody the essentials of reform. Moreover, in this analysis, reform is not construed to be the degree of institutional change within each legislature from one time period to another. It is true that the study acknowledges that very recent changes in the structure and processes of some state legislatures (say, Illinois) have markedly improved their evaluation in terms of the five standards. Therefore reform should be perceived as a static, multidimensional index of the institutional *quality* of each state legislature at a given time. And as the study argues, the quality of institutional arrangements need not be defended in terms of the outputs generated by such legislative systems.

There may seem to be no obvious connection between legislative reform and legislative results—between better staffing or office space or salaries and the ability and willingness of a legislature to deal with the large public problems before us. Nothing can, in fact, guarantee that a well-paid, well-staffed, well-housed legislature will make the right decisions. Neither can anything guarantee that a governor, or a president, or a policeman, or a judge, will make the right

223

decisions. There is no way of guaranteeing anything that depends on human choice. Indeed, the argument for democracy as a form of government is not that under it we always reach the "right" decisions; rather, whatever the "rightness" of our decisions, a democracy enables us to make them more freely and fairly than any other form (Citizens Conference on State Legislatures, 1973).

Scholars have begun to use this analysis as an approximate, but meaningful, benchmark of the quality of state legislatures. Dye argues that the CCSL has ranked the assemblies on the basis of "legislative professionalism" (Dye 1977). Patterson (1976) suggests that "their very thorough study made it possible to map variations among all fifty states in their general levels of organizational capability." Indeed, though no political scientist has previously attempted such a comprehensive evaluation of all state legislatures, scholars have used various data to measure the degree of professionalism in state legislatures. That is, attention has been given to such indices as number of legislators, compensation levels, expenditure on legislative services, number of committees, and number of days in session (Sharkansky and Hofferbert 1969).

Given these parameters by which the concept of legislative "reform" is defined, this research will address three empirical questions about the quality of legislative systems in the states. Implicit in this discussion, moreover, is the assumption that reforms in the institutional arrangements of state legislatures will affect public policies to the extent that variations in the "quality" of legislative systems are found to affect governmental outputs. At the outset, socioeconomic and political variables will be correlated to legislative quality to determine whether certain societal conditions favor professionalism in state legislatures. Second, this chapter will go beyond the assumptions of the Citizens Conference on State Legislatures to examine whether legislative quality does affect legislative outputs. And third, but most importantly, the relative impact of legislative professionalism on outputs will be evaluated in terms of more conventional socioeconomic and political variables. Overall, therefore, this chapter will correlate legislative quality with environmental inputs and with policy outputs to determine the empirical linkages supportive of and resulting from legislative quality.

Given the ordinal ranking of all 50 legislatures on the five performance standards, this statistical analysis is based on Spearman's rank-order correlation. All data on inputs and ouputs, though interval, can be easily converted to ordinal rankings for purposes of comparison. The level of statistical significance is calculated on the basis of a Z score (Kirkpatrick 1974).

Societal Determinants of Legislative Quality

Table 17-1 gives the rank-order correlations between legislative quality and 26 socioeconomic and political variables, drawn from the *Statistical Abstract of the*

United States and the *Congressional District Data Book*. If legislative professionalism is an output of given societal conditions, then the data affirm three hypotheses in the literature. And most significantly, the analysis again indicates that economic development factors are more important determinants of outputs than purely political variables. First, the correlations support the hypothesis that good-government movements have developed in middle-class environments. Socioeconomic status (SES), urbanism, and industrialization are all facets of economic development, but SES is most important to legislative professionalism in the states. The correlations with education, white-collar employment, income, and the "cultural enrichment factor" (Hofferbert 1968) are clearly strongest. Urbanism and residence in "standard metropolitan statistical areas" show significant correlations with legislative quality but at lower levels than those SES factors. Moreover, the "industrialization factor" (Hofferbert 1968) is insignificant, and employment in manufacturing industries is negatively associated with professionalism.

Second, Elazar's thesis—that states with "moralist" political cultures exhibit good-government attributes—is affirmed using an indicator of political cultures based upon the distribution of religious denominations in the states (Johnson 1976). Third, an index of diversity (Sullivan 1973), which excluded race but included education, income, occupation, housing, ethnicity, and religion, correlates with legislative reform. Sullivan excluded race on the grounds that empirical research shows that nonracial diversity in the states generates demands on the political system and also increases social tolerance. But to the contrary, racial diversity "breeds fear and contempt," with accompanying negative effects on the politics and public policies in states. Two other correlations in Table 17-1 confirm Sullivan's hypothesis. The tendency toward legislative professionalism in states with smaller black populations is statistically insignificant; high-quality legislatures are found in those states with a reduced income differential between blacks and whites (Dye 1969). It can be argued that large income differentials between the races may prompt the dominant white elite to maintain a closed legislative system, by obstructing reforms, to deny access to the black community and to protect white economic privilege.

Three measures of numerical apportionment (Dauer and Kelsay 1955; David and Eisenberg 1961; Schubert and Press 1964) have no statistical impact on legislative quality. Similarly, low and statistically insignificant correlations are found between three indices of voting turnout (Milbrath 1971; Ranney 1976) and legislative professionalism. But the degree of two-party competition, especially within state legislatures, exhibits significant correlations with legislative quality on five of six party competition indices (Ranney 1976; Hofferbert 1964; Sharkansky and Hofferbert 1969; Dawson and Robinson 1963). Since the competition-turnout factor of Sharkansky and Hofferbert includes measures of both party competition and voting turnout, either may produce the effect. Given the insignificant correlations with voting turnout noted above, however,

Table 17-1
Correlations between Ranking of States
on Socioeconomic and Political Variables
and Ranking of State Legislatures on Quality

Variable	Quality
Percent high school graduates of persons aged 25 and over, 1970	.404
Percent of total employed in white-collar occupations, 1960	.580
1970 percent of families with $15,000 or more income in 1969	.441
Per capita income, 1969	.430
Hofferbert's cultural enrichment factor, 1960	.404[a]
Dye's "Gini" index of general economic inequality, 1960	−.253*
Percent living in urban places, 1970	.377
Percent living in standard metropolitan statistical areas, 1970	.297**
Hofferbert's industrialization factor, 1960	.088*[a]
Percent of total employed in manufacturing industry, 1970	−.286*
Johnson's index of "moralist" political culture, 1960	.406[a]
Sullivan's diversity index, 1960	.373
Percent black, 1970	−.242*
Dye's index of racial economic inequality, 1960	−.553
Dauer-Kelsay representation score, 1955	−.088*[b]
David-Eisenberg index of urban underrepresentation, 1960	−.061*
Schubert-Press apportionment score, 1962	.026*
Milbrath's mean percent turnout for gubernatorial and senatorial elections in non-Presidential elections, 1952–1960	.176*[a]
Ranney's mean percent turnout for Presidential, congressional, and gubernatorial elections, 1962–1972	.197*
Ranney's percent turnout in 1968 Presidential election	.227*
Percent of membership of lower house of state legislature from majority party, 1962–1970	−.423[a]
Percent of membership of upper house of state legislature from majority party, 1962–1970	−.376[a]
Ranney's party competition index, 1956–1970	.373
Hofferbert's party competition index, 1932–1962	.349**[a]
Sharkansky-Hofferbert competition-turnout factor, 1960	.345**[a]
Dawson-Robinson party competition index, 1938–1958	.253*[c]

One asterisk indicates statistical insignificance; none shows significance at .01 level, and two asterisks indicate significance at the .05 level. Unless stipulated, correlations are based on an N of 50 states; the "a" indicates an N of 48; the "b" indicates an N of 47; and the "c" indicates an N of 46.

one might suspect that two-party competition also operates in this instance. The existence of a two-party system rather than one-party hegemony may encourage both antagonists to favor more open, democratic, and professional methods of decision making to protect their mutual interests whenever the balance of power in the state legislature shifts.

Table 17-2
Correlations between Ranking of State
Legislatures on Quality Attributes and
Ranking of States on Policy Outputs

Output Variable	Quality
Walker's policy innovation index	.351**[a]
Jacob-Vines index of legal professionalism	.558
Schlesinger's index of governors' formal powers	.315**
Sharkansky and Hofferbert professionalism-local reliance factor, 1960	.166*[a]
Total number of all types of local government, 1972	.320**
Total state/local government payroll, 1970	.319**
Sharkansky and Hofferbert highways-natural resources factor, 1960	.011*[a]
Total number of state parks and recreation areas, 1970	.506
Per capita state/local government general revenue from taxes, 1970	.561
Per capita state/local government total general revenue, 1970	.465
Percent of state/local government general revenue from federal government, 1970	−.327**
Per capita direct general expenditures of state/local government, 1970	.442
Sharkansky and Hofferbert welfare education factor, 1960	.508[a]
Average monthly payment per family for aid to dependent children, 1970	.450
Average weekly benefits for unemployment insurance, 1970	.418
Average per pupil expenditure in average daily-attendance public school, 1970	.408
Average monthly payment for aid to permanently and totally disabled, 1970	.361**
Average monthly payment for aid to the blind, 1970	.419
Average monthly old-age assistance payment, 1970	.267*
Per capita expenditures of state/local government for health and hospitals, 1970	.288**
Per capita expenditures of state/local government for public welfare, 1970	.292**
Per capita expenditures of state/local government for education, 1970	.417
Per capita expenditures of state/local government for highways, 1970	.131*
Number of bills introduced into 1971–1972 session of state legislatures	.217*
Number of bills enacted by 1971–1972 sessions of state legislatures	.030*
Percent of introduced bills enacted by 1971–1972 sessions of state legislatures	−.357**

One asterisk indicates statistical insignificance; none shows significance at .01 level, and two asterisks indicate significance at the .05 level. Unless stipulated, correlations are based on an N of 50 states; the "a" indicates an N of 48.

Impact of Legislative Quality on Policy Outputs

The impact of legislative reform—as a political input—on state policies can also be evaluated (Table 17-2). Most output measures come from the extended listings provided by Dye, Sharkansky, and Hofferbert, and these 26 outputs are among those indices repeatedly studied in the literature. States with professionalized legislatures tend to exhibit a history of policy innovation; such states adopted various public policies, such as highway departments, civil rights commissions, and councils on the performing arts, earlier in their history than did most other states (Walker 1969). High-quality legislatures are also found in states ranking high on legal professionalism, as mesured by standards adopted by the American Bar Association and the American Judicature Society (Vines and Jacob 1971). And states with professional legislatures tend to institutionalize strong formal powers in their governors, as indexed by tenure, appointment power, the veto, and budgetary authority (Schlesinger 1971). In this context, it appears that various good-government reforms tend to coalesce in state government. However, the composite index of professionalism-local reliance factor (Sharkansky and Hofferbert 1969) showed a low, insignificant correlation with legislative quality. Again, however, it is not clear which indices effect this correlation; this factor combines six variables, including compensation of judges, number of bills introduced to the assembly, and state-local revenues spent by localities.

My analysis of single indices does affirm the hypothesis Sharkansky and Hofferbert offer when they constructed a factor to measure local government reliance. States with quality legislatures rely less on federal grants-in-aid, and their state and local governments collect more revenue per capita and, in particular, collect more revenue per capita from taxes. But interestingly, and perhaps unexpectedly, professional state legislatures enact a lower percentage of bills introduced (Council of State Governments 1974). It should be noted, however, that relatively few bills pass the more professional (so political scientists argue) United States Congress (Froman 1967). This finding should prompt analyses of actual decision making in high- and low-quality state legislatures. One can speculate, nonetheless, that professionalism may undermine quid pro quo bargaining among dominant legislative elites and introduce wider rank-and-file participation and greater access to affected publics. As indicated, quality does not affect the absolute number of bills legislators introduce or the absolute number of bills state legislatures approve.

Finally, a very strong, significant correlation between legislative quality and the welfare-education factor (Sharkansky and Hofferbert 1969) is reflected also in the many single indices of educational and welfare expenditures. That is, professional assemblies are found in states with higher rates of spending for dependent children, for unemployment insurance, for public schools, for the disabled, for the blind, and for old-age assistance. Similarly, quality legislatures are found in states whose local state governments expend more resources for health and hospitals, for public welfare, and for education. On the other hand, quality in state legislatures does not affect state and local expenditures for highways, and its correlation to the highways-natural resources factor (Sharkansky and Hofferbert 1969) is statistically insignificant. This finding appears compatible with Sharkansky and Hofferbert's analysis of state outputs; they found a "lack of dependence on political factors for highway and natural resources policies."

Comparison of Legislative Quality and Voting Turnout, Party Competition, and Socioeconomic Variables as Determinants of Policy Outputs

Those eight output indices which correlated *most strongly* with legislative quality (Table 17-2) are included, for comparative analysis, in Table 17-3. The same eight outputs are also correlated with most SES and political variables used in Table 17-1. Here one can determine the relative importance of legislative quality in affecting policy outputs.

The correlations between legislative quality and policy outputs are higher in every case when they are compared to the three apportionment indices. The professionalism correlations also are stronger than all three measures of voting turnout for the majority of outputs studied here, but as noted earlier, they are stronger than only two of six party competition indices in the majority of cases. In particular, note again the very strong relationship between two-party competition within the state legislature and policy outputs, as compared to professionalism. This difference may be explained by the hypothesis that quality—once attained—becomes a stable, predictable component in the legislative system. Therefore actors in the legislative struggle are able to develop strategies in line with the newly created organizational features of the assemblies. In contrast, the degree of two-party competition within any assembly may continually change and thereby alter the tactics and strategies of decision makers who make policy. When legislative quality is compared to the seven socioeconomic variables, however, six SES conditions (all except urbanism) generated higher correlations with policy outputs in the majority of cases studied.

Overall, therefore, policy outputs are most strongly influenced by socioeconomic conditions in the states. The degree of two-party competition ranks second in importance, and legislative quality is third. Voting turnout is significantly correlated with policies in most cases, but not as strong as legislative quality in the majority of instances. And finally, apportionment seems to have no real impact, for the vast majority of correlations among three apportionment indices and outputs are statistically insignificant.

Summary

To conclude, this chapter focused on the multifaceted concept of legislative quality (or professionalism), as the Citizens Conference on State Legislatures defined it, to determine whether it correlated with either environmental condi-

Table 17-3
Correlations between Ranking of States on Legislative Quality and Socioeconomic-Political Variables and Policy Outputs[a]

	State/Local Tax Revenue per Capita	Legal Professionalism	Welfare-Education Factor	Number of State Parks and Recreation Areas	State/Local Revenue per Capita	Average Payment for Dependent Children	State/Local per Capita Expenditure	State/Local Unemployment Insurance Payment
Legislative Quality	.561	.558	.508	.506	.465	.450	.442	.418
$15,000 income	.828	.743	.611	.384	.566	.652	.619	.768
Urban	.565	.547	.495	.314	.328	.334	.345	.591
High school	.623	.377	.512	.113	.706	.438	.719	.410
"Moralist" culture	.526	.316	.540	.207	.606	.540	.645	.357
White-collar	.622	.575	.532	.230	.616	.417	.588	.530
Diversity index	.816	.718	.661	.445	.628	.758	.657	.693
Cultural enrichment	.621	.369	.584	.172	.660	.352	.680	.409
1952–1960 voting turnout	.492	.273	.506	.144	.497	.558	.571	.321
1962–1972 voting turnout	.408	.193	.481	.262	.414	.526	.445	.224
1968 voting turnout	.350	.182	.468	.227	.322	.513	.399	.290
Dawson-Robinson index	.537	.455	.497	.140	.404	.521	.513	.487
Hofferbert index	.645	.579	.589	.232	.554	.558	.577	.644
Ranney index	.593	.441	.550	.428	.496	.567	.550	.446
Competition turnout	.435	.338	.623	.278	.407	.517	.429	.396
Lower house majority party	-.759	-.592	-.641	-.322	-.585	-.589	-.610	-.698
Upper house majority party	-.726	-.535	-.493	-.220	-.660	-.530	-.678	-.605
David-Eisenberg index	.013	.029	.091	.180	-.050	.243	.009	-.002
Schubert-Press index	.038	.124	.002	.229	-.063	.216	-.028	.018
Dauer-Kelsay index	-.193	-.039	.115	.134	-.232	.108	-.225	-.199

[a]The 160 correlations are based on varying N's; 77 are based on 50 states, 67 on 48 states, 8 on 47 states, and 8 on 46 states. Tests of significance reflect the size of the N involved, however, and I have calculated that any correlation of .286 or higher within this table is statistically significant at least at the .05 level.

tions or policy outputs. Linkages between societal conditions, legislative quality, and public policies were found. Quality legislatures exist in states with higher socioeconomic status, a "moralist" political culture, and greater nonracial diversity. The existence of racial heterogeneity hinders legislative professionalism in the states, however. The SES variables are more important than any political inputs to the legislative system, that is, party competition, voting turnout, and apportionment. Two-party competition was stronger, however, than voting turnout or apportionment. Similarly, SES variables correlated more strongly with policy outputs than any political variables, including legislative quality. In terms of their relative importance, SES variables rank first, followed by two-party competition, legislative quality, voting turnout, and apportionment. These conclusions are consistent with research by Dye and Sharkansky, each of whom determined that socioeconomic conditions are generally more important than political factors in shaping the nature of state political systems and in affecting their policy outputs.

Nonetheless, this analysis indicates both that the quality of legislative institutions does affect system performance and that quality is more important than other political inputs, such as voting turnout or apportionment. Though based on a very subjective and approximate evaluation of professionalism in state legislatures, this analysis shows its positive impact on legislative outputs. It also suggests that "reforms" in the institutional and procedural framework of state legislatures which increase their level of professionalism should have beneficial effects on the quality of public policies enacted. To this extent, it may be profitable for political scientists to begin with the CCSL framework and to prepare a more quantitative set of indices for the numerous facets of a legislative system that impinge on lawmaking. With more vigorous statistical measures at hand, scholars can then begin to use advanced statistical tools, such as regression or factor analysis, to introduce this institutional component into models designed to explain and predict system performance. At present, comprehensive statistical models based on numerous socioeconomic and political variables fail to explain all variance in state government outputs. For example, despite their exhaustive analysis of SES and political variables through factor analysis, Sharkansky and Hofferbert (1969) acknowledge that much variation in state politics and policy remains unexplained: "This unexplained variance may reflect the importance of particularistic, unpatterned happenings that fashion and lend excitement to political institutions. The effort to explain why politics and policies differ from one state to the next may be helped considerably by examining the dimensions lying beneath readily measured variables." Though not idiosyncratic, the degree of legislative quality—as an index of institutional attributes—may well be that additional, missing variable essential to a more complete understanding of comparative politics and policies in the American states.

References

Adamany, D.W. 1972. *Campaign Finance in America*. North Scituate, Mass.: Duxbury Press.

Agranoff, R. 1976. *The Management of Election Campaigns*. Boston: Holbrook Press.

Alexander, H.E. 1976. *Financing Elections: Money, Elections, and Political Reform*. Washington: Congressional Quarterly Press.

American Enterprise Institute for Public Policy Research. 1977. "Regulation of Political Campaigns—How Successful?" Washington, D.C.

Asher, H.B. 1975. "The Changing Status of the Freshman Representative." In N.J. Ornstein (ed.). *Congress in Change: Evolution and Reform*. New York: Praeger.

Bachrach, P., and M. Baratz. 1962. "Two Faces of Power." *American Political Science Review* 56:947-52.

Barone, J., et al. 1976. *The Almanac of American Politics, 1976*. Boston: Gambit.

Ben-Zion, U., and Z. Eytan. 1974. "On Money, Votes, and Policy in a Democratic Society?" *Public Choice* 17:1-10.

Bernick, E.L., and C.W. Wiggins. 1977. "Executive-Legislative Power Relationships: Perspectives of State Lawmakers." Presented at the Annual Meeting of the Midwest Political Science Association.

Bibby, J.F. 1966. "Committee Characteristics and Legislative Oversight of Administration." *Midwest Journal of Political Science* 10:78-98.

Blalock, H.M., Jr. 1972. *Social Statistics*. New York: McGraw-Hill.

Blondel, J. 1973. *Comparative Legislatures*. Englewood Cliffs, N.J.: Prentice-Hall.

Bolling, R. 1966. *House Out of Order*. New York: Dutton.

Bowler, M.K. 1976. "The New Committee on Ways and Means: Policy Implications of Recent Changes in the House." Presented at the Annual Meeting of the American Political Science Association.

Broder, D. 1971. "The Men of Ways and Means." *Washington Post* (April 29): A 18.

Bullock, C.S., III. 1973. "Committee Transfers in the United States House of Representatives." *Journal of Politics* 35: 85-120.

Bullock, C.S., III. 1976. "Motivations for U.S. Congressional Committee Preferences: Freshmen of the 92nd Congress." *Legislative Studies Quarterly* 1: 201-12.

Bullock, C.S., III. Forthcoming. "House Committee Assignments." In L.N. Rieselbach (ed.), *The Congressional System: Notes and Readings*. North Scituate, Mass.: Duxbury.

Burnham, J. 1959. *Congress and the American Tradition*. Chicago: Regnery.

Burns, J.M. 1963. *The Deadlock of Democracy*. Englewood Cliffs, N.J.: Prentice-Hall.

Burns, J.M. 1965. *Presidential Government*. New York: Houghton Mifflin.

Campbell, D.T. 1969. "Reforms as Experiments." *American Psychologist* 24: 409–29.

Campbell, D.T., and J.C. Stanley. 1963. *Experimental and Quasi-Experimental Designs for Research*. Chicago: Rand McNally.

Carroll, H.N. 1966. *The House of Representatives and Foreign Affairs*. Boston: Little, Brown.

Citizens Conference on State Legislatures. 1973. *The Sometime Governments*. Kansas City.

Clark, J.S. 1965. *Congress: The Sapless Branch*. New York: Harper and Row.

Comptroller General of the United States, Report to Congress. 1977. *Review of the Impoundment and Control Act of 1974 after Two Years*.

Congressional Quarterly Almanac. 1958. 1973. 1974. 1975. 1976. Washington: Congressional Quarterly, Inc.

Congressional Quarterly Weekly Report. 1972. 1975. 1976. Vols. 30, 33, 34. Washington: Congressional Quarterly, Inc.

Council of State Governments. 1974. *The Book of the States, 1974-75*. Chicago.

Council of State Governments. 1976. *The Book of the States, 1976-1977*. Lexington, Ky.

Cover, R.D., and D.R. Mayhew. 1977. "Congressional Dynamics and the Decline of Competitive Congressional Elections." In L.C. Dodd and B.I. Oppenheimer (eds.). *Congress Reconsidered*. New York: Praeger.

Crain, W.M., and R. Tollison. 1976. "Campaign Expenditures and Political Competition." *Journal of Law and Economics* 19:177–88.

Cummings, M.C., and R.L. Peabody. 1963. "The Decision to Enlarge the Committee on Rules: An Analysis of the 1961 Vote." In R.L. Peabody and N.W. Polsby (eds.). *New Perspectives on the House of Representatives*, 1st ed. Chicago: Rand McNally.

Dauer, M.J., and R.G. Kelsay. 1955. "Unrepresentative States." *National Municipal Review* 44:515-75, 587.

David, P.T., and R. Eisenberg. 1961. *Devaluation of the Urban and Suburban Vote*. Charlottesville, Va.: Bureau of Public Administration, University of Virginia.

Davidson, R.H.; D.M. Kovenock; and M.K. O'Leary. 1966. *Congress in Crisis: Politics and Congressional Reform*. Belmont, Calif.: Wadsworth.

Davidson, R.D., and W.J. Oleszek. 1976. "Adaptation and Consolidation: Structural Innovation in the U.S. House of Representatives." *Legislative Studies Quarterly* 1:37-67.

Davidson, R.H., and W.J. Oleszek. 1977. *Congress against Itself*. Bloomington: Indiana University Press.

Dawson, P.A., and J.E. Zinser, 1976. "Political Finance and Participation in Congressional Elections." *Annals* 425:59-73.

Dawson, R.E., and J.A. Robinson. 1963. "Inter-Party Competition, Economic Variables, and Welfare Policies in the American States." *Journal of Politics* 25:268-89.

de Grazia, A. 1965. *Republic in Crisis: Congress against the Executive Force*. New York: Federal Legal Publications.

Dexter, L.A. 1969. *How Organizations Are Represented in Washington*. Indianapolis: Bobbs-Merrill.

Dodd, L.C. 1977. "Congress and the Quest for Power." In L.C. Dodd and B.I. Oppenheimer (eds.). *Congress Reconsidered*. New York: Praeger.

Dodd, L.C., and B.I. Oppenheimer. 1977a. "The House in Transition." In L.C. Dodd and B.I. Oppenheimer (eds.). *Congress Reconsidered*. New York: Praeger.

Dodd, L.C., and B.I. Oppenheimer (eds.). 1977b. *Congress Reconsidered*. New York: Praeger.

Drew, E. 1975. "A Reporter at Large: The Energy Bazaar." *New Yorker* (June 21):35-72.

Dye, T.R. 1969. "Inequality and Civil Rights Policy in the States." *Journal of Politics* 31:1080-97.

Dye, T.R. 1977. *Politics in the States and Communities*. Englewood Cliffs, N.J.: Prentice-Hall.

Eidenberg, E., and R. Morey. 1969. *An Act of Congress: The Legislative Process and the Making of Education Policy*. New York: Norton.

Ellwood, J.W., and J.A. Thurber. 1976a. "The New Congressional Budget Process in the House of Representatives: Some Hypotheses." Presented at the Annual Meeting of the Southwestern Political Science Association.

Ellwood, J.W., and J.A. Thurber. 1976b. "Some Implications of the Congressional Budget and Impoundment Control Act for the Senate." Presented at the Annual Meeting of the American Political Science Association.

Ellwood, J.W., and J.A. Thurber. 1977a. "The New Congressional Budget Process: The Hows and Whys of House-Senate Differences." In L.C. Dodd and B.I. Oppenheimer (eds.). *Congress Reconsidered*. New York: Praeger.

Ellwood, J.W., and J.A. Thurber. 1977b. "The New Congressional Budget Process: Its Causes, Consequences, and Possible Success." In S. Welch and J.G. Peters (eds.). *Legislative Reform and Public Policy*. New York: Praeger.

Erikson, R.S. 1971. "The Advantage of Incumbency in Congressional Elections." *Polity* 3:395-405.

Erikson, R.S. 1976. "Is There Such a Thing as a Safe Seat?" *Polity* 8:623-32.

Eulau, H. 1967. "The Committees in a Revitalized Congress." In A. deGrazia (ed.). *Congress: The First Branch of Government*. Garden City, N.Y.: Doubleday.

Federal Register. 1977. Washington: Government Printing Office.

Fenno, R.F., Jr. 1965. "The Internal Distribution of Influence: The House." In D.B. Truman (ed.). *The Congress and America's Future*. Englewood Cliffs, N.J.: Prentice-Hall.

Fenno, R.F., Jr. 1973. *Congressmen in Committees*. Boston: Little, Brown.

Fenno, R.F., Jr. 1975. "If, as Ralph Nader Says, Congress Is 'The Broken Branch,' How Come We Love Our Congressmen So Much?" In N.J. Ornstein (ed.). *Congress in Change: Evolution and Reform*. New York: Praeger.

Fenno, R.F., Jr. 1977. "U.S. House Members in Their Constituencies: An Exploration." *American Political Science Review* 71:883-917.

Ferejohn, J.A. 1977. "On the Decline of Competition in Congressional Elections." *American Political Science Review* 71:166-76.

Ferejohn, J.A., and M.P. Fiorina. 1975. "Purposive Models of Legislative Behavior." *American Economic Review Papers and Proceedings* 65:407-15.

Fiorina, M.P. 1977a. *Congress: Keystone of the Washington Establishment*. New Haven, Conn.: Yale University Press.

Fiorina, M.P. 1977b. "The Case of the Vanishing Marginals: The Bureaucracy Did It." *American Political Science Review* 71:177-81.

Fisher, L. 1970. "The Politics of Impounded Funds." *Administrative Science Quarterly* 15:361-77.

Fisher, L. 1975. *Presidential Spending Power*. Princeton, N.J.: Princeton University Press.

Fisher, L. 1977a. "Congressional Budget Reform: Committee Conflicts." Presented at Annual Meeting of the Midwest Political Science Association.

Fisher, L. 1977b. "Congressional Budget Reform: The First Two Years." *Harvard Journal of Legislation* 14:413-57.

Fox, D.M., and C.P. Clapp. 1970a. "The House Rules Committee and the Programs of the Kennedy and Johnson Administrations." *Midwest Journal of Political Science* 14:662-72.

Fox, D.M., and C.P. Clapp. 1970b. "The House Rules Committee's Agenda-Setting Function, 1961-1968." *Journal of Politics* 32:440-44.

Fox, H.W., Jr., and S.W. Hammond. 1977. *Congressional Staffs: The Invisible Force in American Lawmaking*. New York: Free Press.

Freed, B. 1976a. "House Leadership Opposes Broadcast Plan." *Congressional Quarterly Weekly Report* 34:623.

Freed, B. 1976b. "Common Cause Lodges Complaint against Sikes." *Congressional Quarterly Weekly Report* 34:885.

Froman, L.A., Jr. 1967. *The Congressional Process: Strategies, Rules and Procedures*. Boston: Little, Brown.

Frye, A. 1975. *A Responsible Congress: The Politics of National Security*. New York: McGraw-Hill.

Gertzog, I.N. 1976. "The Routinization of Committee Assignments in the U.S. House of Representatives." *American Journal of Political Science* 20:693-712.

Gray, V. 1973. "Innovation in the States: A Diffusion Study." *American Political Science Review* 67:1174-85.

Grumm, J. 1971. "The Effects of Legislative Structure on Legislative Performance." In R.I. Hofferbert and I. Sharkansky (eds.). *State and Urban Politics*. Boston: Little, Brown.

Hager, B. 1977. "House Resumes Work on Lobby Disclosure." *Congressional Quarterly Weekly Report* 35:683-84.

Hammond, S.W. 1976. "The Operation of Senators' Offices." In U.S. Senate, Commission on the Operation of the Senate. *Senators: Offices, Ethics and Pressures: A Compilation of Papers*. Washington: Government Printing Office.

Heard, A. 1962. *The Costs of Democracy*, rev. ed. Garden City, N.Y.: Doubleday.

Hedlund, R.D., and H.P. Friesema. 1972. "Representatives' Perceptions of Constituency Opinion." *Journal of Politics* 34:730-52.

Hedlund, R.D., and K.E. Hamm. 1976. "Conflict and Perceived Group Benefits from Legislative Rules Changes." *Legislative Studies Quarterly* 1:181-200.

Hedlund, R.D., and K.E. Hamm. 1977. "Institutional Development and Legislature Effectiveness: Rules Changes in the Wisconsin Assembly." In A.I. Baaklini (ed.). *Comparative Legislative Reforms and Innovations*. Albany: State University of New York Press.

Hinckley, B. 1971. *The Seniority System in Congress*. Bloomington: Indiana University Press.

Hinckley, B. 1977. "Seniority 1975: Old Theories Confront New Facts." *British Journal of Political Science* 6:383-99.

Hofferbert, R.I. 1968. "Socioeconomic Dimensions of the American States, 1890-1960." *Midwest Journal of Political Science* 12:401-18.

Hofferbert, R.I. 1964. "Classification of American State Party Systems." *Journal of Politics* 26:550-67.

Huntington, S.P. 1973. "Congressional Responses to the Twentieth Century." In D.B. Truman (ed.). *The Congress and America's Future*, 2d ed. Englewood Cliffs, N.J.: Prentice-Hall.

Jacobson, G.C. 1976. "Practical Consequences of Campaign Finance Reform: An Incumbent Protection Act?" *Public Policy* 21:1-32.

Jewell, M.E., and C. Chi-Hung. 1974. "Membership Movement and Committee Attractiveness in the U.S. House of Representatives, 1963-1970." *American Journal of Political Science* 18:433-41.

Jewell, M.E., and S.C. Patterson. 1977. *The Legislative Process in the United States*, 3d ed. New York: Random House.

Johannes, J.R. 1974. "Statutory Reporting Requirements: An Assessment." Presented at the Annual Meeting of the Midwest Political Science Association.

Johnson, C.A. 1976. "Political Culture in the American States: Elazar's Formulation Examined." *American Journal of Political Science* 20:491-509.

Jones, B.D. 1973. "Competitiveness, Role Orientations and Legislative Responsiveness." *Journal of Politics* 35:924-47.

Jones, C.O. 1970. *The Minority Party in Congress*. Boston: Little, Brown.

Jones, C.O. 1975. "Somebody Must Be Trusted: An Essay on Leadership of the U.S. Congress." In N.J. Ornstein (ed.). *Congress in Change: Evolution and Reform*. New York: Praeger.

Jones, C.O. 1976. "How Reform Changes Congress." Presented at the Symposium on the Impact of Legislative Reform on Public Policy, University of Nebraska.

Kaiser, F.M. 1977. "Oversight of Foreign Policy: The House Committee on International Relations." *Legislative Studies Quarterly* 2:255-79.

Kammerer, G.M. 1951. *Congressional Committee Staffing Since 1946*. Lexington, Ky.: University of Kentucky.

Katz, D., and R.L. Kahn. 1966. *The Social Psychology of Organizations*. New York: Wiley.

Keefe, W.J., and M.S. Ogul. 1973. *The American Legislative Process*, 3d ed. Englewood Cliffs, N.J.: Prentice-Hall.

Kelly, J. 1974. *Organizational Behavior*, rev. ed. Homewood, Ill.: Irwin.

Kingdon, J.W. 1973. *Congressmen's Voting Decisions*. New York: Harper and Row.

Kirkpatrick, S.A. 1974. *Quantitative Analysis of Political Data*. Columbus, Ohio: Merrill.

Kostroski, W.L. 1973. "Party and Incumbency in Postwar Senate Elections: Trends, Patterns, and Models." *American Political Science Review* 67: 1213-34.

Kuklinski, J.H., and R.C. Elling. 1977. "Representational Role, Constituency Opinion, and Legislative Roll Call Behavior." *American Journal of Political Science* 21:135-47.

Legis 50/The Center for Legislative Improvement. 1976. *Toward a New Decade of Legislative Reform*. Englewood, Colo.

Lott, W.F., and P.D. Warner, III. 1974. "The Relative Importance of Campaign Expenditures: An Application of Production Theory." *Quantity and Quality* 8:99-105.

Lowi, T.J. 1969. *The End of Liberalism*. New York: Norton.

Lyons, R. 1977. "A Persuasive Speaker." *Washington Post*, April 3: A1.

McKelvey, R.D. 1976. "Intransitivities in Multidimensional Voting Models and Some Implications for Agenda Control." *Journal of Economic Theory* 12: 472-82.

McKeough, K.L. 1970. *Financing Campaigns for Congress: Contribution Patterns of National-Level Party and Non-Party Committees*. Princeton, N.J.: Citizens' Research Foundation.

Maffre, J. 1971. "Congressional Report/New Leaders, Staff Changes Stimulate House Foreign Affairs Committee." *National Journal* 3:1314-22.

Malbin, M. 1977. "Congressional Committee Staffs: Who's in Charge Here?" *The Public Interest* 47:16-40.

Manley, J. 1970. *The Politics of Finance*. Boston: Little, Brown.

Masters, N.A. 1961. "Committee Assignments in the House of Representatives." *American Political Science Review* 55:345-57.

Mayhew, D.R. 1974a. *Congress: The Electoral Connection*. New Haven, Conn.: Yale University Press.

Mayhew, D.R. 1974b. "Congressional Elections: The Case of the Vanishing Marginals." *Polity* 6:295-317.

Milbrath, L.W. 1971. "Individuals and Government." In H. Jacob and K.N. Vines (eds.). *Politics in the American States*, 2d ed. Boston: Little, Brown.

Miller, W.E., and D.E. Stokes. 1963. "Constituency Influence in Congress," *American Political Science Review* 57:45-57.

Mills, J.L., and W.G. Munselle. 1975. "Unimpoundment: Politics and the Courts in the Release of Impounded Funds." *Emory Law Journal* 24:313-53.

Mondale, W. 1976. "Reviewing the Rule XXII Change." *Congressional Record* May 4, 1976, S6417-19.

Mueller, J.E. 1973. *War, Presidents, and Public Opinion*. New York: Wiley.

Munger, F.J., and R.F. Fenno, Jr. 1962. *National Politics and Federal Aid to Education*. Syracuse, N.Y.: Syracuse University Press.

Norton, C. 1976. "Congressional Review, Deferral and Disapproval of Executive Action." Washington: Congressional Research Service.

Ogul, M.S. 1976. *Congress Oversees the Bureaucracy*. Pittsburgh: University of Pittsburgh Press.

Oppenheimer, B.J. 1977a. "The Rules Committee: New Arm of the Leadership in a Decentralized House." In L.C. Dodd and B.J. Oppenheimer (eds.). *Congress Reconsidered*. New York: Praeger.

Oppenheimer, B.J. 1977b. "The Rules Committee in the New House." Presented at the Annual Meeting of the Midwest Political Science Association.

Orfield, G. 1975. *Congressional Power: Congress and Social Change*. New York: Harcourt Brace Jovanovich.

Ornstein, N.J. 1975a. "Causes and Consequences of Congressional Change: Subcommittee Reforms in the House of Representatives, 1970-73." In N.J. Ornstein (ed.). *Congress in Change: Evolution and Reform*. New York: Praeger.

Ornstein, N.J. (ed.). 1975b. *Congress in Change: Evolution and Reform*. New York: Praeger.

Ornstein, N.J., and D.W. Rohde. 1977. "Shifting Forces, Changing Rules and Political Outcomes: The Impact of Congressional Change on Four House Committees." In R. Peabody and N.W. Polsby (eds.). *New Perspectives on the House of Representatives*, 3d ed. Chicago: Rand McNally.

Ornstein, N.J., and D.W. Rohde. 1978. "Congressional Reform and Political Parties in the U.S. House of Representatives." In J. Fishel (ed.). *Parties and Elections in an Anti-Party Age*. Bloomington: Indiana University Press.

Palda, K.S. 1975. "The Effects of Expenditures on Political Success." *Journal of Law and Economics* 18:745-71.

Parker, G.R. 1977. "Some Themes in Congressional Unpopularity." *American Journal of Political Science* 21:93-109.

Patterson, S.C. 1976. "American State Legislatures and Public Policy." In H. Jacob and K.N. Vines (eds.). *Politics in the American States*, 3d ed. Boston: Little, Brown.

Peabody, R.L. 1963. "The Enlarged Rules Committee." In R. Peabody and N.W. Polsby (eds.). *New Perspectives on the House of Representatives*, 1st ed. Chicago: Rand McNally.

Pfiffner, J.P. 1977. "Executive Control and the Congressional Budget." Presented at the Annual Meeting of the Midwest Political Science Association.

Pierce, L.C. 1971. *The Politics of Fiscal Policy Formation*. Pacific Palisades, Calif.: Goodyear.

Plato. *The Laws*. T. Saunders, tr. 1970. London: Penguin Books.

Plott, C.R. 1976. "Axiomatic Social Choice Theory: An Overview and Interpretation." *American Journal of Political Science* 20:511-96.

Polsby, N.W. 1971. "Strengthening Congress in National Policy-Making." In N.W. Polsby (ed.). *Congressional Behavior*. New York: Random House.

Polsby, N.W.; M. Gallaher; and B.S. Rundquist. 1969. "The Growth of the Seniority System in the U.S. House of Representatives." *American Political Science Review* 63:787-807.

Poole, F. 1975. "Congress v. Kissinger: The New Equalizers." *Washington Monthly* 7:23-33.

Price, D.E. 1971. "Professionals and 'Entrepreneurs': Staff Orientations and Policy Making on Three Senate Committees." *Journal of Politics* 33:313-36.

Price, D.E. 1974. "The Ambivalence of Congressional Reform." *Public Administration Review* 34:601-08.

Price, D.E., et al. 1975. *The Commerce Committees*. New York: Grossman.

Price, H.D. 1971. "The Congressional Career—Then and Now." In N.W. Polsby (ed.). *Congressional Behavior*. New York: Random House.

Price, J.L. 1968. *Organizational Effectiveness: An Inventory of Propositions*. Homewood, Ill.: Irwin.

Ranney, A. 1962, "The Utility and Limitations of Aggregate Data in the Study of Electoral Behavior." In A. Ranney (ed.). *Essays on the Behavioral Study of Politics*. Urbana: University of Illinois Press.

Ranney, A. 1976. "Parties in State Politics." In H. Jacob and K.N. Vines (eds.). *Politics in the American States*, 3d ed. Boston: Little, Brown.

Ray, D. 1974. "Membership Stability in Three State Legislatures: 1893-1969." *American Political Science Review* 68:106-13.

Ray, D. 1976. "Voluntary Retirement and Electoral Defeat in Eight State Legislatures." *Journal of Politics* 38:426-33.

Reese, T.J. 1975a. "Ways and Means Votes Show Mediocre Record on Tax Reform." *Tax Notes* (June 9):4.

Reese, T.J. 1965b. *Tax Notes* (June 30):3, 8.

Rhodes, J.J. 1976. *The Futile System*. McLean, Va.: EPM Publications.

Riegle, D., with T. Armbrister. 1972. *O Congress*. New York: Popular Library.

Rieselbach, L.N. 1977a. *Congressional Reform in the Seventies*. Morristown, N.J.: General Learning Press.

Rieselbach, L.N. (ed.). 1977b. "Symposium on Legislative Reform." *Policy Studies Journal* 5:394-491.

Ripley, R.B. 1976. "Party Leaders, Policy Committees, and Policy Analysis in the United States Senate." In U.S. Senate, Commission on the Operation of the Senate. *Policymaking Role of Leadership in the Senate: A Compilation of Papers*. Washington: Government Printing Office.

Robinson, J.A. 1963. *The House Rules Committee*. Indianapolis: Bobbs-Merrill.

Rohde, D.W. 1974. "Committee Reform in the House of Representatives and the Subcommittee Bill of Rights." *Annals* 411:39-47.

Rohde, D.W., and K.A. Shepsle. 1973. "Democratic Committee Assignments in the House of Representatives: Strategic Aspects of a Social Choice Process." *American Political Science Review* 57:889-905.

Rohde, D.W.; N.J. Ornstein; and R.L. Peabody. 1974. "Political Change and Legislative Norms in the United States Senate." Presented at the Annual Meeting of the American Political Science Association.

Rohde, D.W., and H.J. Spaeth. 1976. *Supreme Court Decision Making*. San Francisco: W.H. Freeman.

Rosenthal, A. 1974. "Turnover in State Legislatures." *American Journal of Political Science* 18:609-16.

Rudder, C. 1977. "The Impact of the Budget and Impoundment Control Act of 1974 on the Revenue Committees of the U.S. Congress." Presented at the Annual Meeting of the American Political Science Association.

Russell, M. 1977. "House Unit Attempts to Halt Committee Growth, but Fails." *Washington Post* (May 19): A4.

Russell, M., and D.S. Broder. 1977. "Hill's Budget Power Survives Jolts from Outside and In." *Washington Post* (May 15): A3.

Scher, S. 1963. "Conditions for Legislative Control." *Journal of Politics* 25: 526-51.

Schlesinger, J.A. 1971. "The Politics of the Executive." In H. Jacob and K.N. Vines (eds.). *Politics in the American States*, 2d ed. Boston: Little, Brown.

Schubert, G., and C. Press. 1964. "Measuring Malapportionment." *American Political Science Review* 58:302-27 and 968-70.

Schwartz, B. 1959. *The Professor and the Commissions*. New York: Knopf.

Sharkansky, I., and R.I. Hofferbert. 1969. "Dimensions of State Politics, Economics, and Public Policy." *American Political Science Review* 63:867-79.

Shepsle, K.A. 1975. "Congressional Committee Assignments: An Optimization Model with Institutional Constraints." *Public Choice* 22:55-78.

Shepsle, K.A. 1978. *The Giant Jigsaw Puzzle: Democratic Committee Assign-*

ments in the Modern House. Chicago: University of Chicago Press.

Shick, A. 1974. "Budget Reform Legislation: Reorganizing Congressional Centers of Fiscal Power." *Harvard Journal of Legislation* 11:303–50.

Shick, A. 1975. "The Appropriations Committees versus Congress." Presented at the Annual Meeting of the American Political Science Association.

Smith, Linda L. 1977. "The Congressional Budget Process: Why It Worked This Time." *Bureaucrat* 6:88–111.

Southwick, T.P. 1977. "House Voting More in 1977, Senate—under Byrd— Less." *Congressional Quarterly Weekly Report* 35:1130–31.

Stokes, D.E., and W.E. Miller. 1966. "Party Government and the Saliency of Congress." In A. Campbell, P.E. Converse, W.E. Miller, and D.E. Stokes. *Elections and the Political Order*. New York: Wiley.

Stouffer, S.A. 1955. *Communism, Conformity, and Civil Liberties*. Garden City, N.Y.: Doubleday.

Sullivan, J.L. 1973. "Political Correlates of Social, Economic, and Religious Diversity in the American States." *Journal of Politics* 35:70–84.

Sundquist, J.L. 1968. *Politics and Policy*. Washington: The Brookings Institution.

Thurber, J.A. 1976. "Congressional Budget Reform and New Demands for Policy Analysis." *Policy Analysis* 2:198–214.

U.S. Bureau of the Census. 1970–1975. *Statistical Abstract of the United States*. Washington: Government Printing Office.

U.S. Department of Commerce. 1963. 1973. *Congressional District Data Book*. Washington: Government Printing Office.

U.S. House of Representatives. 1975. Committee on International Relations Subcommittee on International Security. *War Powers*. Washington: Government Printing Office.

U.S. House of Representatives. 1976a. Clerk. *Reports to Be Made to Congress*. Washington: Government Printing Office.

U.S. House of Representatives. 1976b. Committee on International Relations. *Survey of Activities*. Washington: Government Printing Office.

U.S. House of Representatives. 1977a. Commission on Administrative Review. *Financial Ethics*. Washington: Government Printing Office.

U.S. House of Representatives. 1977b. Commission on Administrative Review. *Results of Louis Harris Poll*. Xeroxed.

U.S. House of Representatives. 1977c. Commission on Administrative Review. *Background Information on Administrative Units, Members' Offices, and Committee and Leadership Offices*. Washington: Government Printing Office.

U.S. House of Representatives. 1977d. Commission on Administrative Review. *Administrative Reorganization and Legislative Management*. Vol. 2 of 2, "Workload Management." Washington: Government Printing Office.

U.S. Senate. 1973. Committee on Rules and Administration. *Federal Election Reform*. Washington: Government Printing Office.

U.S. Senate. 1976a. Committee on Government Operations, Subcommittee on Oversight Procedures. *Legislative Oversight and Program Evaluation: A Seminar Conducted by the Congressional Research Service*. Washington: Government Printing Office.

U.S. Senate. 1976b. Temporary Select Committee to Study the Senate Committee System. "Implications of the Congressional Budget and Impoundment Control Act for the Senate Committee System." In *The Senate Committee System*. Washington: Government Printing Office.

Uslaner, E.M. 1974. *Congressional Committee Assignments: Alternative Models for Behavior*. Beverly Hills, Calif.: Sage Publications.

Uslaner, E.M. 1977a. "Party Reform and Electoral Disaggregation: A Paradox in Congress." *Policy Studies Journal* 5:454-59.

Uslaner, E.M. 1977b. "Cyclical and Secular Models of Congressional Voting: Party Cohesion and Disarray in the House of Representatives, 1947-1970." Mimeographed.

Verba, S., and N.H. Nie. 1972. *Participation in America: Political Democracy and Social Equality*. New York: Harper and Row.

Vines, K.N., and H. Jacob. 1971. "State Courts." In Jacob and Vines. *Politics in the American States*, 2d ed. Boston: Little, Brown.

Wagner, J.R. 1976. "New Federal Election Law Has Its Critics." *Congressional Quarterly Weekly Report* 34:3032-35.

Walker, J.L. 1969. "The Diffusion of Innovations among the American States." *American Political Science Review* 63:880-99.

Walker, J.L. 1974. "Performance Gaps, Policy Research, and Political Entrepreneurs." *Policy Studies Journal* 3:112-16.

Welch, S., and J.G. Peters (eds.). 1977. *Legislative Reform and Public Policy*. New York: Praeger.

Welch, W.P. 1974. "The Economics of Campaign Funds." *Public Choice* 20: 83-99.

Welch, W.P. 1976. "The Effectiveness of Expenditures in State Legislative Races." *American Politics Quarterly* 4:333-56.

Westefield, L.P. 1974. "Majority Party Leadership and the Committee System in the House of Representatives." *American Political Science Review* 68: 1593-1604.

Wilson, J.Q. 1966. *The Amateur Democrat*. New York: Free Press. Originally published in 1962.

Index of Names

Index of Subjects

About the Contributors

John Berg is an assistant professor of government at Suffolk University. In addition to his interest in legislative policy making, he is currently pursuing studies of neighborhood politics in Boston and of the political thought of John Dewey.

E. Lee Bernick is an assistant professor of political science at Iowa State University. His publications include several monographs on legislative decision making and articles in *Legislative Studies Quarterly* and *Public Administration Review*. His current teaching and research interests are in the areas of legislative process, public administration, and state and local government.

Charles S. Bullock III is professor of political science at the University of Georgia. His research interests include Congress, policy analysis, and civil rights. He is coauthor of the recently published *Public Policy and Politics in America* (1978).

Gary W. Copeland is completing his dissertation at the University of Iowa in political science. His dissertation explores the effects of campaign spending on the voting behavior of individuals.

David N. Farnsworth is a professor of political science at Wichita State University, with research and teaching interests in United States foreign policy. He has specialized in the Congressional role in foreign policy decision making.

Keith E. Hamm is an assistant professor of political science at Texas A&M University. His major research interests include state legislatures with emphasis on various aspects of the policy-making process.

Susan Webb Hammond is assistant professor, School of Government and Public Administration, American University. She has served on the staffs of the Senate Commission on the Operation of the Senate (The Hughes Commission) and the House Commission on Administration Review (The Obey Commission) and has published articles on congressional staffing, office operations, and oversight. She is coauthor of *Congressional Staffs: The Invisible Force in American Lawmaking* (1977).

Ronald D. Hedlund is professor of political science, University of Wisconsin-Milwaukee. His interests include the effects of various kinds of changes in the legislative organization on policy decisions and policy performance. His recent publications include "Institutional Development and Legislature Effectiveness: Rules Change in the Wisconsin Assembly," in *Comparative Legislative Reforms* *and Innovations* (1977) and "A Path-Goal Approach to Explaining Leadership's Impact on Legislator Perceptions," *Social Science Quarterly* (1978).

Fred M. Kaiser is a senior analyst in American national government with the Congressional Research Service and had served as Special Staff Consultant with the House International Relations Committee. This article is a companion to "Oversight of Foreign Policy: The House Committee on International Relations," *Legislative Studies Quarterly*, vol. II (1977), and extends his interests in congressional structure and oversight and the national security/foreign policy arena.

William G. Munselle is an assistant professor of political science at the University of Florida. A specialist in Congress, the presidency, and congressional-executive relations, he has published articles in the *Emory Law Journal* and *Policy Studies Journal.*

Bruce I. Oppenheimer is associate professor of political science at the University of Houston. He is the author of *Oil and the Congressional Process* (1974), coeditor of *Congress Reconsidered* (1977), and a frequent contributor of articles on Congress to professional journals.

Samuel C. Patterson is professor in the Department of Political Science at the University of Iowa, and associated with its Comparative Legislative Research Center. He is coauthor of *The Legislative Process in the United States* (3d ed., 1977) and *Comparing Legislatures* (1978).

David E. Price, associate professor of political science and policy sciences at Duke University, served on the staffs of Senators E.L. Bartlett and Albert Gore. He is the author of *Who Makes the Laws?, The Commerce Committees,* and several articles on congressional policy making. His more recent work considers critical traditions in American political thought and the terms they suggest for policy evaluation.

David W. Rohde is associate professor of political science at Michigan State University. His primary research interests are congressional elections and the effects of institutional rules on behavior and policy outcomes.

Catherine Rudder is administrative assistant for Congressman Wyche Fowler, Jr. (D-Ga.). Her academic interests include congressional reform, budgeting, and policy. She is a former Congressional Fellow and has written on elections, the revenue committees, and presidential impoundments.

Kenneth A. Shepsle is professor of political science at Washington University, St. Louis. His research interests include mathematical modeling and legislative decision-making. His book, *The Giant Jigsaw Puzzle: Democratic Committee Assignments in the Modern House*, was published this year by the University of Chicago Press.

John E. Stanga, Jr., is an associate professor of political science at Wichita State University with teaching and research interests in the areas of public law and American politics.

Raymond Tatalovich is associate professor of political science at Chicago State University. His major fields of academic interest include legislative process, public policy analysis, and administrative politics.

James A. Thurber is associate professor of government and public administration at American University. He was formerly legislative assistant to Senator Hubert H. Humphrey and most recently a professional staff member for The Temporary Select Committee to Study The U.S. Senate Committee System. He has published several articles on congressional budget reform and legislative behavior.

Eric M. Uslaner, assistant professor of government and politics, University of Maryland, is engaged in studies of reform in the contemporary Congress, the effects of issues in Congressional elections, and the representation of various elite groups in the American states. He has coauthored *Patterns of Decision Making in State Legislatures* (1977) and has published articles in the *American Political Science Review, American Journal of Political Science, Journal of Politics, Behavioral Science*, and *Political Methodology*.

Charles W. Wiggins is a professor of political science at Iowa State University in Ames. His research and publications have been in the fields of state legislatures, political parties, interest groups, and public policy. He is currently working on a manuscript on state legislative committee systems.

About the Editor

Leroy N. Rieselbach received the A.B. from Harvard College and the Ph.D. from Yale University. He is currently professor of political science at Indiana University. Dr. Rieselbach has been Postdoctoral Fellow at The Mental Health Research Institute, University of Michigan, and research associate, Center for International Affairs, Harvard University. His publications on the legislative process include *The Roots of Isolationism* (1966), *The Congressional System: Notes and Readings* (1970), *Congressional Politics* (1973), *Congressional Reform in The Seventies* (1977), and articles in the *American Political Science Review, Midwest Journal of Political Science, Public Opinion Quarterly*, and *Policy Studies Journal.*